Animals' Best Friends

Animals' Best Friends

PUTTING COMPASSION TO WORK FOR
ANIMALS IN CAPTIVITY AND IN THE WILD

Barbara J. King

The University of Chicago Press
Chicago and London

The University of Chicago Press, Chicago 60637
The University of Chicago Press, Ltd., London
Published 2021
Printed in the United States of America

30 29 28 27 26 25 24 23 22 21   1 2 3 4 5

ISBN-13: 978-0-226-60148-9 (cloth)
ISBN-13: 978-0-226-60151-9 (e-book)
DOI: https://doi.org/10.7208/chicago/9780226601519.001.0001

Library of Congress Cataloging-in-Publication Data

Names: King, Barbara J., 1956– author.
Title: Animals' best friends : putting compassion to work
for animals in captivity and in the wild / Barbara J. King.
Description: Chicago : University of Chicago Press, 2021. |
Includes bibliographical references and index.
Identifiers: LCCN 2020036666 | ISBN 9780226601489
(cloth) | ISBN 9780226601519 (ebook)
Subjects: LCSH: Human-animal relationships. |
Compassion.
Classification: LCC QL85 .K532 2021 | DDC 590—dc23
LC record available at https://lccn.loc.gov/2020036666

♾ This paper meets the requirements of ANSI/NISO
Z39.48-1992 (Permanence of Paper).

For my loved ones, friends, and colleagues
who give everything to animals.

Joy can only remind you why you fight.

— JEFF VANDERMEER, *Dead Astronauts*

Contents

1

Cultivating Compassionate Action

"If you turn your back on these calves, they will mount you!" Standing in one of the cow barns at Farm Sanctuary in Watkins Glen in Upstate New York, I heard shelter director Susie Coston's voice ring out through the warm August air. During Farm Sanctuary's 2018 hoedown, an annual open-house weekend, Coston led a small group of invited speakers and our families around the property to meet some of the 735 resident animals. Calves who had been bottle fed at the sanctuary, like the one named Alexander Beans who reclined near me, often feel such warmth for people that they jump up and "embrace" a visitor in an excess of youthful exuberance. It's meant well—but it can hurt, because at six months these calves may weigh over three hundred pounds.

Keeping my eyes open and my back unturned as I walked among the calves, I reached under a chin here and there to offer a caress. Eyes were upon me, and not just Coston's: a cow called Bonnie stood just outside the barn door. Bonnie fixed a protective gaze on us visitors as we weaved among the youngsters. Famous in the world of rescued farm animals, Bonnie was born at a beef farm in Holland, New York. At four months old, her herd went up for sale when the farm owner died. A man soon showed up with a trailer to take away the cows, including Bonnie and her mother, to his own farm. The herd reacted with distress and fear.

Making a fateful decision, Bonnie bolted. She ran into nearby woods, and there she stayed for almost a year, an escapee who became known to local residents through brief glimpses and trail-cam images. Even at such a young age, Bonnie showed resourcefulness in surviving out in the forest, a wholly unfamiliar environment to her. Her most inspired choice was to join up with a herd of deer. Bonnie and the deer ate, slept, and traveled together. Trail-cam images show this wasn't a lonely cow trailing haplessly after deer but a truly mutual acceptance. Whether Bonnie missed her mother we will never know, but through her wits, she found a new family for herself.

Bonnie's second wise decision was to accept help from a human. Many local people admired Bonnie's bold escape, but one woman named Becky went a step further and took action. Each day in the early morning, she walked out into the woods with a sled piled with food and bedding for Bonnie. Slowly, Bonnie came to trust her. In this way—surrounded by the bodily warmth of her deer companions and the kind caring of Becky—Bonnie survived a cold and snowy winter.

Forest living was not sustainable for Bonnie in the long term. The harsh winters were bad enough, but some local people considered her a pest and announced they would eat Bonnie if they could. The notion of this animal becoming a family's supply of steak was too much for Coston and the Farm Sanctuary staff, who mounted a rescue. Twice the rescuers set out from Watkins Glen at 3:30 a.m. to be at the "breakfast spot" where Bonnie met Becky at 6:30. Twice Bonnie eluded capture. Her trust in Becky did not generalize to trust in other humans (with good reason). But gradually Bonnie became accustomed to entering a small corral constructed by the sanctuary team as a feeding area. On the third rescue attempt, rescuers darted Bonnie with a stronger sedative. That worked. Bonnie was transported back to Watkins Glen, where she permanently resides now. Gazing at Bonnie's body posture and facial expression that August day, I could see for myself what a presence she has.

For so many of us who love animals, our dogs and cats, bunnies and ferrets, and snakes and fish are family members. We care for them through everyday acts of devotion to make their lives better. Opportunities to transform the lives of animals beyond our pets can be found, too, all around us; the trick is to uncover those opportunities and decide if we wish to act on them.

At Farm Sanctuary I used my sense of touch to soothe and be soothed by animals rescued from industrialized farms or other places where they had been abused or neglected. For two hours, animals of species whose thinking and feeling capacities I had written about for years snuffled, shuffled, and walked up to me—or sometimes away from me in a desire *not* to interact, as sanctuary residents are free to do. Unexpectedly, the strongest bond I felt was with a goat called Cynthia. A goat of the La-Mancha breed, Cynthia responded blissfully when I stroked her head, neck, and chin; she turned firmly into my hand as a signal that I should not, please, think of stopping. Her former life on a Hudson Valley farm had been rough; according to Farm Sanctuary, she had arrived "lice-covered, anemic, weak, and quiet." Eventually Cynthia recovered to become healthy, energetic, and in love with loving attention.

Like the cow Bonnie and the calf Alexander Beans who kindly did not mount me that morning, in sanctuary Cynthia has a life with a dual nature. She is recognized for the unique individual she is with all her moods, likes, and dislikes. Simultaneously she is a symbol of the powerful effect that compassionate action has on animal lives.

One morning just after Christmas 2017, thirteen elk fell through the ice into eight feet of frigid water in a reservoir near the Alpine Feed Ground, not far from Jackson, Wyoming. Morning commuters saw the herd suddenly go under. Stopping on the side of the road, a group of them mounted a rescue effort that soon came to include officials from the Wyoming Game and Fish Department and the Lincoln County Sheriff's Office.

One of the passersby who joined in, Dusty Jones, later spoke to the media about the event: "We began cutting a little path toward the shore so the animals could walk out but they were so cold they couldn't move. That's when we just started grabbing them and pulling them out."

Video of the rescue shows a group of men tying ropes around a thrashing and obviously frightened elk cow in the water, then hauling her out. The men run after another elk, now free of the water, in order to remove the rescue rope from her neck before she flees. Powerful animals who may easily weigh five hundred pounds, elk cows are no easy force of nature to handle, especially when they are adrenalized by fear. The effort required courage and hard cooperative labor. All thirteen elk were rescued.

A month earlier and over eighty-five hundred miles away from Wyoming, a baby elephant fell into a well while trying to cross a river in the town of Thattekad in India's state of Kerala. Just as with the elk, "regular people" and government officials came together to help, this time with the aid of a mechanical digger in a five-hour rescue operation. The elephant infant's kin had crowded around in distress; when finally the baby was able to walk up an incline of soil packed down by the rescuers for this purpose, a joyful family reunion occurred. Parts of this rescue, too, were captured on video. At the end, as the little herd moves away to cross the river, one of the adult elephants turns around and calmly raises her trunk toward the rescuers, who ululate in celebration. Was the raised trunk a gesture of gratitude? Knowing what I do about elephants' intelligence, I think it's perfectly possible.

In any given week, stories about animal rescues go viral on the internet. Some are as large-scale and dramatic as the elk and elephant examples, as when hour-by-hour updates come in from teams trying to rescue whales in the ocean who become entangled in fishing equipment. Others are smaller-scale: a family chooses an elderly cat to bring home from the animal shelter, or a driver, already late for work, stops to move a turtle to safety from the middle of the road.

When we see animals in trouble, concern wells up in us. We may worry for our neighbor's dog chained outside in subzero temperatures, a bored-looking gorilla at a zoo, or a wild orca population in grave danger of extinction. Our compassion may blossom for a truckload of chickens headed to slaughter or for a spider crushed by a friend just because he finds arachnids to be creepy. The contexts are almost endless, and while that reality is sad, it also creates space for action. As Hope Ferdowsian puts it in her book *Phoenix Zones*, when we allow ourselves to see the urgency in situations of suffering, we are given a chance to make a difference. In our everyday lives we constantly make choices that affect animals for good or ill. When we tune in to the animal lives threaded through our own, opportunities for positive outcomes expand and flourish. That process catches us up in a net of rewards: our world may transform as we *see* how animals rejoice in good days and endure bad ones; love their families and friends and grieve their losses; and struggle to overcome physical and emotional challenges. When each of us takes positive steps to help, the collective impact is enormous, an arc in which we strive to create a better world for animals.

Decades ago, I fell in love with anthropology and decided to observe monkeys and apes as a career; over the years since then, I've come to advocate for animals rather than only study them. The ethical questions involved become thornier over time, I found, embracing a broad swath of the animal kingdom and only rarely equipped with clear answers. That lengthy grappling has led to this book, where I take up compassionate action for animals in five different contexts: our homes, the wild, zoos, our food system, and research facilities such as biomedical laboratories. Taken together, the chapters that follow offer a cornucopia of ways in which each of us can work toward becoming animals' best friends.

To begin, I offer two stories from my own life, each centered on rescue. In the first, an American hiker goes missing in a national park. In the second, bears are held captive in order for people to harvest and sell their bile. The contrast between the two opens a window on ways to think through some tangled issues about compassion, action, and our own readiness to get involved.

*   *   *

In spring 2013, I learned by telephone that I had a fast-moving malignancy, a tumor that makes up only 5 percent of all uterine cancers. The words my doctor uttered, "serous papillary carcinoma of the uterus," combined with the survival statistics I soon found on the internet, caused nausea to set in.

Months of pealing phones ensued. Conversations centered on medical appointments, coping methods for treatment side effects, and good wishes expressed by family, friends, and work colleagues. Though I always felt gratitude for this multifaceted care, at times I wished that the telephone would just hush. And then one day the following year, it did hush—when I wanted just the opposite.

Solo hiking in Utah, my husband Charlie was late checking in with me. Our tried-and-true routine for Charlie's annual trips to the desert Southwest had been in place for over two decades: as he prepared his hiking gear each morning, Charlie informed me about the trail he would hike, the hour at which he expected to depart the trailhead, and the hour at which he anticipated finishing up. A case of overkill, perhaps—a succumbing to anxious overthinking of what could possibly happen? It seemed that way sometimes; no hiking emergency had ever materialized. We kept at our system anyway.

The year before, no hiking trip had been possible as together we negotiated a maze of my treatment: six hours of surgery by a surgeon-robot team; six rounds of infusions of chemicals that my nurses handled only with gloves; twenty-five external-beam radiation sessions taken while flat on a table in a room that featured painted beach scenes and energized rock music; three internal-radiation sessions featuring large radioactive canisters that are repressed in my memory as I never again want to think about them; and months of recovery. Now, no longer bald or fatigued, I was excited about a chance to run the house for a week and care for our rescued cats while Charlie hiked. Besides, unlike Charlie, I wasn't going *entirely* solo: our Sarah was home from college for the summer. Though busy with work and friends, they would pitch in as needed.

Then, the phone silence. That morning Charlie had started out at 9:30 Utah time to hike a 8.3-mile loop trail in Canyonlands National Park around a feature called Upheaval Dome, planning to come off trail by 5:00 p.m. As that hour came and went, I willed myself to remain patient. By 9:00 p.m. Virginia time, though (7:00 for Charlie), a pit of uneasiness had lodged in my stomach. The ranger station at Canyonlands had already closed for the day, but the police dispatcher in Moab was able to connect me with the National Park Service ranger, Lofton Wiley, stationed in the park. Wiley calmly asked question after question beyond the basics of Charlie's name, age, and appearance. What brand and style of hiking shoes did he wear? Could I estimate his stride length? Wiley strongly suspected that Charlie was lost rather than badly injured, a prediction to which Sarah and I clung tightly over the next hours.

From that point forward, things happened at a rapid pace. In the 337,000-acre park, rangers located Charlie's car in the lot where I'd known it would be. Right then and there, our information-sharing system paid its weight in gold. Around 2:00 a.m. Virginia time two teams of search-and-rescue personnel set out to seek Charlie, one walking clockwise, the other counterclockwise around the loop. A dog named Shalla accompanied one of the teams, with Charlie's scent lodged in her acutely sensitive nose: a Moab-based search-and-rescue team member had gone to the hotel and retrieved Charlie's T-shirt and spare shoes for Shalla to sniff. Most dramatically, or so it felt to me listening on the telephone, a helicopter was flown in from Salt Lake City to commence an air search.

During the long night hours during which Sarah and I worried about Charlie, he was lying on the trail dehydrated, fatigued, and disoriented—lost, just as Ranger Wiley had predicted. We learned this only later, of course. Around 7:30 the previous evening, just as the telephone's silence had begun to oppress, he had finished the food and water he had packed for a day hike. Quite aware that he was lost, he didn't realize that he had begun to walk *backwards* on the trail, away from the direction he needed to go. He slept on the trail as best he could, taking sensible precautions for his safety. At more than one point, as he took in the beauty of an unpolluted night sky, Charlie heard the helicopter overhead and waved his arms. The helicopter didn't spot him, and the two search teams didn't either. Rescue hiking is slow and intensely focused work: neither team covered the full loop, which is why another team was scheduled to go out at dawn.

At first light, Charlie entered a wash. Extremely thirsty, he was about to dig underground for the freshest water available.

Before he could do this, a helicopter flew near then hovered in the air nearby; the pilot called out, "Are you Charles Hogg? We've been talking with your wife." First by copter, then by car, Charlie made his way to the ranger station, where he offered profuse thanks to the whole rescue team. His gratitude included Shalla, who was then allowed to "find" him, a joyful outcome important to this working dog's sense of accomplishment.

In retrospect I see the entire event, spanning just about eleven hours in total, as a lava flow of compassion. Sarah and I felt it for Charlie throughout the night, and he felt the same for us; certainly the rescuers must have felt it for their lost man on the trail, and the three of us felt a version of it for them, along with respect and gratitude. When I recounted this story to family and friends, and later for readers of my National Public Radio blog posts, responses were a mix of fascination and relief. Pretty much anyone can relate to this kind of close call; over and over I heard expressions of caring and requests for more details. I couldn't help but think back to the year before and a different rescue story.

On the hospital ward following the lengthy surgery to remove my cancerous uterus, plus assorted other organs and twenty-nine lymph nodes, I felt like a bear. This was not a drug-induced hallucination or nightmare that brought bear images into my brain. No, this was different, a sustained waking state in which all species boundaries fell away and I knew myself to *be* a bear. It wasn't a grizzly or black bear, those massive mammals I had glimpsed with awe on trips to Yellowstone National Park in Wyoming. Nor was it a bear confined in one of the zoos I have visited over the years. This bear dwelled in a tight cage, tethered to a catheter just as I was. In the bear's case, the catheter was affixed to the gallbladder so that her bile could be harvested for sale.

Across China and Vietnam in their terrible thousands, black

bears (also known as moon bears) are kept in bile farms in torturous conditions, as brown bears and sun bears may also be.
The bottom line is greed: harvested bear bile brings big money
when sold as a medical remedy for liver diseases including cancer and cirrhosis. This "farming" practice is rooted in beliefs
in ancient traditional medicine, though the remedies remain
almost wholly unproven and synthetic alternatives are now
available. The bile is touted also as a libido booster.

In my postsurgical hospital bed, I was alone; Charlie and
Sarah had departed for home. As the soft, bulky boots encas-
ing my legs pumped air in and air out with a rhythmic whoosh,
working to prevent postsurgical blood clots, it seemed that I
had landed on the shores of a strange cancer world. In the long
darkness, I felt not-myself and all-bear. Of course everything
being done *to* me, and everything that was *about* to be done to
me via chemotherapy and radiation, was in aid of my well-being:
in this way, my situation was quite different from that of the
bears. Neither that difference nor any other came through to
me that night, though. None of my response was cerebral. I was
one big exposed nerve root of empathy for suffering bears.

How could I tell anyone about this experience? Certainly
I couldn't inform the night nurse that her patient had transmuted into a bear. The next morning I couldn't find the words
to describe even to Charlie what had happened. In my culture
people just don't turn into bears, and my feelings were too intense to relive in the telling. Only much later did I tell him.
Later still, I described that night in a piece for *Undark* magazine
and discovered then and there how differently family, friends,
and strangers reacted to this story compared to the one about
Charlie lost in the desert. No one wanted more details; many
people wished they hadn't learned any to begin with. "I hadn't
heard before of these bile bears, and I wish I could unlearn what
I now know about them" was the gist of many responses.

That's not indifference speaking, at least not typically. A weight descends on caring people who learn about animals in pain, a weight of a different size and pressure from any that attached to Charlie's close call in Utah. Taking in the bears' misery and taking in Charlie's night of discomfort differ qualitatively, and not only because after a single night Charlie's plight ended with a banana and a happy rescue dog. Even if the helicopter pilot had not spotted Charlie that morning, and Charlie had gotten into real trouble from the combination of dehydration, heat, and disorientation, it's unlikely that anyone would turn away from my words feeling so pierced by them that they wished to purge them from memory.

Comparing the responses to these two rescue stories, I can't readily navigate the maze of questions that surface. Can it be that caring deeply for animals may shut down our willingness to grasp that they are hurting? Or perhaps instead it becomes possible to compartmentalize and tamp down our concern in the case of animals who are not our companions, whom we don't readily know how to help? After all, people flock to horse races, dolphin shows, and roadside zoos even as reports of animal pain in those places emerge regularly. At the same time, though, I'm surrounded by colleagues and friends who devote their lives to responding to animals—all kinds of animals—in need, and many of my global heroes do the same.

Working through the plight of the bile bears, and what can be done to help, highlights both the opportunities and the obstacles that accompany compassionate concern. Like any animal confronted with the worst of humanity, a bile bear tells us with her body and her eyes, and sometimes her voice, how hard it is to try to endure the unendurable. Yet the bears cannot advocate for themselves or set up a plan that boosts the chances of their rescue; they can't work to enlist the help of others. Humans *do* help, thankfully. A rescue organization headquartered in Hong

Kong called Animals Asia fights on behalf of the bile bears and *wants* us to take on learning about them, as hard emotionally as that may be. Over six hundred of the bears so far have been rescued from bile farms and taken to Animals Asia's sanctuaries, one in Chengdu, China, and the other in Tam Dao, Vietnam.

In these sanctuaries, large outdoor enclosures with comfortable dens greet the bears. I wonder if the space isn't slightly vertiginous for them upon first sighting, after so long in confined spaces. Of course, though, the animals don't arrive hale, hearty, and ready to explore. Many of the bears require special medical care after their rescue; the bile-harvesting procedures, especially those involving catheters, sometimes cause serious infections. Sometimes rescue comes too late: the most badly damaged bears simply don't make it.

Jill Robinson, the founder and CEO of Animals Asia, told me that confined bile bears may come down with septicemia, or blood poisoning. Just as the catheter was a point of embodied connection for me with the bears, it's septicemia that does this for Robinson. "My mother died of septicemia," she told me. "I never knew her, as she died when my sister and I were babies, and my heartbroken father rarely spoke about her except to say that she was the best woman in the world, and that she died screaming in agony. He never married again. Today when I see the bears suffering and dying from this horrible disease it brings me full circle—remembering a woman I never knew, but would have loved to, and knowing how much the bears must be suffering as she did then."

Robinson puts her strong feelings to use. It's not only that Animals Asia brings about individual bear rescues. More than ten thousand bears dwell on farms in China alone, and another five hundred in Vietnam; six hundred rescues make a dent in the problem but do not come close to solving it. In 2017 Animals Asia announced hopeful news: Vietnam pledged to end bile farming altogether and to work with Animals Asia to place its remaining bears in sanctuaries. Practitioners of traditional medicine in Vietnam said they will cease all prescriptions that incorporate bear bile by 2020, a goal that Animals Asia tells me is on track at the year's midpoint. To ensure that these declarations of intent amount to more than just pretty public-relations statements is a formidable task. Similar measures in China, where so many more bile farms exist than in Vietnam, will be critical to the bears' welfare too.

Most readers of this book neither live in China or Vietnam nor adopt the practices of traditional medicine that sustain the market for bear bile. What's the point, then, of cultivating compassion for these bears? How can those of us so far removed possibly help with a situation that involves two Asian governments and thousands of animals over whom we have no control? Here we come again to the heart of this book: almost always there's a way to help. In Charlie's case, when he was stranded in Canyonlands National Park, I became part of his rescue team even from halfway across the country. With the bears, anyone who wishes can join in with an international team effort.

Direct action on behalf of the bears might involve sponsoring an individual rescued bear or volunteering in aid of Animals Asia. It's a contribution too just to spread the word that these bile farms exist and that a concerted campaign is under way to dismantle them. Even when it doesn't involve a shape-shifting night in the hospital as it did for me, sharing concern for the bears may bring mixed results. That "No thanks, I don't want to know" reaction—rooted in caring too much or too little, either way—will ensue from some quarters. Yet especially when it's possible to *also* share news of bears' resilience and recovery, storytelling about the bears can be powerful indeed.

A three-minute video depicts an Animals Asia team setting off by boat for the island of Ba Mun in Vietnam's Halong Bay, where two moon bears had been held for four years. The camera swings to reveal two small adjacent and barren cages. In one is the bear Simon, visibly ill, with open-wound injuries. Robinson calls him a "broken bear," lame, blind, and suffering from brain damage. Together with the second bear, a female named Sam, Simon is carried onto the boat—no easy feat to manage given the bear's weight—then ferried to the Vietnam sanctuary. Three months later, Simon died. Despite this sad outcome, think of what Simon gained through this rescue: he died surrounded by love, not alone in a dark cage as an object ripe for harvest. Sam is now, as Animals Asia says, "living for two," shy but able to explore the grassy outdoors in safety.

Cameras caught the moment when moon bear Snow, rescued in 2016 from a bile farm in Buon Ma Thuot city, invited another bear to play for the very first time at the sanctuary. Snow, who had been found by the rescue team rocking back and forth in his bile-farm cage and missing his tongue, ambles up to a bear named Poe who relaxes outdoors in a tub of water. A tangle of bear fur is the happy result, a milestone moment because play in traumatized animals is a sign of emotional recovery. Sharing these mini-films conveys the message that there *is*, after all, a good reason to learn about these bears: captivity kept secret is captivity that benefits only the bear abusers.

Compassion for faraway bears finds a meaningful outlet too when it spills over to include bears held in bad conditions closer to home. An Asiatic black bear called Dillon was held in a small concrete and steel cage for some years at a sportsmen's club in the town of Millmont in western Pennsylvania. Reporting in 2020, the *Philly Voice* online noted that Dillon had been allowed to grow to a "morbidly obese" size and suffered from shattered nerves. "He was surrounded daily by the crackling of recreational gunfire and developed nervous rocking behavior that became evident to anyone who visited him," explains reporter

Michael Tanenbaum. Dillon's situation caught the public's attention. In large part through activism efforts by PETA, he is recovering in safety at the Wild Animal Sanctuary in Keenesburg, Colorado.

Bears need cool water to thermoregulate, especially in summer. Roadside zoos that go unrecognized by the accrediting body American Association of Zoos and Aquariums (AZA) often fail to provide this basic need to their bears. In 2017 I wrote about conditions for Asian bears in an unaccredited zoo in Winchester, Virginia, and for American black bears at another such facility in Myrtle Beach, South Carolina. At that time I spoke with Mindy Babitz, captive bear welfare consultant and member of the steering committee of the AZA Bear Taxon Advisory Group. Babitz described for me the consequences for bears when they aren't permitted to carry out evolved behaviors that are key to their health and well-being: "When bears are not housed in adequate environments and not given the opportunities to express natural behaviors, frustration and stress result. Chronic frustration and stress can lead to abnormal behaviors, changes in brain chemistry, and poor health (mental and physical)."

Conditions for some US-confined bears exist, then, on an uncomfortable continuum with the bile bears held in Vietnam and China. The surprising fact of the matter is that the Animal Welfare Act in the United States includes no bear-specific regulations—nothing in the Act (excepting some regulations for polar bears) takes into account bears' species-specific needs for space and thermoregulation. Bears' brains need stimulation as much as their bodies need space in which to live as bears: these big mammals have impressive minds. Dipping into the science of bear behavior can be very motivating for animal lovers who want to act on behalf of bears in need.

Wild bears sense, store in memory, and then recall the location of foods across a wide region—part of the reason campers and other visitors to wilderness areas, like national parks, are instructed to keep food stored away from a bear's reach. Animals' intelligence should not be the sole reason for our concern, yet it is painful to imagine the degree to which captivity weighs on such sensitive animals. Working with three sibling American black bears at Alabama's Mobile Zoo, males Brutus and Dusty and female Bella, psychologists Jennifer Vonk and Michael J. Beran showed that bears have a degree of numerical competence. Participating in the experiment only when they wished to do so, the bears used their noses to press a touch screen to solve problems set up on a computer cart. In the process they distinguished sets of items based on both surface area and number. This result, the authors say, matches in some ways the performance of monkeys. (Bears are far less social than monkeys, making this result—if confirmed in testing of more bears on more cognitive tasks—a thorn in the side of hypotheses that link a high degree of social grouping with increased intelligence.)

In her book *Smiling Bears*, Else Poulsen describes reasoning behavior by Sissy, a twenty-seven-year-old polar bear at the Detroit Zoo. The context in this case was not carnivore mathematics but instead how to communicate across species lines to bring about a pleasurable soaking bath. Sissy was recovering from dental surgery that had left her somewhat sore; Poulsen offered her some water with a hose in order to distract and soothe her. As the water streamed out, Sissy began to do things that puzzled Poulsen. "Staring into my eyes," Poulsen writes, "she slapped her right front leg with her left paw. . . . Without dunking her paw in the water stream she rubbed her front right leg with her left paw, showing me a washing motion. She completed the demonstration by again slapping her right leg." Poulsen aimed the water stream on the bear's right foot, but Sissy slapped her leg again. At this point the bear's intent became clear: Poulsen hosed the bear's leg, Sissy washed herself, and from that point forward, Sissy would slap the part of her body she wished for Poulsen to hose down. That action by Sissy again suggests a bear-to-primate comparison: to me it sounds akin to the ways chimpanzees and gorillas may gesture to their social partner by indicating a specific part of their body at which they want an action (grooming, for instance) to unfold.

Poulsen worked with bears at two North American zoos: Calgary in Canada and Detroit in the US. Zoo staff baked nutritious cakes for nursing bear moms, offered watermelons and herring-filled barrels as enrichment items, encouraged seasonal denning by providing enticing material, and planned safe and smart bear-to-bear introductions. But Poulsen's positive experience with the treatment of zoo-confined bears, as we have seen, is far from universal. Roadside zoos provide little, if any, of this loving care (see chapter 4).

Bears, then, point us back to my theme: opportunities for compassionate action exist where harms exist. When we "think bear," what first pops into our head may involve the majesty of wild grizzlies, or suburban encounters as bears are pushed closer to our homes, or even sports teams and Smokey the Bear animations. Bile-bear realities take us further. If we don't support the incarceration of bears for the painful extraction of their bile, can we apply our concern also to bears in trouble elsewhere? To what new destinations may that widening circle of compassion lead? The possibilities that I explain in the next five chapters for improving animals' lives bring me an enduring sense of hope.

*   *   *

Originally I had thought to center the concept of empathy for animals at the heart of this book. Yet as I brushed up on the discourse about empathy, both popular and scholarly, I found it to be more chaotic than useful. On the one hand, there's a co-opting of "empathy," a deploying of the term as a cultural meme that doesn't fit with serious reflection and an intent to work for change. I've done it myself—tossed off "I feel your pain" to a friend, uttered with a light inflection and followed by a rapid move to the next topic of conversation. On the other hand, empathy workshops and self-help books exhort us to walk a mile in another's shoes in ways that may start to feel onerous. If we take that walk, the story goes, we can become better people, as if empathy were mostly about moral self-improvement through a series of "shoulds." Too often empathy becomes stripped of meaning, or commodified and weaponized as primarily about our failings.

Further, the scholarly literature on empathy is deep and complex and has attached quite different meanings to the term. Empathy is often defined by psychologists as the ability to understand and share the feelings of another. Each of us probably has had memorable experiences that match up with that definition. Years ago when Sarah stepped onto stage to sing their first soprano solo in their high school's production of *Fiddler on the Roof*, knowing that they were nervous, I became nervous too. "Butterflies in the stomach" was way too gentle a zoological term for the force let loose in my torso. Fiercely swooping fruit bats, maybe? Manta rays leaping around in ocean waves? Sarah sang beautifully, and eventually I relaxed. More prolonged was the parental empathy exhibited by Olympic gymnast Aly Raisman's mother and father as they watched her compete during the 2016 games in Rio de Janeiro. Now-famous video clips published by NBC on August 12 of that year show the pair's outsize reactions in split screen with Raisman's floor, uneven bar, and balance-beam routines, and are equal parts amusing and excruciating to watch.

CULTIVATING COMPASSIONATE ACTION 19

Other perspectives on empathy, though, take up not just *feeling with* but also *acting with or acting for* others. One framework that resonates with me is Lori Gruen's writing about "entangled empathy" as a way of attuning to the highly specific needs and desires of other individuals, whether people or animals, in order to improve our ethical relating with them. If we aim only to walk in the shoes of others, Gruen says, we risk diverting close attention from differences between our ways of being in the world and others' ways. We thus risk missing what matters most to see. In *Entangled Empathy: An Alternative Ethic for Our Relationships with Animals*, Gruen notes that "many, perhaps most, current discussions of what we owe animals fail to attend to the particularity of individual animal lives and the very different sorts of relationships we are in with them. . . . Theories that generalize over differences will obscure the distinct experiences of others." The ways in which we may relate with a chicken won't be the same as the ways in which we relate with a chipmunk or a chimpanzee, she points out. Gruen intends for entangled empathy to bring about improved lives for animals through acutely attentive ethics.

Pick up psychologist Paul Bloom's book *Against Empathy: The Case for Rational Compassion* and you'll find a remarkably different perspective: "If we want to be good and caring people, if we want to make the world a better place, then we are better off without empathy." In its place Bloom would like to see "conscious, deliberate reasoning," because empathizing with another individual sometimes leads us to make choices that hurt rather than help, bringing about an outcome completely opposite to our best intentions. It causes us to weight what is in front of us, happening now, more heavily than what may happen some years down the road.

Clearly, "empathy" carries a lot of baggage these days. Endeavoring to bring about positive change for animals is the goal that motivates my writing. While some perspectives on empathy take up a similar goal, others do not. By contrast, "compassionate action" explicitly centers that goal. For my purposes in this book, "compassionate action" is the better, less confusing term.

* * *

When we connect emotionally with others and wish to help them, it's possible to end up in an emotional landscape of anxiety or severe sadness. In *Phoenix Zones*, Ferdowsian explains that "our bodies absorb the visceral costs of compassion in an imperfect world." I have wondered: How well can any of us function if we take on others' pain every day, including that felt by animals, especially if we can't alleviate it right away? Can our bodies, and the mental well-being that is integrally connected with our bodies, withstand that kind of cost? Is this why people who responded with interest and concern to the story of Charlie's night lost in the Utah wilderness shut down when told about the bile bears?

As I began to work years ago in animal-rescue networks, the scope of the problem became clearer. People who devote themselves to compassionate action for animals may burn out or experience symptoms of severe depression. The *Canadian Veterinary Journal* reports statistics that suggest the rate of suicide in the veterinary profession is close to twice that of the dental profession, more than twice that of the medical profession, and four times the rate in the general population. These figures are staggering. They don't prove a causal link; no basis exists for a claim that veterinary professionals kill themselves at an alarming rate *because* they take on suffering that is related to their life's work with animal patients. The explanation may involve—instead of or in addition to—risks for mental illness in people who choose to enter the profession, or some other factor altogether. Yet the increase in risk compared with that for doctors is at the very least suggestive. Burnout and fatigue among animal-rescue workers is now increasingly recognized as a serious problem, in part due to what writer Kasia Galazaka describes as the "almost Sisyphean nature of animal rescue." The work is simply never done: there's always another animal to help, equally as deserving as the last one already helped, and equally unable to help herself in a human world without human intervention.

To think that we can cultivate compassionate action for animals in ways that never induce heartache would be wonderful, but that is just a dream. For most of us most of the time, I think, the joy outstrips the sad moments, and that may be enough. Helping animals can overwhelmingly enrich our lives, bringing us closer to understanding the other creatures all around us and to the knowledge that we are doing our part to make things better for them. That it doesn't come without risk is a reality that I want to keep in mind, yet it's just as important to recognize the fantastic lift that helping animals may bring into our lives. Rescuing dozens of cats over the years—some of whom you'll meet in the next chapter—has added immeasurably to my own good life, as has joining with other activists to work on behalf of animals thought to be food or confined to laboratories. I know well the "happiness lift" that follows in the wake of helping animals and can't imagine life without it.

Let's begin now a journey of cultivating compassionate action, right in our own homes. Surely you have always secretly longed to live peaceably together with spiders—haven't you? That's where we will begin.

Author's Note, June 2020

Rarely has the intertwined fate of human and other animal populations been brought home to the world as vividly as during the COVID-19 pandemic. This 2020 statement from the US Centers for Disease Control (CDC) makes clear the animal origins of the virus: "The SARS-CoV-2 virus is a betacoronavirus, like MERS-CoV and SARS-CoV. All three of these viruses have their origins in bats. . . . Early on, many of the patients at the epicenter of the outbreak in Wuhan, Hubei Province, China had some link to a large seafood and live animal market, suggesting animal-to-person spread. Later, a growing number of patients reportedly did not have exposure to animal markets, indicating person-to-person spread." An origin in bats doesn't mean that direct transmission from bats to humans necessarily occurred; just as SARS-CoV was transmitted from bats to palm civets to humans, the COVID virus most likely jumped to humans through an intermediate animal host, perhaps pangolins.

I completed the writing of *Animals' Best Friends* about six months after COVID-19 outbreaks initially took hold in China and began to spread globally. At certain points in the following chapters I mention implications of this pandemic for human–wildlife interactions, human food consumption, and the fate of animals used for invasive experimentation in laboratories. Even though it's too early to offer a full assessment of what this pandemic means for human–animal relationships in the long term, this much is already clear: enacting compassion for animals will include paying close attention to this and other emerging viruses for decades to come.

2
Animals at Home

About ten years ago, I walked into the bathroom at home one evening and saw on the floor, at the baseboard near our sink cabinet, two enormous spiders. They simply sat there, side by side; I felt that they were staring at me. An irrational feeling? Maybe, though astronomers and arachnologists later teamed up to announce that some spiders' vision is so terrifically acute that they can see the moon.

Whether they could make me out or not, my coming upon these two startled me so badly—their size, their stillness, their side-by-side doubling—that I fetched a shoe and beat the spiders to death. Then I flushed them down the toilet.

This incident has stayed with me because I am ashamed of what I did. With the exception of mosquitoes, ticks, termites, cockroaches, and fleas, not to mention full-scale invasions of ants (which we have experienced) and bedbugs (which we have not), our house is a rescue zone for insects and arachnids. Over the years we have borne innumerable spiders out of the house and into the yard, each one riding along in the designated "rescue glass" topped by a piece of paper. When a tiny animal risks becoming a cat's protein snack or accidentally flattened under resident bipeds' feet, a rescue instinct kicks in. Except it's not really an instinct at all, because I wasn't born with it.

When I grew up in New Jersey in the 1960s, no family I knew would bother to save any bug, and mine didn't either. At the sight of any sizable insect or spider, I blanched and would shriek for my father, who would arrive with a jolly if ironic "Great hunter!" exclamation, then squash the tiny being in a tissue. It was all a good joke, with never a thought spent on the lives lost. I'm not proud of that either, but it was a different time; my childhood love for my cats and dogs connected up in no way with spiders. My mother visibly feared spiders and insects, declaring them dirty, and so to me they seemed akin to tiny, unknowable, and (worse yet) unpredictable miniature aliens. In terms of who was welcome to coexist with us in the house, spiders dwelled on the far wrong side of the delight–disgust divide.

Decades later, I weaponized my shoe against those side-by-side spiders in my own home on an evening when I was alone in the house and spooked by them. Yet I did know better by that time; I had learned. That's why I am ashamed. Before taking action I didn't pause to attempt a species ID, but I knew the spiders weren't black widows, the sole venomous spider native to Virginia—the size, shape, and color were all wrong for that. Brown recluse spiders, a species whose bites may cause tissue damage and subsequent infections, are rare in Virginia, and I doubt that two showed up together in my house. Probably the pair were wolf spiders, the largest in Virginia measuring up to 1.5 inches in body size and 4 inches in leg span. (Not truly "enormous," then, but they loomed large to me in the moment.)

In her book *The Chicken Chronicles*, the great American writer Alice Walker describes the "automatic" state we may fall into when confronted with insects or spiders. "In 'automatic,'" Walker writes, "bugs of any kind are suspect," because we have been trained to associate them (as I was) with germs, disease, and trouble of any number of kinds. This training may even be evolutionary in nature. Avoiding venomous spiders, and some insects and snakes too, may have aided our primate ancestors' survival and reproduction. But any basic biologically based avoidance impulse like this is greatly magnified by cultural learning, as occurred in my childhood home. The end result is that many harmless beings are met with our outsize dread.

Walker, too, killed a spider one day. She rushed at one small creature and scooped her up into the toilet in one fluid motion, believing her to be a cockroach. Too late did Walker realize, as the water swirled in the toilet, that it was instead a female spider with her young attached. Once released from "automatic," Walker was seized by regret. If she had it to do over, she realized, she would have placed the mother and baby spiders outside on the grass.

As it turns out, the "house to yard rescue" plan isn't always as spider-friendly as it's intended to be. In *Dr. Eleanor's Book of Common Spiders*, Christopher M. Buddle and Eleanor Spicer Rice say that it's not necessarily the best outcome for the spider. What if it is much hotter or colder outdoors in the yard than the ambient temperature in the house? More fundamentally—this was the eye-opener for me—the great outdoors may not be the spider's natural home at all: "Remember, many spiders found in our homes are actually in their preferred habitat already."

Now there's a goal for compassionate action: to transform our homes into natural spider zones! But of course not all of us are arachnophiles. It may help to think of dual benefits to sparing the lives of nonvenomous spiders in our homes: we save a life with value all its own, and we add value to a small ecosystem. Spiders may hoover up the pesky, germy insects that we don't much want around (and more on those in a moment). Entomologist Matt Bertone puts it this way: "Killing a spider doesn't just cost the arachnid its life, it may take an important predator out of your home."

Spiders, unlike insects, have two body segments (not three)

and eight legs (not six). Small appendagelike pedipalps extrude from their heads with which they sense the world and move objects around. Between thirty-five and forty-five thousand spider species live in the world today. That's a good guess, at least; paradoxically, for all our high-tech science, no one really knows the number. Writing for the *New York Times* in 2018, the biologist and good friend of ants E. O. Wilson estimates that about 20 percent of animal and plant species on Earth are known to us, leaving 80 percent as yet undiscovered. "It is fair to call the Earth a little-known planet," Wilson declares.

What is known about spiders tells us that their behavior is far more complex than that spider-fearing Jersey-girl self of my past could have imagined. Here's one startling finding: Spiders can count. That is, some spiders can count. A research team led by biologist Rafael L. Rodriguez disturbed the webs of wild orb-web spiders (*Nephila clavipes*) in Costa Rica and found that these spiders rank among the animals (like bears) who are in some way mathematically endowed.

Nephila spiders are sit-and-wait predators who affix prey to the hub of their web, attaching it securely by means of a silk line. Film buffs may remember the scene in the original 1958 *The Fly* where a man, transmuted into a fly and caught fast in a spiderweb, screams for help as the spider approaches with the intent of making him into a meal. Recalling this image, we may feel sympathy for Nephila's wrapped-up prey and at the same time recognize that Nephila has to eat, after all. Whenever a new prey animal is ensnared, the wrapping-up process continues, resulting in what Rodriguez et al. term a multi-item "larder."

The larder becomes a site of experimental intervention when scientists work to see if these spiders have a capacity for counting, or numerosity. Going in, Rodriguez and his team already knew some significant facts. If prey items are removed from the web by other spiders or even by the wind, the Nephila commence a search: they move about and tug on the web, exploring for a longer period when they have lost larger individual prey items or multiple prey items. Some researchers have begun to talk about such behavior as an "extended cognition," meaning that spiders don't just build webs but may also *think with* webs. This notion makes sense to me intuitively. Right now as I type these words onto a computer screen, I am *thinking with* my laptop, attending and responding to how the words appear on the screen. I can easily imagine a spider's active manipulation of her web to gain sensory feedback as she goes about her day.

Crafting a new research question, the team focused on "how the quantity of prey is represented in the memory," as they put it in an article in *Animal Cognition*. Specifically, the researchers wanted to see if spiders responded to experimental larder alterations in ways that indicated they had counted and remembered what existed in the larder. Or could there be a simpler reason? For example, if spiders searching their web for removed prey come across plant debris on the web and stop searching, that would indicate they had not held in their minds a number of prey items. If instead they move on and keep searching, that would be evidence for memory and counting.

A supply of mealworm larvae and a steady hand were the tools needed to carry out this research on adult female spiders. In the first experiment called the "prey count" test, the spiders were allowed to accumulate a larder. The biologists then stepped in to empty it entirely by removing the whole collection, either one, two, or four prey items. In the second experiment called the "prey size" test, the spiders obtained a single prey item of either small, intermediate or large size and then that item was removed. (Are you conjuring up a somewhat poignant image of a spider who suddenly realizes all her labor is for naught and her larder is empty? If so, welcome to my brain.)

The spiders searched the web longer when their pillaged larders had contained more prey items or larger single prey items, and searching increased more steeply as prey counts went up. Thus they gave special weight to prey numerosity. The specifics of their behavior too point to a capacity for numerosity. The spiders don't, for instance, get distracted by plant debris on the web. This evidence taken together, Rodriguez et al. write, "considerably expands the taxonomic and ecological diversity of numerosity in animals, with this report being the first for a spider other than jumping spiders (family Salticidae)."

Here then is a groundbreaking finding achieved without plucking animals from their home territories or harming them in any way (other than disturbing briefly their prey consumption process). The team's focus on these spiders' natural behavior in their Costa Rican home environment strikes me as highly ethical. And the mention of numerosity in Salticidae? My pulse quickened.

Jumping spiders could be emissaries to all the world's arachnophobes. For one thing, they are cute. If you doubt me on this, check out the Facebook group "Jumping Spiders (Salticidae)." The group is officially a closed one, but that just means an administrator's approval is required to sign up; I was readily approved and welcomed to join the other fans (now numbering over 23,000) who share, or just enjoy, photographs and stories about jumping spiders and their behaviors. One day we were treated to photographs of a light-colored jumping spider with splashes of elegant gold around the eyes. Group member Shaham Tamir wrote, "This cute small jumper showed up in my kitchen today and was photographed on a teapot lid. Photographed in Israel." Often these spiders do just show up spontaneously—in the kitchen, out in the yard—and other times they are purchased from spider suppliers. Many of them are named as pets: I've "met" Ignatz, Missy, Phineas, Annakin, and Khalessi online. Sometimes a photograph is posted of a newly encountered spider with request for a taxonomic ID. Participants often debate what species the little one may be according to his or her appearance and geographic location.

Mating displays of males are captivating to watch, even if you're not a female jumping spider. Individuals of two taxonomic groups (Habronattus jumping spiders of North America and Maratus "peacock" jumping spiders of Australia) can see bright colors, and the bodies of some of the males are splashed with vivid reds, purples, yellows, and oranges. Through an arresting combination of color and movement, these males dance to attract the attention of a female. A three-minute video of an Australian peacock spider wooing a mate conveys the flavor: The little (think ladybug-sized) male sits calmly on a surface, then vigorously thrusts one leg on each side up in the air. He moves his legs at clean angles like a baton-bearing attendant flagging an aircraft in to the gate, all while shaking his abdomen flag, a body part that's basically a rainbow flag of red, blue, black, and orange. The rhythm of the dance, at times smooth and other times jerky, is a choreography of spider hopes and desires.

*　*　*

Only months after joining the Facebook group, I was perched on a green lawn chair in my yard, enjoying a book on a summer afternoon. I noticed a tiny eight-legged body rushing back and forth on one chair arm. A closer look confirmed my suspicion: my first up-close sighting of a jumping spider! I took admiring photographs just as I do when spotting a fascinating bird or mammal. No mating dance was forthcoming since, after all, I was the only female around. Still, this encounter made for a breakthrough in my ability to recognize a small package of arachnid beauty right on my home turf.

Jumping spiders are smart. We already know they have

a handle on numeracy. Their intelligence combines with a uniquely sharp visual-spatial acuity; that the light of the moon may reach their eyes just delights me no end. Their four pairs of specialized eyes allow depth perception and color vision too. These characteristics make them good experimental subjects for studying invertebrate visual cognition in the lab. Here I risk the appearance of waffling. Didn't I just say that research in spiders' natural environments makes for a preferable ethics? The research I'm about to describe takes a 180-degree turn from an approach of noninterference, yet as far as I can tell causes little to no harm to spiders beyond the disorientation of relocating them to confinement. Biologists Tina Peckmezian and Phillip W. Taylor first cooled female jumping spiders in a refrigerator (to make them calm), then affixed small magnets on their bodies. The next day they placed the spiders on a 3D-printed spherical treadmill in front of a display screen. At this point, the spiders' visual world altered: on the screen they saw projected a virtual-reality (VR) environment, one that they could proceed to walk through. (An arachnid equivalent of the film *The Matrix*?)

The VR world in question was what's called a closed-loop VR, meaning that the spiders' own movements caused contingent changes in what happened next on the screen. The projected scenes were set against a flat ground plane that was made to look like tree bark in both texture and color.

Right away it became clear that the spiders acted pretty much in their natural ways in the VR world, as measured against their behavior in the RW (real world). In one experiment, for instance, spiders in RW encountered one of two conditions: either a beacon (a red pillar or green cross) placed behind their nest site, or no beacon. Once put in VR, the spiders with beacon experience made more visits to the beacons—which were positioned in the same place relative to their own orientation as had been the case in RW. They also spent more time near the beacons than spiders who hadn't first learned about beacons in RW. The spiders had, in other words, transferred successfully their learned association between beacons and nest sites from one type of environment to the other.

Some people keep spiders as pets, as we have seen with the jumping spiders. Caretakers of home-dwelling tarantulas are equally passionate about their larger charges. Still, I'd say it's safe to wager that most of us don't first think "Spiders!" when we are prompted to consider animals in the home. Here they are with us, though, spinning a web in a bedroom corner, popping up unexpectedly in the bathroom, or joining us on outdoor lawn furniture. These multi-eyed and -legged bodies in our homes as well as the wild and laboratories carry a lesson: the more we grasp how animals negotiate their worlds, the less alien they may seem to us. That hope doesn't mean we should seek (or impose) human patterns onto other species. Nor does it imply that it's necessarily fair to spiders to interrupt their lives, cool them in refrigerators, and ask them to hang out on treadmills to satisfy our curiosity. Yet, the benefits of relatively noninvasive experiments like the ones I have described here may be considerable. From grasping their results may emerge a greater awareness that the quashing of a spider by wadding one up in a tissue—or hitting one with a shoe—extinguishes a life that, at some level, was lived thoughtfully.

Happily, I'm come a long way since that spider-killing incident in the bathroom. No longer do I kill wolf spiders who appear in the house, and I thoroughly enjoy observing spiders outdoors. Late in the summer of 2019, a large female orb-weaver spider (genus *Argiope*) constructed a web right outside my writing-study window. I became attached not only to a daily practice, gazing from both sides of the window to observe her hunting and web-repair skills, but indeed to the spider herself.

I named her Portia because I had just read *Children of Time* and *Children of Ruin*, the astoundingly good science-fiction novels by Adrian Tchaikovsky in which a sentient spider called Portia plays a major role in the world-building action. With family and friends, I shared pictures of "my" Portia on social media and announced with excitement to them the appearance of her egg sac at summer's end. This event presaged her disappearance and apparent death; I missed her presence for many weeks. My affection for Portia went wholly unrequited, of course, yet the very act of feeling it was meaningful for me.

A year before, a spider was memorialized in a beautiful piece written by Avi Selk for the *Washington Post*, based on research by zoologists Barbara Main and Leanda Mason. In an enchanting way, Selk traces forty-three years of one small life. Spider 16, as she was named, was birthed in a burrow under an acacia tree in southwestern Australia's North Bungulla Reserve. When she was six months old, her mother unsealed the silk-sealed tunnel to the burrow, and out ventured 16. The likelihood is that most of her two dozen or so siblings died in the blazing heat or in a predator's jaws, but 16 didn't. She dug a circle down into the soil and, in beautiful intergenerational continuity, lined it with a silk covering hinged on one side like a door. (This type of spider, *Gaius villosus*, is one of the "trapdoor" spider species.) She added an array of sticks around that door, a platform across which her future insect prey would walk and alert her by vibrations to their presence. Over the ensuing years, 16 enlarged the burrow but stayed rooted to that spot. "For as long as she lived," Selk writes, "this would be her only home."

Like all adult female *Gaius villosus*, 16 emerged to mate, then retreated to her home to lay and shelter her eggs; in the earth's depth, the mom and spiderlings-to-be could ride out droughts and fires. We can't know how many spiderlings 16 sent out into the world or how many survived. Sometime in 2016, Mason discovered the burrow empty for the first time: 16 was gone. Judging from the hole in the silk door, most probably she had been killed by a parasitic wasp. As far as we are aware, no spider has ever lived longer than the forty-three years of 16's life.

When I shared Selk's piece on Twitter, it was shared and re-shared in a rippling effect across my network of animal, book, and science people. The spider called 16 touched people's emotions in a big way. Even though she is known by a number rather than a name, 16's individuality shines through and invites us to adopt a new vocabulary in talking about spider lives.

My enchantment with 16's life story loomed large in part because, at the time of her media stardom, I had just weeks before visited the *Art and Science of Arachnids* exhibit at the Virginia Living Museum in Newport News not far from my home. At this facility, dually accredited as a zoo and a museum, staff biologists had the year before released a ninety-pound loggerhead sea turtle back to the ocean in cooperation with a North Carolina aquarium. The turtle, named Coco, had been taken as a youngster from the wild and raised at the Living Museum as part of the Sea Turtle Loan Program, in which weak or ailing juveniles are raised in captivity. Coco, after two years at the museum, was released as a healthy animal back into the Atlantic Ocean. This modification of the traditional zoo approach to displaying animals is admirable, and the Living Museum takes in other special-needs animals too. The ones I met on a guided tour by curatorial director George Mathews in 2017 included former pets like an otter who had been almost completely confined to a household bathtub and a bobcat whose tendons had been severed; two red foxes rescued from a roadside zoo, where they dwelled only on concrete; a great blue heron with a deformed bill that made eating difficult unless food was prepared; and two bald eagles injured when they flew into power lines and a building, respectively. None of these animals could safely live on their own in nature.

The arachnid exhibit, too, aimed to help animals by showcasing beautiful spiders and information about them designed to override a knee-jerk "Gross!" or fearful response. As I wandered the small (some *too* small) display cases, the vibrant pink of the Mexican red knee tarantula and the striking patterns of the Brazilian red and white tarantula wowed my eyes. A young boy exclaimed excitedly to his family about one spider he observed intently for long minutes; during a half hour's visit I heard only one or two "Ewwww" comments. Text panels offered facts on arachnid conservation, arachnids in medicine and as food, and even arachnids in film and literature, folklore, and culture. With the exception of one panel about spider silk production ("spiders use silk for housing, web construction, defense capturing prey [*sic*], protecting eggs, and traveling"), no discussion of spider behavior was on offer. This was an unfortunate gap. We need a new way to talk about the tinier beings among us.

* * *

If we endeavor to acquire a new vocabulary for the Earth's invertebrates, and from it grow new paths for compassionate action, what might happen next? If we start with spider appreciation and protection, are we poised on the proverbial slippery slope? Is ant rescue in our homes important too? On the very first page of the book I wrote about animal grief, I invoke ants as a primary counterexample to the expression of emotion in nonhumans. Sure, ants may respond to their companions' death, but they do so simply, instinctually, I wrote, without learning and without emotion. They collect a dead individual's body and move it to a sort of ant graveyard much the same way a robot would. In fact, if you paint a healthy ant with oleic acid, its companions will come and carry it away too, even as the one borne away struggles to get free: the oleic acid is a hard-and-fast trigger for the grave-yard carry.

Research published in 2018 by ecologist Erik Frank reveals, however, a caretaking complex in African Matabele ants that re-flects a commitment on the part of the ants to tend their group-mates' wounds—at least if the injuries aren't too severe. Frank spent three years doing field experiments in Ivory Coast in West Africa and saw that when these ants go out en masse to hunt ter-mites, some individuals inevitably meet up with the termites' jaws and lose a leg in the process. Through his work in the field supplemented by a phase in which the ants were brought into the laboratory, Frank discovered that if ants lose only one or two legs, they are able to assume a stand position and signal for help, a process aided by the release of pheromone chemicals. When this happens, they are carried home and their wounds cleaned by their companions. "If you can stand up you are still useful," Frank told the *Guardian* newspaper. The injured ants even help their rescuers by tucking in their remaining legs, making for an easier rescue carry. When ants are missing more legs, they are unable to signal properly and are left behind to die.

The *Guardian* ran its story about this research with a head-line about "paramedic ants" and a valorizing lead about the "victors" in battle hauling their wounded "back to base for life-saving treatment." Yet Frank makes crystal clear that this sophisticated carry-and-rescue system is not a cognitive one. That sets it solidly apart from the kind of spider cognition that I've described earlier, when individuals make choices that are thought-based rather than triggered by inborn biological pro-grams.

Still though, wound-tending in ants! Why should the ability to think through a given situation be a litmus test for animals worthy of compassionate action? The challenging questions pile on one after the other. If ants rescue each other, wouldn't that be the least our species could do for theirs? Shouldn't we make the same effort for them as I'm recommending for spiders?

Here I must come clean: I am not willing to mount an individual-by-individual rescue effort when ants invade my house, trailing in their hundreds through a room to converge on some dropped bit of food. The logistics make ant rescue unwieldy, to say the least. Nor can I bring myself to follow E. O. Wilson's advice to feed ants who show up in the kitchen. In his memoir *Tales from the Ant World*, Wilson recommends offering ant-sized portions of honey, sugar water, chopped nuts, or canned tuna to house ants, then "reflecting upon what you see" when a scout ant rushes back toward the nest with the food. On the contrary, I endeavor to ant-proof our house as much as possible, sweeping up tiny sweet lures from the floor. I'm also unwilling to spare the lives of disease-bearing insects like fleas, ticks, and mosquitoes. According to UNICEF, three thousand children worldwide die from mosquito-borne malaria every day, and over 300 million people annually suffer from its effects. Regarding Lyme disease, the CDC reports that in the United States alone, around three hundred thousand cases occur per year. Adding in the toll taken by other insect-borne diseases ranging from Zika to dengue fever, even with the availability of modern antibiotics it's clear that there's little room for sentimentality when it comes to insects as vectors of disease. I have suffered with two unpleasant episodes of tick-borne disease in the US and with one bout of malaria in Kenya. Those experiences contributed to my conclusion that at times compassion for insects must be superseded by public-health measures.

Drawing a line between those who deserve rescue and those who don't may be more enlightened than my childhood practice of consigning all insects and spiders to instant death. Still, it remains open to charges of hypocrisy. Ants, after all, don't belong in the disease-vector group (on occasion they may transmit food-borne illness, but the risk usually is low). The stance I advocate for here favors human convenience as well as health over a thorough commitment to compassionate action for living beings. This point will surface again and again throughout this book in the course of considering animals in different contexts: a goal of compassionate action for animals needn't be pushed to a point of purity, such that anything less than perfection becomes a failure. How many of us realistically could emulate the Jains of India, who historically extended the principle of ahimsa, nonviolence, to each and every living creature? Jains devoted themselves wholeheartedly to their goal, moving with extreme awareness and care through the world because they wished never to harm an insect even by stepping upon one by mistake. This stance is impractical today, to say the least. In its place, we can set ourselves a task that is big in aspiration and realistic in scope: an aim to minimize harm when and where we can, including when we host insects and arachnids in our homes.

*   *   *

When jumping spiders, or any spiders, are kept in species-appropriate enclosures and handled with care, they make good pets. If captivity is harmful full stop, then certainly, confining spiders is harmful. But all-or-nothing arguments are spectacularly useless in deciding cases of animal confinement (see chapter 4). When chimpanzees or capuchin monkeys, or lions or tigers, are kept as pets for private amusement, it's a recipe for catastrophe. The well-being of large-brained mammals like these cannot be addressed in home environments, and the risk of injury or worse to their caretakers is high. Keeping spiders in a spacious enclosure with access to species-typical food and mates, or simply allowing spiders to roam around the basement or bedroom freely, does not compare.

Into the yawning gap between monkey-keeping and spider-keeping falls the keeping of pets like dogs and cats. Over one hundred million more pets than people live in the United States, and these dogs, cats, rabbits, fish, and assorted other creatures bring daily companionship, and sometimes much more. In her memoir *How to Be a Good Creature*, Sy Montgomery calls her border collie Tess a "lifetime dog," an animal in whose company you feel right and happy, an animal with whom you share intense mutual attunement. After Tess died, Montgomery never stopped missing her and yet eventually came to feel the same rightness and happiness when she was with Sally and Thurber, border collies who came into her life at later periods. Our companion animals, Montgomery writes, "enlarge our hearts. They leave us a greater capacity for love." The joy of sharing life with animals we love is hard to do without, once it becomes as central to us as food and shelter.

Given my long involvement with cat rescue, I can't help but bring in cats here. Can animals who evolved as hunters of moving prey be truly content when confined indoors? Do catnip mice, or laser-pointer dots and moving iPAD images that can be chased but never caught, meet their needs? What pros and cons inform a discussion of keeping cats indoors instead of allowing them to roam? How should the welfare of birds and wildlife, including small mammals, be factored into this discussion? Through contemplation of these questions, I have come to experience a fresh arc of compassion for cats and also for their prey.

If binaries ruled the world, being a "cat person" or a "bird person" would amount to the only choices, and I would land squarely in the feline camp. Cats festoon our house and yard like exquisite works of art in an indoor-outdoor sculpture garden. They rest in a sun patch, hiss throughout an argument with a coresident cat, or lazily play with a "fish kicker," the salmon-shaped toy that's hot in our house this season. Living indoors with us are extroverted "greeter cat" Nicholas Longtail, sweet-natured Flame, whip-smart and "freakishly strong" (says our veterinarian) Marie, shy Diana, and even shyer Bootsie. All but Bootsie had been abandoned at the site of a feral cat colony two miles from our house; their early-life experiences remain opaque to us. Bootsie's history we partially know, and it takes my breath away every time I contemplate it.

Charlie and I first met Bootsie at our local spay-neuter clinic, where he hunkered down under a thick pad inside his litter box. Only two frightened eyes peeped out. All his life of ten years, Bootsie had lived alongside his mother and brother with a human family. When the family's circumstances changed, all three animals were turned in to a shelter. Assessing Bootsie alone of the trio as shy to the point of evident distress, shelter workers separated him from his mother and brother. He was sent on to the quieter clinic in hopes that there he might calm. This plan, Charlie and I could plainly see, wasn't working. Separated both from his human companions and from his mom and sibling, Bootsie was grieving a double loss.

For me, his situation was too much to bear. Just weeks before, my mother had died at the age of eighty-eight. I was feeling sad and disoriented in the way that even middle-aged adult children may feel orphaned when all at once they no longer have a living parent. Immediately I felt a bond with Bootsie. Charlie and I brought him home with the intention of working with him in order to gain his trust. Eventually, we figured, he would relax somewhat, and we would then put him up for adoption. At first we confined him to my writing study. Day by day, Bootsie ventured out a little farther from his lair under the bed, receptive to our hushed words and gentle stroking of his fur. As it turned out, the path toward adoption was straightforward, because we soon enough realized what was inevitable all along. *We* became the adopters; he was ours permanently. Bootsie and I grieved together, and gradually recovered together too.

These days, Bootsie's favorite things include food treats between meals, sleeping in sun patches stretched out at full length, batting little plastic jingly balls around the house in wild trajectories, and kneading industriously on the laps of the three people he trusts: Charlie and me daily, and Sarah when they come home to visit. Even we scare him, unintentionally, if we make sudden movements or when we alter his feeding routine in some way; back under furniture he goes until he feels safe again. Traces of trauma live on close to the surface in Bootsie, and that may be the way it will always be. Most of the time, though, he's a content and affectionate cat.

Four more cats reside outdoors in our backyard enclosure, a big grassy area penned in on all sides. A two-story wooden shelter and large shade bushes to explore (and in which to hide) make this space a comfortable one for D.T., Daniel, Dexter, and Kayley, who allow us occasional touches when they are in the mood. By the time these cats came to us, having been abandoned in one way or another, none could be socialized for home living. Our tenth cat is Ivan, our single free-roamer. Following a memorable attempt to enclose him, which failed when he became a panicked ball of slashing canines and claws inside the enclosure, he spends the great majority of his hours lounging in our yard, and during cold nights, nestled in blankets in a room next to our garage. There's no getting around the fact, though, that Ivan saunters through neighboring land at will.

Each of these cats is spayed or neutered, and each is part of our family, though the indoor cats are more intimately integrated with our everyday lives. The ashes of other cats, loved equally in their day, reside in wooden boxes on the mantel in our den; bones of others rest outdoors beneath the ground in a small burial area adjacent to the enclosure.

I wonder so often about these cats' inner lives. What is Marie dreaming about when, during a nap, her paws twitch and her mouth moves? What is Diana feeling when she hears a knock on our door and rushes to hide in the dark of a kitchen cabinet? Does Bootsie think about his mom and brother still?

Peruse a bookstore's shelves or a library's holdings of academic journals, and it's evident that scientific wisdom about cat cognition and emotion lags far behind that for dogs. Dogs, many of them anyway, make agreeable participants in all kinds of social experiments situated in dog parks and canine laboratories. When thirty-six pet dogs were brought by ethology researchers Charlotte Duranton and her colleagues to an open area in Maisons-Laffitte, France, with their owners, the dogs by all accounts enjoyed the experiment as much as did the people. The experiment's protocol was straightforward. After fifteen free minutes to do whatever they liked, the owner-dog pairs participated in three testing conditions presented to them in random order: stay-still (owner didn't move for ten seconds), normal-walk (owners walked at normal speed for ten seconds), and fast-walk (owner walked fast for ten seconds).

In all cases, according to Duranton et al.'s article in *Animal Cognition*, the dogs matched their pace closely with that of their owner, even when people hustled along at an artificially speedy pace. This finding of dog-to-human attunement is notable especially because the dogs were unfettered, off leash, and thus free to do as they pleased. They received no praise or cues of encouragement from the people to whom they were attuned. Yet it was clearly important to these dogs to bring about a synchrony between their movements and those of their human partners. Intriguingly, the dogs spent more time gazing at their owners in the fast-walk condition than in the other two conditions. It's easy to imagine some of the dogs arriving at a sort of quizzical mental state: their everyday walks had routinely unfolded at a more leisurely pace, punctuated by conversational interludes when their people and other dogs' people met up along the way. Why now, they might well have wondered, the sudden rush?

It's even easier to imagine the dogs' positive emotional state, even in this mildly novel situation: they got to do cool stuff alongside the people who mattered to them. When I interviewed lead researcher Duranton for an NPR commentary about this research, she told me, "All dogs were very cooperative when participating in the study, but one dog, Izzy, was particularly enthusiastic, and when the owner was walking fast, she was running so fast and then suddenly she was rolling in the grass, out of joy."

I mention this study about canine synchronization, and these three dozen happy dogs, for a few reasons. It is one representation—see Alexandra Horowitz's wonderful books for others—of the exploding interest in how our companion animals make decisions in their everyday lives. It relieves a tiny bit of my species bias in focusing here on cats. It invites a new thought experiment: cats, with their well-earned reputation for haughty independence, wouldn't act similarly—would they?

No batch of thirty-six unleashed cats has been invited to the French outdoors, or anywhere else to my knowledge, in order to test for stride-matching with their humans. Twenty-four cats and their owners in Italy *were* asked by Isabella Merola and her colleagues to participate in a study designed to replicate an earlier project carried out by researchers with dogs. Here the main event centered on an electric fan decorated with plastic green ribbons, set up in a room with a screen at one end that hid a video camera. The screen acted as a barrier for the cats (though they could see behind it) at the only available exit from the room.

The goal of the experiment was to assess whether cats take their cues from the owners about the beribboned fan. It may be tempting to think in terms of black-and-white horror-movie images here, as if the fan *lurked* in the room radiating evil intent, but of course it was just a fan. No cats spontaneously became cartoons of themselves by arching their backs and spitting at the fan. The cats' responses, however, *did* track those of their owners. As reported in *Animal Cognition*, here's what the owners were instructed to do: First, regard the fan neutrally. Then, depending upon which group you have been assigned to, respond positively by making an approach to the fan with a happy expression and relaxed voice tone, or depart the region of the fan in a fearful manner. In either case, alternate your gaze between the fan and your cat.

Did the cats do their own thing, remaining indifferent to their owners' emotional responses? Not at all. Over three quarters (79 percent) looked between the owner and the fan during the neutral phase, when they first had to cope with this strange and uncertain situation. This percentage closely matched the results for dogs in a similar setup. From that point forward, cats whose owners responded fearfully were significantly more likely to alternate their gaze between the screen and the fan than were cats in the positive group. (Recall that the screen was the only way out of the room.) These cats also began moving earlier than cats whose owners acted relaxed and happy, perhaps related to their unease about this peculiar object that clearly was unnerving the person whom they trusted.

This study takes a bite out of species-based stereotypes. Sure, some cats may deploy affectionate head butts and dreamy gazes with their humans purely in the service of eliciting food and backrubs. They may not be devoted to us precisely in the way that dogs are: come home from a vacation and your cats may not greet you with a delighted full-body tackle. A tough kernel of truth resides in the favorite analogy of a former dean of mine at William & Mary, for whom managing the competing interests of hundreds of university faculty members was on a par with "wrangling cats." Yet a typical cat, at least according to the Merola study, uses his or her bond with a human to help figure out what's going on in an unfamiliar situation.

This response only makes sense, after all: cats are, like dogs, good learners and highly attuned to their environment. Oscar the cat became famous for his awareness of the approaching death of elderly persons in the Rhode Island nursing home where he lived; over and over again, he would curl up next to elderly people shortly before their deaths. Through this selective behavior, he correctly predicted the end of life in over one hundred cases. Sometimes cats do wear their hearts on their sleeve. Pilar, a black cat with whom I was especially close for eleven years, responded with astounding insight and care to me on days when the aftereffects of chemotherapy laid me low. One Christmas afternoon I spent alone reading and dozing on our big red couch, after a morning with Charlie and Sarah and during the hours they celebrated at a nearby family member's house. I wasn't really alone, though: Pilar lay by my side (thankfully for a reason different from Oscar's). Pilar's devotion isn't best described as doglike; she was just showing one way to be a cat.

Cats think about things, and here too researchers are exploring the details. Spiders and bears aren't the only animals to show evidence of numerosity, as evidenced by twenty-two cats in Mexico. Observed in their own homes by Oxana Banszegi and her colleagues, these cats were watched at the outset to assess their favorite food. Would they prefer raw minced beef or canned tuna, or remain loyal to the canned food that they were fed every day? Once each cat made his or her selection, that food item was incorporated into the test procedure for that individual animal. Several experiments were run to assess the cats' understanding of quantity. In order to participate, owners had to agree to deprive their cats of food for four hours before the testing commenced. (A wry note in Banszegi et al.'s *Animal Cognition* article explains that some cats could not be motivated to participate unless they lacked food for twice that long. Every species has its underachievers, or maybe better put, its defiant freethinkers.)

The experimental results show that cats generally chose the larger quantities. When it comes to preferred food, more is logically better, after all, for a hungry animal. It's the exceptions that are most intriguing to think through, including these described by the researchers: "If the difference is small (as in the 1 vs. 2 times bigger condition) they are either unable or not motivated to discriminate, and if the difference is large (as in the 1 vs. 5 times bigger condition) the choice may be determined by the animals actively rejecting the larger item." In other words, it may not always be more *enough* food to register or to matter, and sometimes "more" may carry costs greater than benefits. Cats' mental gymnastics with numbers (described more comprehensively in the journal article than I do here) cannot be understood without attending to the cats' obligate carnivory. Why, then, would cats reject five items of preferred food when the alternative was only a single piece of food? Are they the dim bulbs of the animal kingdom who don't "get" math after all? Not so: cats, Banszegi et al. suggest, may be wary of the largest items because big prey can be hard to manage, prone to fighting back, and altogether not worth the trouble. In this light, the cats' refusal to choose the bigger quantity under certain conditions shows that they are strategic and discriminating.

Here I see a bridge between research into cat behavior and issues of ethics that relate closely to compassionate action. The math at *our* house works out specifically to this: nine-tenths of our cats remain enclosed, either in the house or at a stone's throw from the house in the large outdoor pen. A 90 percent grade in responsible cat ownership is pretty darn good, but not perfect. Our enclosed cats are protected from the dogs and occasional coyotes who roam in our area (as well as modern-day predators like Priuses and SUVs). At the same time, they can't hunt birds and other wildlife. Part of the reason we enclose cats, then, is for the sake of wild animals who may become their prey. It's an issue—cat predation on wildlife and the suggestions of what to do about it—that has sparked a new way of thinking for me in the last few years. Unlike the situation with spiders, I have lived with and adored cats since childhood. Only when I became embroiled in cat rescue and the "cat wars" debates, though, did I fully grasp how crucial it is to help wildlife *and* domestic cats, including homeless cats.

In a statement that gained worldwide media attention in 2016, Peter P. Marra and Chris Santella explained how to best control cats' predation in their book *Cat Wars: The Devastating Consequences of a Cuddly Killer*: "While individual pet owners must take responsibility for their cats, it is everyone's responsibility to address the challenges of managing free-range cats to limit their impact on wildlife, both as predators and vectors of disease. From a conservation ecology perspective, the most desirable outcome seems clear—remove all free-ranging cats from the landscape by any means necessary." This provocative language riled cat advocates, including me. "By any means necessary" is a chilling phrase because it underwrites a campaign of lethal eradication.

Could my use of "chilling" be a cat lover's overreaction, based on a single quote taken out of context? Am I misconstruing what the authors mean with that "by any means necessary" language? After all, Marra and Santella go on to say that removing all cats from the landscape is "hardly practical." Yet a second passage from *Cat Wars* wipes away any lingering ambiguity: "In high-priority areas [the authors say these exist in every state] there must be zero tolerance for free-ranging cats. If the animals are trapped, they must be removed from the area and not returned. If homes cannot be found for the animals and no sanctuaries or shelters are available, there is no choice but to euthanize them. If the animals cannot be trapped, other means must be taken to remove them from the landscape—be it the use of select poisons or the retention of professional hunters."

Poisoning and shooting homeless cats is viewed by Marra and Santella as fair practice because, they say, cats kill between 1.3 billion and 4 billion birds annually in the contiguous United States alone. That estimate doesn't include small mammals and other wildlife. In the wake of these statistics, and of Marra and Santella's recommendations for killing cats, a fierce debate erupted in conservation biology that still rages. Some scientists and cat advocates insist that the statistics in *Cat Wars* are inflated well beyond reality. In Australia there's a similar debate: estimates of feral cats on that continent range from 5 million to 18 million, and estimates of wildlife killed by those feral cats varies so wildly that numbers as high as 20 billion "native animals" to 164 billion a year are bandied about.

A first step forward is to acknowledge that no one participating in this contentious discussion has access to reliable numbers when it comes to feral cat populations or impacts of these cats on wildlife. We just don't, and to base any specific eradication policy on preliminary numbers is problematic. How can compassion help? We can refuse any kind of panicked and extreme "by any means necessary" talk or, worse, policy based on it. We can recognize that feral cats are singled out as demons in this context, when roaming dogs too threaten wildlife. "Of the around 200 species said to be threatened by feral and free-ranging dogs," the BBC reported in 2019, "30 are classed as critically endangered, 71 endangered, and 87 vulnerable in the IUCN Red List of at-risk species." And we can see that it's because of human domestication practices initially, coupled with irresponsible breeding and pet-keeping practices more recently, that dogs and cats are "invasive" across varied habitats in the first place. Feral cat overpopulation occurs in large part because people abandon cats who then reproduce outdoors in uncontrolled ways.

When I wrote about this issue for NPR, ethicist William Lynn told me that the claims in *Cat Wars* amount to alarmism, especially considering that humans are the greater cause of harm to birds and other wildlife. Specifically, Lynn finds that Marra and Santella "overgeneralize the findings of specific, local studies to the world at large. In terms of logic, this involves both the fallacy of composition (all the world is like the part where cats and wildlife have been studied), and the fallacy of hasty generalization (if cats are a problem for wildlife in this place, then they must be a problem in every place)."

It's easy enough to frame this debate in a polarizing way. If we ask, do cat advocates care only for their feline friends and nothing about birds and other wildlife? or, are *Cat Wars* supporters completely lacking any compassion for cats? no way forward is likely to emerge. (See chapter 3's discussion of compassionate conservation, and the role of the individual animal versus the ecosystem in conservation initiatives.) It's possible to seek instead a chance to dig deeper, by refusing in the first instance to hurl insult and make monsters of "the other side" in this fraught conversation.

Besides slowing down the rhetoric, what else might help? Speaking nicely to others is not enough. Cat advocates like me need to look hard at the toll cats take by hunting other animals. That humans' impact is the bigger one I do believe is true. Our penchant for land grabs of bird habitats for agricultural and urban needs, which results in the shrinking of wetlands and other areas crucial to bird survival plus the erecting of more buildings into which flying birds may crash, means that our species shoulders the bulk of the blame. Yet starting off on this foot as a "cat person" talking to a "bird person" misses an opportunity to seek a patch of common ground. In working to create such a space, the evolved nature of the cat becomes a critical focus.

As Banszegi's numerosity study reminds us, cats are obligate carnivores. They cannot thrive in the absence of meat eating, and their evolved nature does cause the deaths of many other animals. I am in no danger of forgetting this, but if I were, I could take out my cellphone and scroll to the photograph I took one Wednesday in spring 2018. It shows a lifeless baby bunny, one Charlie first noticed being carried across our yard in cat Ivan's jaws. When Charlie ran forward, Ivan dropped the tiny rabbit, who was not visibly wounded but who was also not breathing. We placed the body on a blanket in a box and rubbed the tiny chest, hoping against hope to revive him or her. This didn't happen. The bunny may have died of a fright-induced heart attack or a neck fracture because of rough handling by Ivan: there was no way to tell. Here is the cost of Ivan's freedom, and our less-than-perfect grade in cat-owner responsibility, made real.

Ivan himself hasn't escaped the costs of predation. Years ago when he was quite young, his mother India was severely wounded in our yard by a larger, unknown animal, perhaps a dog or coyote. We raced India to the vet as soon as we found her in that condition, but her injuries were grave. Putting her down was the kindest choice, and suddenly Ivan was motherless. Life in the outdoors can be very tough indeed.

At this next statement, some cat lovers may balk. I have come to think that it is an overall ethical good for humans to intervene in the expression of cats' evolved nature. Keeping pet cats indoors is crucial. If our admiration for cats leads us to romanticize their independent nature and their need to play out their instinct for wanderlust, then compassion has led us astray. A worry that cats inevitably will fall victim to crippling boredom if cooped up indoors is a shortsighted ethic. I have found it a bracing challenge to create activities that help keep housecats amused. Our indoor five enjoy—each according to his or her own personality—watching outdoor birds while perched on the sill of a large window; chasing and throwing around catnip mice, "tiger tails," and plastic balls; and most consistently of all, interacting with and tracking what's going on with the other four. This intercat vigilance amounts to a busybody type of monitoring like that of sixth graders who can't keep out of each other's business at school. Their social preoccupation with each other at times devolves into fits of shrieking when one cat is cornered or irked. Once in a while two cats will indulge in sweet body-to-body nestling or grooming. Cats may be kept entirely indoors like these five of ours, or in well-designed enclosures like our outdoor four, or in a popular type of "catio" arrangement that features indoor-outdoor access. This decision is up to the family to which the cats belong. The result is likely to be noticeable cat contentment plus a small but valuable contribution to wildlife conservation.

What should happen with unowned or community cats, including feral cats who cannot be socialized and adopted? Here the answer is more complex. No one wants to see an increase in the population of these cats. This fact does make for common ground with bird advocates, and yet I find it's not often recognized as such. Population control of unowned cats (indeed of all cats) is a goal shared by all stakeholders in the "cat wars" conversation. Moving on from that starting point, though, the ground becomes hotly contested. Becky Robinson, the founder and president of Alley Cat Allies, told me by telephone in 2018 that killing feral cats as a way to control the predation problem does not work. Trapping and "euthanizing"—a word neither Robinson nor I like in this context because "euthanasia" means good death—healthy cats only makes way for more cats. "Here in the United States when it comes to decades of rounding up and killing cats," Robinson explained, "the animal agencies that have stopped that practice are the first ones to say it hasn't worked because of the vacuum effect: more cats move in and breed again."

Writing about the vacuum effect—what they term "compensatory immigration" in *Conservation Letters* in 2016—Tim S. Doherty and Euan G. Ritchie of Australia's Deakin University discuss the result of a cat-culling program in southeastern Australia. In defiance of what had been expected, feral cat numbers *increased* in the area during the program. A likely explanation is that the dominant, least fearful cats were the ones trapped and removed. Their absence then enticed younger and subordinate cats to come forward, colonize those same areas, and hunt in them. Lethal-management proponents might respond that still, the *overall* number of cats is reduced in a situation like this; cat advocates in turn insist that killing cats just brings about a sort of Groundhog Day result that enables the presence again and again of *bold, hunting-focused* cats.

In a paper published in 2019 in *Conservation Biology*, I joined with William Lynn and other coauthors to argue that sensationalism over cats' impact on wildlife is unwarranted. Evidence ranges from the findings in Australia I've just mentioned to unexpectedly low rates of predation by cats in one study in the US; we do caution against the overgeneralizing of results from any single study, because ecological factors vary greatly across locations. The group of us concluded this: "As ethicists and scientists who value the lives of individual animals as well as the preservation of biodiversity, we recognize that non-native species may, in specific circumstances, pose a threat to native wildlife and human health. This does not excuse, however, conservationists overgeneralizing their science and losing their moral compass by profiling cats as a threat in all ecological or public health circumstances. The nuanced scientific evidence we do have—and the ethical dialogue that has just begun—cautions against a moral panic over cats."

What opportunities exist to help cats, given this complex situation? A method called trap-neuter-return, or TNR, is the strategy that cat advocates recommend for keeping unowned cats under control. In this system, feral cats are trapped with choice food as bait in a special cage. Charlie, a master cat trapper, uses salmon or mackerel, and a spring trap that the cat trips upon stepping inside to seek the fish. Sometimes with extra-shy cats he resorts to a drop trap propped up on a stick; standing at a distance, he pulls a string, causing the small cagelike trap to tumble down over top of the cat. Captured cats are then maneuvered into a carrier using a special "fork" tool, a delicate process with frightened animals, but I've seen him do it time and again successfully.

The cats are taken to a clinic—spay-neuter or veterinary, mobile or brick-and-mortar—to undergo sterilization surgery. There the cats receive a rabies injection. A tiny piece of skin at the end of one ear is removed, thus creating the universal "ear tip" signal of a spayed or neutered cat. Once the T and the N phases are complete, and following a period of recovery for the cats from the surgery, the R part ensues: the cats are released back to the very same spot where they were trapped.

TNR works, its advocates say, and they provide examples in a range of towns or cities to prove it. It definitely *doesn't* work, bird advocates retort, and they cite instances where TNR failed to control feral-cat populations. The truth at the present moment is probably somewhere in the middle, not because of any inherent flaw in TNR but instead because it takes serious time and money to make TNR work, more time and money than many communities have been so far able to summon. A hit-and-miss plan in which a few well-intentioned folks round up, spay or neuter, then return a few cats (or even half the local cats) isn't good enough.

Support of TNR efforts in our own communities can bring about real change for the better, for cats, birds, and wildlife. The unowned cats who are out there hunting and killing for a living are fundamentally no different from the cats who curl up with us when we read a book or take a nap. They are not vicious or murderous animals. True, they don't care for being petted or for playing with intoxicant-laced toys. They didn't grow up to trust and value those things. They of course do think and feel, and *could have been* among those cats passing the numerosity tests at home or checking in with their owners' moods around fans. Their luck didn't break that way. On what basis could we decide that these cats are unworthy of our compassionate action simply because they were born wild as obligate carnivores?

A big stumbling block exists to this vision of kindness for homeless cats, I know. I've written as if cat advocates can readily expend many hours and dollars on TNR initiatives to reduce the numbers of cats and their hunting pressure on wildlife—whether found to be low, medium, or high in a specific location. This is not true, either globally or across the board in my country. In communities where people lack safe shelter or enough to eat, TNR campaigns will rank low on a list of goals. Many other campaigns for animals vie for time and attention as well. Still, here is an opportunity for compassionate action that is worth considering: are community resources for TNR available, or ripe for creating? Animal lovers may come together in common cause around the fact that TNR can help cats *and* birds *and* other wildlife.

Even as I was first drafting this section, an acquaintance declared to me on Facebook (September 15, 2018) his certainty about the solution to the hunting by feral cats: "The most serious threat to birds and small mammals in the US and Australia is the feral cat population—no option other than to kill them." I was sorry to read this violent view and offered to my correspondent some of the points made here in explaining why I don't agree. Open discussion is itself an opportunity. When I was invited by the organizers of the William & Mary Global Film Festival in Williamsburg to introduce and lead a Q&A on the Turkish film *Kedi*, my answer was "yes, if." I would happily discuss this film about homeless cats if a staff member from the local Heritage Humane Society animal shelter would be invited too, so the two of us could address how to help such cats in our own region. That is indeed what happened.

A gorgeous film, *Kedi* showcases the beauty of Istanbul and its people, whose faces shine with love for the roaming cats who visit homes, bakeries, restaurants, and open-air markets in the city. People scrimp and save in order to pay for the cats' food and medical care; they try hard to protect them from harm. Director Ceyda Torun does a marvelous job of bringing the cats' lives into focus as valuable in their own right. Yet the sight of litter after litter of new kittens, blooming all over the city, was disturbing. Though TNR campaigns do go on in Istanbul (none were mentioned in the film), clearly they are not widespread enough to be effective. After the movie, I stood in front of hundreds of cat (and film) fans to lead a discussion, aided by input from the Heritage Humane Society representative. The cat–human relationship is as beautiful as it is ancient, yet as I suggested that evening, a romanticizing of homeless cats doesn't help anyone.

Birds are among the most amazing wild lives around. Birds may love and grieve: Canada geese and storks fuse emotionally with their long-term mates. Crows and ravens are cerebral tool-users, and the songbirds who grace our ears with glorious music are incredibly clever learners. Raptors like owls and hawks hunt with astonishing skill, some capable of spotting medium-sized prey a mile away. As the Peregrine Fund puts it, "That would be like spotting a rabbit across more than 17 football fields lined up in a row!" Birds, all of these birds, deserve our compassionate care, and that care includes spay-neutering and enclosing all the cats we possibly can. To be a "bird person" and "a cat person" simultaneously is no trick of magic: kindness enacted toward animals is not a limited good.

*   *   *

To think of spiders as residing *with us* in our homes may create a fresh path for compassionate action. Thinking through our behaviors with cats, whether pampered or homeless, may accomplish the same thing. We see anew how blurred is the boundary between home life and wild life. Let's turn now to some truly wild places and the animals who live there.

3

Animals in the Wild

For seventeen days in the summer of 2018, an orca named Tahlequah captivated much of the world's attention. On July 24, in the waters off Canada near Victoria, British Columbia, Tahlequah gave birth to a calf, the first baby born in her pod in three years. For thirty minutes, the calf lived—and then she didn't.

Tahlequah's response to her baby's death brought global attention: day after day, through waters calm and rough, she carried her dead calf on her body. If the calf slipped off and into the water, Tahlequah (also known as J35 to scientists) dived, again and again, to retrieve it. Tahlequah's refusal to part physically from the body of her baby became a signal of her emotional distress. By about day five, the story jumped from a relatively local one in British Columbia and Washington State, the pod's home waters, to an international sensation. Stories in Spanish and Korean supplemented the coverage in North America and Britain. The focal point was Tahlequah's life in the J pod, one of the three pods that make up the southern resident orca (or killer whale) population, and her actions with the lifeless body of her calf. Was Tahlehquah grieving?

Grief is, I believe, the right word to use for Tahlequah's emotional state: her behavior tells us that. The reports of whale biologists at the scene emphasized how much Tahlequah labored physically to keep her calf with her. Through all her dives and thousand miles of swimming, Tahlequah never gave up, at times lagging behind her pod and at other times surrounded by her pod mates.

Throughout the decades of my anthropology outreach, the strongest response I have received to my work has centered on animal grief. In the pages of my book on the topic and of *Scientific American* magazine, at college campuses and on the main stage of TED's flagship conference in Vancouver, I have made my case: many different kinds of animals love or feel great fondness for their relatives, mates, and friends, and grieve when they die. These animals include chimpanzees and dairy cows, elephants and peccaries, Canada geese and ferrets, dogs and cats. Every month I receive letters or media requests regarding stories of animal love and grief. Tahlequah's grief, unfolding over those seventeen summer days right before the eyes of the world, offered an especially poignant opportunity for fostering a better understanding of the science of animal emotions.

Tahlequah's behavior meets the definition I set forth in *How Animals Grieve*. Right after the death of her baby, Tahlequah veered away from her normal routine in ways that signaled not mere stress but an expression of emotional upset that was prolonged. Orcas like Tahlequah create an ocean culture that centers on social connection among pod mates: the community, in some real sense, is the organism. In another population studied by scientists, the orcas learn to hunt communally with such precision that, working together, they create waves to wash seals—only certain species, because orcas reject others—off their ice floes and into the sea where they can be readily consumed. Orca intelligence is such that chances were virtually nil that Tahlequah didn't understand, in some orca way, that her baby was no longer living and breathing. At the same time, we have no way to assess whether orcas possess a concept of death. As Frans de

Waal notes in *Mama's Last Hug*, it may be that some animals understand the finality inherent in the death of others but have no conception of mortality involving the self. In any case, we can't know what animals are thinking, and my definition of grief doesn't require that we do. It relies instead on seeking symptoms of the visible expression of grief in a survivor, such as social withdrawal; failure to travel, eat, or sleep normally; and vocalizations, facial expressions, or postures reflective of distress.

Convincing examples of mourning by whale and dolphin mothers pepper the science journals, including in a review article senior-authored by Giovanni Bearzi in *Zoology*. Reviewing records for cetaceans in the wild and captivity from 1970 to 2016, Bearzi and his colleagues found evidence for "post-mortem attentive behavior," including mothers who keep their dead calves afloat, in nearly a quarter (22.8%) of the eighty-eight species of dolphins and whales. Here is a good context in which to evaluate whether Tahlequah grieved her calf's death. Yes, the behavior she exhibited in her thousand-mile swim was unusual, but even so, the cetacean database allows us to see that exhibiting grief is precisely how some orca individuals behave. From the work on animal grief and mourning now available, we see that the expression of emotion around the death of a family member, partner, or friend is commonplace among some animals. As I am fond of saying, "Grief and love don't belong to us." We humans share the capacity for expressing these emotions with many other animals.

Some grieving people, statistically more often women, are diagnosed with "broken heart syndrome": their heart suddenly and acutely weakens, leading to chest pain and shortness of breath, and in some cases death. Cardiologist Sandeep Jauhar describes the case of a woman who, two weeks after her husband's death, suffered these cardiac symptoms. An ultrasound showed her heart working at half strength, even without any evidence of heart disease such as clogged arteries. "Two weeks later," Jauhar writes, "her emotional state had returned to normal, and so too, an ultrasound confirmed, had her heart."

I don't buy the claim that this woman's emotional state normalized in fourteen days. Grief lingers; grief comes in waves. Still, I understand what Jauhar is getting at: her immediate crushing sorrow eased, and thus so did her cardiac trauma. Grief (and other kinds of extreme stress too) may affect us in catastrophic ways. "Takotsubo cardiomyopathy" is the technical term for broken-heart syndrome, coined by Japanese doctors who noted that the heart muscles of patients suffering from it assume an unusual shape, one that reminded them of an octopus-trapping pot called a *takotsubo*.

No one yet knows if octopuses feel grief, but I do know that animals who grieve don't always recover from their crushing sorrow. Jane Goodall told the world this, when, in 1972, she described how within a month of the death of old chimpanzee female Flo, her eight-year-old son Flint died too. At least in part, Flint's death can be attributed to the depression he suffered at losing the individual who meant the most to him. Could there be an animal analogue to takotsubo cardiomyopathy? Ripe for questions like this, the emerging field of evolutionary thanatology will enable, in the words of researchers James R. Anderson, Donna Biro, and Paul Pettitt, "a more explicit evolutionary consideration of all aspects of studies of death and dying across the biological and sociological fields."

Even now, though, the fact of animal grief opens a window through which we may see the lives of wild animals with sharper clarity. As Tahlequah's sorrow became clear, the tenor of the international conversation changed. The first step had been to see Tahlequah as an individual animal embedded in a family circle: born to Princess Angeline (J17), Tahlequah has a living brother, Moby (J44), and sister, Kiki (J53). Tahlequah herself became a mother in 2010 to Notch (J47) and is aunt to Star (J46). Thanks to good science reporting, more and more people became curious about this entire family and its pod, and the sad fact that these southern resident orcas live in crisis mode. According to Ken Balcomb of the Center for Whale Research, in the three years prior to Tahlequah's baby's death, 100 percent of the pregnancies in J pod had failed to produce living calves.

The ongoing hit to survival and reproduction among these marine mammals reflects a complex ecology: The orcas' fate is tied up with that of Chinook salmon, their primary food. (As I have noted, orcas are fussy eaters. In *The Cultural Lives of Whales and Dolphins*, whale biologists Hal Whitehead and Luke Rendell report that orcas who eat baleen whales often select and consume just the tongue and lips from that multi-ton animal.) And Chinook salmon numbers are down for an interconnected set of reasons. Waterways in the Columbia River system have been dammed, affecting fish survival, and overfishing has contributed as well, to the extent that all of us who consume fish from Pacific Northwest waters play a role in this ecological web.

Tahlequah's remarkable dedication to her dead calf became a springboard: compassion for this mammalian mother expanded to become compassion for her pod and her population in the Pacific Northwest. The *Seattle Times* environmental reporter Lynda Mapes wrote regularly about Tahlequah's ordeal. Her paper also recounted the outpouring of distress expressed by people who had closely tracked Tahlequah's situation. Headlined with "'I Have Not Slept in Days': Readers React to Tahlequah, the Mother Orca Clinging to Her Dead Calf," the piece includes poems for this orca mother, artwork about her plight, and descriptions of the distress and disturbed sleep experienced by their creators.

Mapes also wrote about a second female in the J pod, Scarlet or J50, a three-year-old who had been a highly active youngster, known for energetic movements in the water. Now in summer 2018, thin and ailing, her body signaled her own terrible starvation and the orcas' overall decline. Malnutrition, probably accompanied by an infection and invasive worms, was the official verdict announced by scientists who observed her; whether Scarlet could possibly live until her fourth birthday seemed doubtful. By early August—the period during which Tahlequah carried her dead calf—Scarlet's cranium was visible, an extraordinarily worrisome sign.

That same month, a coalition of scientists and members of the indigenous Lummi Nation readied themselves to offer live Chinook salmon, a dose of protein laced with antibiotics, to Scarlet from a boat. This kind of coordinated intervention aimed at marine wildlife requires an emergency government permit, which was obtained. It wasn't until early September, however—long after Tahlequah had allowed the remains of her baby to drift away in the sea, and weeks more time for Scarlet to weaken—that a dose of antibiotics was successfully administered to the young orca. It wasn't enough.

Balcomb of the Whale Research Center is the person responsible for recording demographic events—births and deaths—of this orca population on behalf of NOAA (the National Oceanic and Atmospheric Administration). On the afternoon of September 13, he declared Scarlet "presumed dead." By that point she hadn't been seen at all since September 7, although her family members were repeatedly observed during the intense searches for Scarlet. That Scarlet was no longer traveling with, or even trailing behind, her family could only mean that her death was a near certainty. Her body was never located.

Here was another blow to the orcas, so soon after the death of Tahlequah's infant. Balcomb's news release on that day conveys his exasperation with the glacial pace of efforts to help the orcas: "The message brought by J50, and by J35 and her dead calf a few weeks ago, is that the southern resident killer whales are running out of reproductive capacity and extinction of this population is looming, while the humans convene task forces and conference calls that result in nothing, or worse than nothing, diverting attention and resources from solving the underlying ecological problems that will ultimately make this once-productive region unlivable for all."

If task forces and conferences calls aren't the answer, what is? What can any of us do? Dam reform in the Pacific Northwest is one avenue under consideration. The rivers of today in the United States, including in the Pacific Northwest, barely resemble the rivers of the past which ran free and unfettered. Four dams in the Snake River impede navigation of the water for Chinook salmon as they attempt to spawn in the riverbed. Were those dams no longer to constrain the salmon's movements, there would likely be a cascade of positive effects: an increase in salmon numbers would lead to an increase in prey availability for the orcas and a leap forward in orca recovery. Critics fear that removal of the dams would threaten the generation of power for the Pacific Northwest. This claim is contested by advocates of undamming, who point out that annual power generation at these dams is relatively weak, dependent on seasonal snowpack, and replaceable by renewable energy sources including solar and wind. Here again we come to Balcomb's frustration: as these issues are debated, the orcas decline further.

Chef Renee Erickson, based in Seattle, announced in 2018 that no more Chinook salmon will be served in the restaurants she co-owns. "The biggest gut wrench is that we have starving orcas," Erickson said at the time. "We are eating the salmon they need to eat." That last statement is no exaggeration. In a paper published in *Scientific Reports*, "Evaluating Anthropogenic Threats to Endangered Killer Whales to Inform Effective Recovery Plans," a group of ten authors including Ken Balcomb specifies ways in which human activity harms these orcas. Here's a key sentence from the paper's abstract: "Primary threats include: limitation of preferred prey, Chinook salmon; anthropogenic noise and disturbance, which reduce foraging efficiency; and high levels of stored contaminants, including PCB." Of these, prey limitation ranks as the most significant factor. If acoustic disturbance were cut in half and the availability of Chinook salmon increased by even just 15 percent, that would be enough, Lacy et al. conclude, to reach an annual population growth for these orcas of 2.3 percent. That rate is a "conservation objective," right now only a dream in the face of zero-growth projections for this population under current conditions.

Acoustic stress and a crash in salmon numbers occur because of collective human activity, and they can shift based on what we collectively choose to do or not do. Rob Williams, lead author of the paper, backs up Chef Erickson's removal of Chinook salmon from her menus: "Don't buy it, don't eat it, don't serve it," Williams told Mapes of the *Seattle Times*. "The whales need it more than we do."

Seeing orcas in the wild is high on my bucket list. Would observing Tahlequah and all of J pod, now, feel akin to mourning? Or would it feel more like an act of devotion, a promise kept not to look away? Could that simple act of looking signal an understanding of what we stand to lose if these orcas vanish into extinction? And it's not only orcas at risk.

Wildlife biologist Karsten Heuer and filmmaker Leanne Allison brought the world's attention to the risks facing caribou who migrate from protected Canadian lands to unprotected Alaskan ones. In spring 2003 they celebrated their marriage with an unusual honeymoon: for over one thousand rugged miles they walked with the 123,000 members of the Porcupine Caribou Herd as they headed toward their calving grounds inside the Arctic National Wildlife Refuge. That vast Alaskan wilderness area was under threat of oil and gas drilling back then—as, despite conservationists' best efforts, it still is. The migration that spring, meant to bring public attention to developmental threats to the region, took on unexpected intimacy. For many miles Heuer and Allison *followed* the caribou, sometimes searching for them in vain. Near the end of their journey, after sleeping unwashed and wild in tents, surviving bear scares and at times running out of food before a scheduled air drop, they *walked with* these large mammals. In *Being Caribou* Heuer writes about the moment, with Allison trekking behind him, when he realized he wasn't walking alone: three bull caribou were right with him, two steps and a hand's breadth away. Heuer told himself to relax. "The bulls seemed to sense this: their eyes softened," he writes, "their breathing quieted, and for a brief, suspended moment we moved in unison, heartbeats and footsteps mingling while we inhaled each other's exhaled breaths."

Of what Heuer and Allison may have felt, being so close to the caribou, I have just the slightest inkling. Four times in recent years I've stationed myself quietly on the side of the road in a summer-lush valley to watch and hear the bison of Yellowstone National Park. The sounds captivate me as much as the sights: grunts of a bison bull as he guards a female during the rut, ripping of grass from the ground as a female eats and allows her baby to scoot in close for a milk snack. I've never walked with the bison—it's not safe to do so. Nonetheless, every encounter lifts me to an ethereal state.

One late-summer day in 2011, Charlie and I observed bison in the Slough Creek area of Lamar Valley as we stood at our car in a little parking area off a gravel road. Closer and closer to us the herd moved. Motionless, we stayed quiet, right at our vehicle doors. It felt surreal. We weren't in the middle of the herd, of course; I would estimate we were close to the park-mandated distance of twenty-five yards away from bison. Still, I felt engulfed. The bison's choice of travel path, ever nearer to us, felt like a beautiful gift bestowed. I nicknamed one magnificent bull Glisten because his nose was shiny in the day's sun. While mate-guarding, Glisten pressed up close to a female and tracked her every step. I kept my eyes fixed on him as the herd passed by and continued on, walking away from us. It was a "wildlife high" I remember with an intense clarity.

Often people ask me, why bison? The answer remains as elusive as knowing why I felt especially close with Cynthia the goat at Farm Sanctuary (chapter 1). When I watch Yellowstone wolves through the spotting scopes of roadside observers who offer me a turn, I enjoy hearing life histories of known individuals, who mates with whom and who rivals whom. Yet my heart doesn't rise in joy quite as intensely as it does with bison. Other folks may politely admire bison yet thrill to the core as they watch wolves. For some people it's rhinos or raptors or spiders who deliver that thrill. "The mind needs wild animals," writes Ellen Meloy in her book about desert bighorn sheep, *Eating Stone: Imagination and the Loss of the Wild*. Yes, and the mind may need some wild animals more than others. Taking compassionate action for animals shouldn't be rooted only in these emotional resonances, of course. Nonetheless, we feel them, and sometimes in ways that surprise others.

When I met veterinarian and nature writer Abbie Gascho Landis at a writer's panel at the 2018 Virginia Festival of the Book in Charlottesville, she struck me as extraordinarily enthusiastic about freshwater mussels. Landis and I were there, along with reporter and writer Maryn McKenna, to talk about animals and food and our recently published books. I took notes as Landis described with fervor the behaviors of animals to whom I'd given precisely zero thought in my life. Healthy waters full of mussels are like river rainforests, Landis explained, teeming with organisms who move around the landscape, eat, reproduce—and filter our water. When female mussels are ready to release the larvae they have brooded, they launch a decorated lure from their bodies. The lure entices fish to come near and strike it, an action that releases the larvae from the female's body. These tiny youngsters hitch a ride on the fish and later detach and float to the riverbed, where their independent life commences.

Back home again, I dove into a copy of Landis's book *Immersion: The Science and Mystery of Freshwater Mussels*. Her engagement with mussels translated perfectly to the printed page. The first time Landis had ever encountered a mussel, she had entered Alabama's Chewacla Creek wearing a wetsuit zipped up over her pregnant belly. In a lovely cosmic coincidence, the mussel she first saw was a female bulging with offspring. The mussel was even using the lure technique right before Landis's eyes. At that moment, Landis was smitten. "This mussel and I were similarly vulnerable," she writes in *Immersion*, "preparing to empty our bodies into the future." This veterinarian who spends her working hours caring for families' dogs and cats became a mussel groupie: "I stalked them from a distance, writing their names in my notebooks: fatmucket, pistolgrip, heelsplitter, shinyrayed pocketbook, spectaclecase, pigtoe, snuffbox. I pored over their bios. Posters of mussels hung in our bedroom."

It was the posters that got me. Decades before I ever thought of studying monkeys in the wild, the walls of my childhood room were hung with posters of The Monkees (singer Davy Jones was my first heartthrob). Nowadays the walls of my writing study feature framed photographs of wild bison. We may surround ourselves visually with what—or with who—sets our hearts to beating just that little bit faster. That it was mussels for Landis delighted me, and not solely because the nearly three hundred mussel species in North American creeks and rivers turn out to be genuinely cool to learn about. As it happened, when I met her

I was in the midst of rediscovering what an engagement with wildlife can mean.

Venturing into "the wild" to encounter animals meant, for most of my life, a certain type of planned, controlled experience carried out at a specific destination. There's a limit to planning and controlling when it comes to wildlife, of course. As I walk a trail or motor around a bend in some nature-rich area, I cannot know which animals will appear before me; baboons in Kenya or grizzlies in the American West wander in ways unpredictable even to a seasoned animal observer. By taking myself out of a daily routine, making my way to a location known for high concentrations of wildlife, I draw a boundary around my animal-watching: I go *there* to *that* place at *that* season, *that* day, and *that* time of day to observe animals.

Some of my most spectacular memories trace back to planned experiences like this: At Yellowstone National Park, the "bison flow" morning I have just described. At Amboseli National Park in Kenya, walking through tall grass behind a group of baboons with my heart in my throat because the monkeys had let loose with alarm calls meaning a lion was nearby, or so the monkeys suspected. In my room at night in the Amboseli Baboon Project House, hearing through the open-mesh screen over my bed a lion's roar in the distance. Then hearing the slow shuffling movements of an elephant munching some delicacy right at my bedroom wall, feet from where I lay. At Kenya's Tsavo National Park, watching a life-and-death struggle with a sense of acute cognitive dissonance: yearning for a Cape buffalo's agony to end as a lion slowly pulled him or her down with sharp claws implanted in the flesh, while admiring the lion's persistence and skill in doing precisely what a big cat has evolved to do. In Everglades National Park in Florida, observing a dolphin's cool and calm technique of spinning a net of sand and silt, stirred up by his or her tail, around fish that will make a good meal. That was cetacean culture made visible, a method of fish capture invented by the dolphins in that region and passed down across the generations. Off the coast of Moss Landing, California, glimpsing that iconic image, a humpback whale's tail flukes breaking the ocean's surface. Our tour leader explained that orcas—the "apex predator" killer whales, kin to Tahlequah and Scarlet of J pod—had blown through the area the day before; humpbacks had dispersed and stayed hidden, except for this single one. Seeing the whale alone meant, I realized, seeing a trace imprinted upon the water of a spectacular predator–prey encounter.

To immerse oneself in this kind of bounded experience brings deep satisfaction. My goal is to hush the ever-present cellphone, slow my step, and anchor my gaze on the animal world. Subtle sights and sounds come into focus. In the best moments, something magical happens, akin to turning a kaleidoscope and seeing the world's design in a fresh way. I *feel with* rather than only *look at* the landscape of animals, taking in those who move through the air, water, and land. My intuition sharpens. Translating animals' movements into meaningful patterns of behavior, often social behavior, comes more readily.

Writers who capture this transformation teach me too. "Mere" reading about the wild should feel like a pale imitation of breathing in wild air and walking a wild path, shouldn't it? Except it doesn't, not when one is in the thrall of master nature writers. Desert bighorn sheep of Utah are exquisitely adapted to the baking heat of Utah's canyons, writes Ellen Meloy in *Eating Stone*. She watches the grace of a group of seventeen as led by an ewe and one by one—"with their muscles, they map the shape of the stone"—they enter an impossibly small crack in the rock and vanish from sight into the canyon's depth. Suddenly I feel that I've been close enough to look into the sheep's eyes and breathe in their wild smell.

My entire sensibility about animals, not to mention my career trajectory in anthropology, was shaped by Jane Goodall's way of writing about the chimpanzees in Gombe, Tanzania. For Goodall these apes were never research subjects to be assigned numbers and studied in order to derive "average" behaviors through the analysis of statistical patterns. Flo was the Gombe chimpanzee whose calm and loving mothering skills influenced Goodall's own; who earned an obituary in the *Times* of London in 1972; and whose death was so grievously mourned by her son Flint. Flint's mental state at the loss of his mother tipped him from sadness into inconsolability. Though more than old enough to care for himself independently, Flint fell into depression when his mother died. Unable to eat, he weakened rapidly. As I mentioned above, he died within a month.

Just as I came gradually to a different understanding of spiders and cats living in our homes (chapter 2), so too has the notion of "wild animals" slowly shifted for me. Like Landis's mussels living in the latticework of the freshwater rivers that snake through many of our cities and towns, wild animals fly, trot, swim, and creep everywhere through our three-dimensional universe. When we walk to the end of our driveway, garden in our backyard, stroll at a local pond, or pass a trash-filled vacant lot on a city street, they are there: unbounded wildlife to be ignored or to be seen, by our choice, on any day (or night), even when we hadn't set out to meet the wild at all. These encounters can lay a foundation for helping the wild animals who go about their days all around us.

Admiration for vacant-lot residents comes to me from science writer Brandon Keim's essay "The Wild, Secret Life of New York City," a chapter in his book *The Eye of the Sandpiper: Stories from the Living World*. Out walking in Brooklyn, Keim converses with a woman who tells him "there's nothing there at all" on a corner property. Keim himself, though, sees the lot as teeming with life, "a pocket grassland where the hand of human development had skipped a beat." That "pocket grassland" stopped me in my bison-loving tracks. If I yearn to fly the two-thousand-some miles from the airport at Richmond, Virginia to Jackson Hole, Wyoming, then drive forty-eight miles farther into Yellowstone National Park to fill my eyes with grazing bison, could I perhaps train my senses to see the magnificence of tiny ecosystems close to home? What outlook of mine keeps the bison tucked into a sacred space in my heart but dismisses from my attention smaller, nearby planetary cotravelers? Most of us, Keim says, see "untended nature" as a place waiting to be filled. We don't see what is in front of us: in the case of that Brooklyn lot, a riot of plants from broadleaf plantain to white snakeroot. Butterflies, bees, and countless other insects, too, and birds. Six percent of New York City lands are vacant, but in most cities the percentage is more than twice as high as that, coming in at around 15 percent. "That's a whole lot of life we're not noticing," Keim observes.

Certainly a butterfly is not a bison. In the service of what goal could we compare a mega-mammal to an insect? Each species adapts to its own niche: that's the primary lesson I imparted to undergraduates in the first days of the course Introduction to Biological Anthropology. Humans are not more evolved than apes, nor are apes more evolved than monkeys—or butterflies. Each animal is shaped by evolutionary forces over time to thrive in its own way (or to try to thrive, while, too often, battling anthropogenic changes to the world).

For me, it's probably true that observing bison in Yellowstone or monkeys in Kenya engulfs all my senses in a way that observing mussels would not. Abby Gashko Landis, she of the mussels posters, would come to a different conclusion, I suspect. Cultivating compassionate action depends in some part on cultivating wonder, and wonder doesn't dwell only in landscapes that are wildlife-viewing destinations. Recall E. O. Wilson's estimate that about 80 percent of our planet's living species have yet to be discovered. Even among the known organisms, Wilson says, an abundance of life thrives without the attention of most of us, except scientific specialists. Wilson is adamant that we should not fall back on terms like "bugs" and "critters" when we contemplate insects, centipedes, mites, spiders, and so on: "They too are wildlife," he declares. It's true: when I gazed at my small jumping-spider friend that day (chapter 2) while reading outdoors, I encountered wildlife.

Some among us excel at seeing the oft-overlooked. A Scottish woman called Fiona Presly enjoyed a remarkable relationship with a queen bumblebee for five months. In her garden one spring day in 2017, Presly noticed two odd things about an insect she eventually named Bee: her lack of wings and a certain disoriented quality to her movements. At first, Presly assumed that Bee needed just a moment's respite; she placed Bee on a flower and provisioned her with some sugar water. Hours later, with bad weather pressing down, the bee remained motionless in precisely the spot in which Presly had put her. At this point, the equivalent of a pet adoption occurred: inside with Presly went Bee. Presly came to feel for the small animal and (back outside) created a garden in which a damaged being could thrive. She enclosed plants with netting so that Bee could walk from flower to flower without winged rivals swooping in to poach her pollen. She supplemented the flower foods with sugar water now and then, and during bad weather transported Bee back inside.

Presly felt attached to Bee; that much is clear. Is it going too far to call this woman-and-bee interaction a relationship, though? Wasn't Bee a passive partner, after all, like the spider Portia in my own summer observations (chapter 2)? My answer is no to both questions, judging from what Presly told the *Dodo* website. "She'd walk toward me and crawl on my hand. She seemed so happy to see me. It made me stop and think—there's something going on here."

Insect cognition is a hot area of research. Recently bees, specifically buff-headed bumbles, were found to learn how to roll a ball by imitation. Behavioral ecologist Olli Loukola, biologist Clint Perry, and their colleagues trained bees to move a tiny yellow wooden ball towards a target on a blue platform. These were timed trials: the bees had five minutes to complete the task. Successful bees could lap up some sugar water as reward. (I too consider small bits of sugar completely appropriate as reward for labor completed, so I can relate.) The research team then set up an experiment in which naive bees watched the experienced ones carry out the ball-rolling task. After three observation sessions, these observers excelled at the task (99% of the time), much more than did bees asked to roll a ball without first watching models (34%) and also more than did bees who watched the ball advance via a magnet (78%). That the bees could learn pretty well by watching magnets attests to an astute insect mind. It's notable, though, that they learned better when models of their own kind were available to them.

Here's the coolest part of all: it wasn't strict copying that the observer bees did but something more clever. The research team reported it this way in *Science*: "On most successful trials, bees used the closest ball instead of the furthest ball (which they had seen the demonstrator moving) and in the generalization test used a differently colored ball than previously encountered, suggesting that bees did not simply copy the behavior of the demonstrator but rather improved on the observed behavior by using a more optimal route." The bees didn't imitate in an automatic-pilot sort of way what they saw; they thought about things, then selected an effective option for how to proceed. Loukola's team offered this conclusion: "That bees solved this novel, complex goal-directed problem—and solved it via observation and using a better strategy than originally demonstrated—shows an un-precedented degree of behavioral flexibility in an insect."

Bee smarts are far easier to demonstrate than bee feelings. The term *happy* applied to Bee or to any insect may result from a besotted animal-adopter going a bit too far with anthropomorphism, I admit. On what basis would we affix human labels to bee emotions? Yet the notion that Bee exhibited a positive emotional state fits with the discovery that bees are prone to what's called optimism bias, an expectation that something good is going to happen. In an experiment run by biologist Perry and his colleagues at Queen Mary University of London and reported, again, in *Science*, bees were trained to distinguish a blue portal (presented with 30% sugar solution) from a green one (presented with unsweetened water). Then bees were divided into two groups, half receiving a sweet treat, this time ramped up to 60% sugar solution, and half nothing. All were released in proximity to a purple portal, what's called an "ambiguous stimulus" because the bees couldn't know what to expect associated with that color (as opposed to what they had learned about blue or green).

Take a moment and try to predict the outcome of this experiment. Which set of bees more rapidly approached the purple door? Any of us who has raided a chocolate stash, then felt a small surge of pleasurable mental energy, may guess the right answer: the sweet-treated bees flew faster to the purple door. (Of course once there, they found nothing, so if bees are capable of disappointment . . .) It's not just that the sucrose on offer ramped up the sucrose-receiving bees' excitement level: when tested, sucrose-receiving and the non-sucrose-receiving bees differed not at all in flight time or speed to reach a feeder. The best explanation is that the bees experienced a brain-mediated optimism bias as they made decisions about what to do with an ambiguous stimulus. When dopamine pathways in the insects' brains were blocked, the bees who received sucrose did not fly faster to the purple stimulus. Dopamine is a chemical associated with positive emotional states, so this finding lends support to the optimism-bias conclusion.

In ethology, "experiencing an emotional state" is one thing and a notion that "Bee the bumblebee felt happy" is quite another: we shouldn't assume automatically that an emotional state felt in an animal's body is registered consciously by the animal as a feeling. Many scientists remain agnostic on whether feelings are indeed part of animals' consciousness at all, as one commenter on Perry's research puts it. Yet it's as misguided to dismiss such feelings in animals as it is to assume them. Doing that, we would lose an opportunity to understand the orca Tahlequah's grief for her dead calf, or the visible expression of sadness or joy our dog feels in her daily life. I liked how Perry put it to me in an email message when I asked him what he thought of Presly's comment about Bee's happiness. "We all have a tendency to describe emotions in human terms, but even more specifically in our own cultural and personal terms," Perry wrote. "It may not be correct to describe what a bee experiences as happy, but then again, the way I understand happiness may not be the same way you understand it. If we take happiness to be a very general basic experience of pleasantness, then perhaps the bee was experiencing this. But at this point we just don't know, and will not be able to know until we can get at the neural underpinnings of emotions."

Does Perry envision any way for scientists to distinguish in bees between an emotional state (like optimism bias) and a subjective feeling (like happiness), or is this distinction not scientifically testable? "At the moment," he replied, "we do not have the ability (cleverness?) to measure the subjective component of emotions in any animal directly. This includes humans, for we are making an assumption that verbal reports from people accurately communicate the subjective feeling of emotions. Our verbal reports are actually indirect inferences of our subjective experience. It is a rather good assumption of something subjective going on, but still an assumption." Here Perry makes an excellent point: in scrutinizing Presly's claims about Bee's feelings so closely, we're going well beyond what we would do were a human the one rescued and cared for. In that case we would believe our eyes in interpreting the person's body language or simply take the person's word about feeling happiness at having found a friend.

What I see as the underlying beautiful truth of Presly's account is this: Bee sought Presly's company because that company felt in some way pleasurable to the insect. One day, long after the friendship was firmly established, Bee crawled into Presly's hand. In that warm palm Bee died, ending a life lengthier than typical for a female of her species. Bees can be highly social creatures—from the ball-rolling experiment it's clear that they often attend to each other's behavior closely—and this particular Bee in her necessary isolation sought out what company she could find. (Bees shouldn't be overgeneralized any more than primates should. Some bees among the world's twenty thousand species are egregiously asocial. As Thor Hansen remarks in his book *Buzz: The Nature and Necessity of Bees*, once a mason-bee mother lays an egg, she walls it up with a supply of food and "moves on without a second thought.")

Whether Bee's impulse was as cognitively rooted as that of the cow Bonnie who ran into the woods and joined a deer herd (chapter 1) cannot be known. We do know that Presly's compassion soared when she sighted Bee, struggling in her wingless state, and she took action based on it. Venturing no farther than our yard if we have one, or a local pond or park, may result in opportunities for aiding wildlife. "Wherever you are, wherever you go," writes Ellen Meloy, "there are untamed creatures nearby that need your attention." What specifically to do? Invite birds into your yard, Meloy says, allow black widow spiders to live in your eaves. (That last would be a tough one for me, I admit, given the presence of powerful neurotoxins in black widow venom.) Pay attention and learn—that counts too. "Admire the male midwife toad, who carries fertilized eggs on his back for a month," Meloy advises.

As I walked on a sidewalk one day along a car-choked street, making my way from the New England Aquarium at Boston Harbor back to my rented apartment in the North End, I came upon a colorful black and green sign announcing a "Pollinator ribbon on the Greenway." Featuring a flower icon, with one of the yellow petals morphed by an artist into a striped bee, the sign was posted at one end of a long planter filled with flowering and fruiting plants. From it, I learned Boston's Greenway Conservancy had in 2016 introduced "a series of new garden spaces intended to connect a corridor of plants designed to attract and support pollinator species." In each, bees, wasps, butterflies and pollinating birds could find spaces designed expressly for them, rich with nectar and pollen: little spaces that together add up to sanctuary.

As I walked, I thought of the corridor in Kenya that extends from Amboseli National Park to Chyulu Hills and Tsavo West National Park, protected by conservationists who intend to keep development in the area under some degree of control. That Kenyan corridor benefits lions, zebras, elephants, and giraffes who wish to move freely. Here in the US, an overpass meant to span ten lanes of California's Highway 101 west of Los Angeles is in its final design stages. If approved and constructed, it will offer safe passage across two segments of the Santa Monica Mountains to endangered mountain lions and other wildlife. According to the *Guardian* in 2019, "it's designed to blend into the mountains so animals won't realize they are on a bridge at all." If all goes well and the crossing opens in 2023 as planned, California will boast the biggest wildlife crossing in the world.

Even in its scaled-down version, the Boston garden spaces offer a welcome aerial pathway across the city for pollinators. Here is a model ripe for adoption in our cities and towns, and even in our neighborhoods through a series of connected, customized gardens.

Tremendous aid to wildlife can come about when we enter parks or traverse nature trails during the bounded experiences I wrote about before. Doing nothing in these locations may itself become an act of spectacular help. Here again the Yellowstone bison are my touchstone. Every tourist season, some park tourists mistake these wild bison for Disney movie props or at least for petting-zoo animals, and approach them on foot in order to take a photograph or to just see what happens. Between the years 2000 and 2015, twenty-five people (including four park employees) were injured—butted, gored, or tossed—by Yellowstone bison either because they actively approached bison closely (80%) or failed to move when bison approached them (20%). Make no mistake, we're talking about *very near* approaches, far nearer than Charlie or I ever got on in our cherished "close" herd encounter: the median human distance just before injury was 3.4 meters. That's slightly over 11 feet: roughly two body lengths of a person, or the length of one elephant trunk to tail. The *range* of human distances before injury is telling, too: from a third of a meter (1 foot) to 6.1 meters. People stayed close enough to the largest terrestrial mammals in the Western Hemisphere to defy any common sense.

The data I have cited come from a 2018 paper in the journal *One Health* senior-authored by Cara Cherry of the CDC (Centers for Disease Control and Prevention), three National Park Service people, and a person on the Bison Ecology and Management Team of Yellowstone National Park. Why the CDC? Careless behavior that provokes or otherwise results in attack by wildlife is not only associated with Yellowstone bison, and in part the research aims at figuring out how to combat it. The authors point out that Yellowstone National Park carries out a vigorous educational campaign, through pamphlets, signage, and videos, to inform visitors (and their own employees) of distance regulations: people must stay 25 yards back from most wildlife and 100 yards back from bears and wolves. As a park visitor, I would judge this campaign to be extensive, yet it doesn't seem to be as effective as it should. In 2015 alone, five people were injured by bison, the highest number of any of the study years. Might behavioral science help shape a different kind of approach? Would detailed investigation of the circumstances of the injuries lead to more effective intervention with the public?

Four findings stand out, based on Cherry et al.'s review of the data. All of the twenty-five encounters occurred in developed areas of Yellowstone; these buttings, gorings, and tossings are not happening in the backcountry. In fact, the area around the famous Old Faithful geyser is the most frequent location. Unsurprisingly given the popularity of nature photography on social media, most people (80% of the cases) were taking pictures when they were injured. Most injuries (60% of the cases) occurred when the person was with three or more others. With this last factor, it's clear that humans can be herd animals too. As Cherry et al. put it, "we tend to look at what others do to make decisions about our own appropriate behaviors. . . . We often look to social norms to understand how to respond in times of uncertainty."

Qualitative data from the study underscore the authors' point. A man who had been gored told Yellowstone rangers that he had originally felt uncomfortable about getting close enough to a bison in order to take a family photograph, but his qualms eased when he noticed others close to the animal. A second injured person, and a third person who witnessed one of the incidents, made similar statements: a perception of safety in approaching near to a bison was associated with other people already standing close to the animal.

This study was small, limited to encounters with one kind of large mammal in one national park. I would wager that the patterns reported would generalize to other wildlife encounters in other areas, a statement that remains speculative until comparative research is done. Nonetheless, here emerges a possibility for a cascading positive action for animals: when outdoors near to wildlife, if we ourselves refuse to move close to the animals, we may increase chances that others too will avoid moving dangerously near. Stress on the animals would decrease, and almost certainly animal deaths too. Even in "protected" areas like national parks and nature reserves, animals are routinely killed when they attack humans, particularly if a person dies in the encounter (as thankfully did not happen to any of the twenty-five injured people in the Cherry study).

Doing no harm is not enough; wildlife management is a topic of enormous complexity, and how and when we should intervene in the lives of wild animals is beyond my scope here. Yet just as a close look at animal lives may invite fresh compassion, so may a compassionate action-based framework invite reframing of old questions. An entire book could be written around the question of whether hunting can ever reasonably be said to coexist with expressing compassion for animals. Here I can only hint at some of the layers of complexity involved, coupled with a suggestion for how ecosystem management and welfare of individual animals need not automatically be thought to be in opposition.

In 2018 a friend who knows my love of bison sent me a link to this Facebook announcement: "Bid online from Sept. 12–20 for the opportunity to harvest a bison from the American Prairie Reserve herd in Montana!" Go to the American Prairie Reserve website page and you will see beautiful animal images coupled with text like this: "From birds to bison, find out what's happening with science and restoration by our biologists, partners, and visiting researchers." On the date I looked, you would also have found this: "American Prairie Reserve will offer six bison harvest opportunities: four to eligible Montana residents and two to the public."

How might we think about the inherent contradictions in working to conserve animals and also working toward killing them? Is this advertised event at the Montana reserve part of the "pay to stay" approach, in which the deaths of a limited number of animals by hunters raise money to help the rest? The goals of the harvest, according to the American Prairie Reserve, are to keep herd numbers in check and to ensure that the bison population is kept in balance with other species on the landscape. The hunt is a controlled one. "To mimic natural predation," the website announcement reads, "hunters will only be allowed to take a specific age class of bison, generally in the range of two-years old or under, which, along with the aged and less fit, are the animals most commonly taken when predators are present in sufficient numbers."

This harvest showcases the fact that our ecosystems are out of whack: as the American Prairie Reserve statement goes on to say, thinning of bison herds would be accomplished naturally if wolves and grizzly bears were thriving in the American West. The killing event, then, becomes an effective argument for restoring ecosystems. My chief purpose in evoking it, though, is to use it as a springboard to look more broadly at the practice of recreational hunting. The notion of people killing healthy animals with guns or bows and arrows may be quite difficult emotionally for those of us whose lives are bound up with helping animals. In reply, hunters may respond that they too help animals, through a careful approach regarding which animals to take down and through payment of hunting fees. These points are debated with as much ferocity as are the perspectives in the "feral cat versus wild bird" wars (chapter 2). Discussing that issue, I said that no one need choose between birds and other wildlife or feral cats when implementing plans for aiding animals. But can we possibly reconcile the "I could never hunt" and the "I hunt to help animals" camps?

I recognize my own strong bias against hunting. Occasionally as I am scrolling through my Facebook feed, a photograph of a deer flashes into my vision. The prize of a recent hunting expedition, the animal is plated, recognizable as a deer only because a friend's caption identifies deer meat being consumed at dinnertime. These images differ in kind from others, posted by strangers, that depict the aftermath of canned "trophy" hunts: hunters posed, gun-toting and grinning, next to a dead lion or giraffe. Those I delete altogether. Even though I don't see the two kinds of hunters as identical (and more on this below), I still choose to hide from further visibility the social-media posts about the plated deer. It's out of the question for me to walk into the woods, hoist a gun, and shoot a deer, and I dislike seeing images shared by others who have done so. Intentionally causing an animal's death, plus physical pain (either momentary or not, depending on the hunter's accuracy) and perhaps emotional pain to her offspring or kin as well, is something I can't do or celebrate.

Can the ethics of the deer-hunting situation be sewn up so neatly, though? Should I be easily content with a wholesale disavowal of it? Musing along the lines of "Would you really let your family go hungry to save a deer's life?" is too superficial a thought experiment to count as serious exploration of the issue. Realistically speaking, subsistence hunting is highly unlikely to become a relevant factor in my life—yet for some hunters, hunting does fulfill an economic need. A second thought experiment hits closer to home: Do hunters who skillfully take down a deer in a controlled hunt, then eat or donate the meat, act more kindly toward animals than do my family members who eat factory-farmed animals? This question acknowledges that some hunters care deeply that they not, through their eating patterns, contribute to the suffering of animals kept on industrial farms. Even this question is too limited, though. It implies a binary of sorts, as if a person must choose between piling her shopping cart with shrink-wrapped cows, chickens, and pigs and heading into the woods to shoot, skin, and cook a deer. Plenty of choices exist between those two poles, as we will see (chapter 5).

Let's dig deeper. What if a controlled hunt is set up by wildlife managers in an area with high deer density and mortality rates known to be high through the winter? In this case, at least some animals killed by hunters are spared the probability of a slow death by starvation. Here we meet Paul Bloom's caution noted in chapter 1: short-term acts of compassion (a refusal to kill an individual animal) may inadvertently cause greater suffering in the long term, in the form of a less-good death for that animal later. Unlike some animal activists, I don't find it an impossible contradiction to state that some hunters care profoundly about wildlife and work hard toward a goal of less animal suffering.

My thinking along these lines has been influenced by Harry W. Greene from Cornell University, an author of books including *Tracks and Shadows: Field Biology as Art* and a hunter of over a decade who has become a friend. Greene and I have specialized, I think it's fair to say, in conversing together about sensitive topics with mutual respect. Here's Greene explaining to me some of his motivations for, and pleasures in, hunting:

> Having spent most of my seventy-five years as a naturalist, more than ten as a hunter, I'm confident that extremely few wild animals have a peaceful death, that instead their endings come from disease, starvation, or violence via predators, collisions with cars, falling off cliffs, fires, etc. Having watched animals as diverse as rattlesnakes and deer die from all three (as well as quite a few people from the first and third), I'd definitely prefer blinking out thanks to an ethical hunter. In other words, they're all going to die, and what I'm imposing is to be the particular reason, at a particular time. Second, for me hunting is never "just" motivated by a single factor, but rather a constellation of needs, some of them instrumental (eating environmentally and medically healthy meat), some of them emotional. As a hunter for meat I feel deeply rewarded by being more part of nature, owning up to the inherent conflicts of my life at the expense of other organisms, and doing so in the company of dear friends who share similar values, especially in landscapes of which I am especially fond.

Greene's words caused me to think long and hard. Admittedly, my first response is to lament the years of potentially healthy living erased from a deer's life by the act of hunting. People close to me have suffered and died over the years, including from protracted illness. Often I have wished for more humane right-to-die laws, yet no one ever seriously thought to relieve those individuals of their suffering by shooting them well ahead of its onset and without their consent. If I value humility, though—and I do—here's the right question to ask myself: who am I to proclaim that my approach to wildlife is somehow ethically superior to Harry Greene's? Read *Tracks and Shadows*;

listen to scores of his former students, many of whom are now professional zoologists, who under his guidance learned about and came to respect snakes, turtles, and a host of other noncuddly animals; or spend a short afternoon with him as I did in the field looking for snakes, and there can be no doubt of his profound knowledge of and love for animals. Years ago I was very sure of myself in thinking that "hunters" and "animal lovers" represented completely nonoverlapping categories. I no longer think this, surprising no one more than myself.

I'm hard-pressed to think of hunting as compassionate action, however, in large part because considering an ethical deer hunt to be the norm in the hunting world would be wrong. Upwards of one hundred million animals are killed annually by hunters in the US alone, with only about six million of the prey animals being deer. The Safari Club International (SCI) boasted in February 2020 of the variety of animals living in North America alone who are ripe for killing, including many species that aren't overpopulated:

> With more than 60 varieties of game animals to hunt, North America can keep a hunter occupied his or her entire hunting career. The SCI Record Book lists six kinds of bears, two bison, two muskox, one unique species of goat, three thinhorn sheep, six kinds of bighorns, six canines, four wild cats, the American alligator, three varieties of elk, four kinds of moose, six different caribou, three mule deer and three blacktail deer, 14 varieties of whitetail deer, two brocket deer, two peccaries, the unique pronghorn, six kinds of wild turkeys, two kinds of walrus and one large and toothy weasel. That doesn't include small game species, such as squirrels and prairie dogs, or the more than 100 species of waterfowl and upland birds found across the continent. Whether it's dangerous game or wary ungulates, fur or feathers, North America has it.

This doesn't sound like an ethically motivated statement to me, but rather one based in recreational pleasure in killing animals. Further, it's by no means the case that animals regularly die a quick, clean death at hunters' hands. In summer 2018 an elk-hunting guide was killed by a mother-and-cub pair of grizzly bears near the border of Yellowstone and Grand Teton National Parks north of Jackson Hole, Wyoming. The guide's client was also injured by the bears. This single hunt expedition became a cascading set of tragedies, starting when the man who paid to go on the hunt shot an elk. Next, he and the hunting guide lost sight of the elk. The newspaper *USA Today* reports that "the two men were attacked by the bears as they field dressed the elk, which they had shot Thursday but were only able to find early Friday." The most likely scenario here, given that an experienced hunting guide could not quickly locate the animal who had been shot, is that the elk fled and died slowly of the inflicted injuries. After the bear attacks in which the hunting guide died, the two bears themselves were killed by Wyoming wildlife managers because they were deemed to have acted aggressively. So much death!

Wolf experts Jim and Jamie Dutcher describe in *The Wisdom of Wolves* the practice of hunters who station themselves just outside the borders of national parks. When wolves or other large mammals cross out of the protected borders of a park like Yellowstone in Wyoming or Denali in Alaska, the hunters are ready with bullets—or traps. A wolf named Limpy (Yellowstone Wolf no. 253), born into the famous Druid Peak Pack in 2000, sustained an injury as a youngster that left him with only three legs. The absence of a fourth leg slowed Limpy not at all: he walked into Utah, was released by wildlife officials back into Wyoming's Grand Teton National Park, and from there trekked back to Yellowstone. Throughout his life he hunted wild deer and elk, never going after ranchers' "livestock." It didn't matter.

In 2008, months after he had again left Yellowstone National Park and entered the surrounding Wyoming countryside, he was shot and killed along with two other wolves near an elk feeding ground. Though we don't know the identity of the person who shot Limpy, we do have statistics from Wyoming's 2017 licensed hunting season: forty-three wolves were legally hunted, and one was illegally hunted. Thirty-two more wolves were killed that same year in areas of Wyoming where no license is needed at all because it's open season on animals who are deemed predators. It's a good bet that a hunter killed Limpy, too.

Ethical hunters exist, as do subsistence hunters who may genuinely have few alternative choices for feeding their families. In addition, indigenous cultural and cosmological practices may be bound up with hunting in ways that may be hard for nonindigenous people to grasp. Whether in these situations a stance of nonviolence toward animals or instead cultural tradition takes precedence is a topic on which there's no homogeneous perspective among indigenous scholars. (For a valuable discussion of these points, see the chapter "Postcolonial" by Maneesha Deckha in the volume *Critical Terms for Animal Studies*.)

Yet the reality is that instance after reported instance shines a light on highly unethical hunting practices. In October 2018 pictures came to light on the internet taken by Idaho Fish and Game commissioner Blake Fischer on a trip to Namibia; he had killed a family of baboons with bow and arrow. In one photograph Fischer kneels, grinning. "Arranged in front of him, resembling a macabre family picture, are the bodies of four baboons," reported the *Washington Post*. "The smallest one's head is lolled back, its mouth slightly agape. Crimson blood stains its abdomen. A quiver of arrows is in the foreground." On the same trip Fischer had also killed giraffe, leopard, impala, sable antelope, waterbuck, kudu, warthog, oryx, and eland. It was the baboons that sparked intense outrage, probably because the whole family was killed together. (Of course the other animals killed came from families of one kind or another, too, and those families were disrupted.)

When I emailed Fischer at his Idaho Fish and Game address, I kept it professional, expressed my thoughts as a person who has observed family groups of baboons in Kenya, and asked: "Is that what hunting is supposed to be about? Just walking in to an area—not local, not a place you know and understand—and taking lives in order to boast about it with images and text?" I expected no answer and got none. In the media, Fischer noted that during his Namibia hunt he had done nothing illegal. Nor were his actions unethical or immoral, he added.

It's no use concluding that Fischer is the hunting community's bad apple. Carry out a Google image search with the words "trophy hunting," or explore photographs associated with the Safari Hunting Club's members, and the parade of grinning hunters and dead animals seems endless. Paying big money to kill exotic animals goes beyond the "viral" cases we may have heard about, like Fischer's killing of the baboon family or the killing of Cecil the lion in Zimbabwe three years prior by American dentist Walter Palmer. It's a thriving subculture, one whose practitioners aim to keep it going. In Fischer's case, cultural transmission of hunting to the younger generation is an explicit theme. From the Idaho Fish and Game "Commission Members" webpage at the time of the furor about his baboon hunt, I learned that Fischer is active in the Big Brothers Big Sisters organization. He aims to reverse the decline in the population of hunters by recruiting youth: "We need to figure out how to turn this around by developing new and better hunter recruitment programs and get youth out in the field and transition them into lifelong hunters," Fischer wrote. This outreach to boys and girls is especially notable when done by someone whose local hunting blurs with trophy hunting in Africa.

Let's return to hunting that is not of the trophy variety. When wildlife-management policies rest on easy acceptance of hunting as a first-line defense for animal overpopulation, alternatives go unexplored. Administering birth control to female animals against the risk of overpopulation is dismissed as too expensive and difficult by some experts, but is this a failure of imagination more than of know-how? In a 2013 article for *Journal of Zoo and Wildlife Medicine*, Allen Rutberg writes this: "A widespread public awareness that deer contraceptives are effective and can control deer populations under some circumstances would threaten one of the fundamental organizational principles of North American wildlife management agencies: that wildlife management and hunting are synonymous." However, writing in the *Guardian* in 2020, George Monbiot says that in order to hit a deer with a contraceptive dart, a person has to get within 40 meters, which can be difficult or impossible in more open areas. Monbiot continues, "Even if you could find some other, ecologically safe means of delivering the chemicals (none exists), suppressing fertility across a population is extremely difficult, perhaps impossible."

For me the question remains: in a culture that broadly accepts *lethal* wildlife management as the norm, how intensive and persistent is the scientific labor to seek alternatives to hunting as population control? I don't have an answer to this question. At NPR I wrote about the Florida Fish and Wildlife Conservation Commission's funding of scientists in 2018 to kill invasive green iguanas by brutal methods. These methods included swinging the animals against trucks and boats in order to bash in their skulls. Even the preferred method of iguana slaughter, pushing metal bolts into the animals' skulls using a special tool, which is considered humane, does not always render the animals quickly unconscious when carried out in the uncontrolled conditions of the field. It's situations like these that lend urgency to the question about alternatives. Brutal treatment of species that are labeled as invasive by our own species—which most definitely should be considered invasive into habitats originally belonging to other animals—would fill a chapter all on its own. Regarding brutal treatment of species considered to be invasive, Marina Bolotnikova and Jeff Sebo write this for Sentient Media in 2020: "In many cases, we use militaristic, catastrophizing language to justify this violence against other animals. Instead of portraying nonhumans as fellow creatures who are simply trying to exist, we portray them as enemy invaders who are coming to destroy our communities. For example, as *The New York Times* wrote last month regarding feral pigs: 'Ranchers and government officials here are keeping watch on an enemy army gathering to the north, along the border with Canada.' The idea of invasive species is political as much as scientific."

In wildlife management and environmental stewardship, now and then a shining idea makes so much sense that it opens a new window on compassionate action. So it is with beavers and ecological restoration. I've already mentioned some books that lit up my understanding of wild animals, and in 2018 Ben Goldfarb's *Eager: The Surprising, Secret Life of Beavers and Why They Matter* did that for me. Sure, beavers always struck me as cute with their big buck teeth and paddle tails. I knew about their industrious dam-building habits. The rate at which they are trapped and killed as pests I hadn't known. Beaver activity may cause flooding of property or farmlands, causing them to be labeled as nuisance animals: over twenty-one thousand beavers were killed by the Wildlife Services division of the US Department of Agriculture in the year 2016 alone. This outcome isn't only sorrowful for the individual beaver families; it's also a wrongheaded decision because these aquatic rodents have an immense role to play in restoring damaging ecosystems. Beavers, Goldfarb writes, are "the ultimate keystone species," "the animal that doubles as an ecosystem." These aquatic rodents help counteract, for instance, the negative effects of global warming. In Colorado's Rocky Mountain National Park, beaver activity on twenty-seven streams stored carbon in amounts equivalent to what 37,000 acres of American forest can do.

Beavers have a positive influence too on the ecological dynamics of Yellowstone National Park. When the "trophic cascade" in the park is described in the media, wolves are typically given the starring role. Reintroduced to the park in 1995, wolves with their predation caused the roaming patterns of elk to shift, which in turn allowed trees like aspen and willow to regenerate and creeks to deepen and thrive. While wolves win the limelight, beavers deserve credit too: relocated first to the nearby Absaroka-Beartooth Wilderness Area and eventually emergent in Yellowstone, they also spur the willows' regrowth; the trees' roots are kept wet by way of beaver dams.

Beaver relocation away from areas where they are perceived as troublesome to those where they may store carbon or otherwise positively reshape the landscape is a win-win conservation strategy: it helps our planet, it helps the beavers. One of the most brilliant aspects of this relocation is the larger lesson it offers: conservation initiatives carried out at the ecosystem level don't need to leave behind the well-being of individual animals. The developing field of compassionate conservation builds on this notion and applies it broadly. Its central premise is that taking into account the welfare of individual animals and working to care for ecosystems need not be at odds. As Daniel Ramp and Marc Bekoff write in *BioScience*, extinction risks are obviously crucial to address. Yet our care for animals shouldn't stop there. "Harm," Ramp and Bekoff write, "also encompasses the suffering experienced by individuals and associated costs to social units and the populations to which they contribute."

Taking into account the grief of Tahlequah the orca, indeed the significance of each individual orca life with all its attendant thinking and feeling, can coexist with work to restore the Salish Sea ecosystem. Even in complex cases, compassion for animals can be brought explicitly into the discussion in serious and interdisciplinary ways. There's no naive hope that each and every animal will be saved; indeed, that's naive in the extreme. Limited funds, time, and space render such a goal impossible, and scientists who approach matters from a stance of compassionate conservation know this. When tough choices must be made—how many bison can the Yellowstone ecosystem support, do we save endangered frogs or birds first in a particular region, how many deer can suburban ecologies handle, what do we do when predators like wolves come into increasing conflict with humans?—decisionmakers will be better served when they are armed with data explaining how alternative management strategies will affect ecosystems and individuals both.

Ethicist William Lynn and scientists Francisco Santiago-Avila and Adrian Treves grapple with questions like these. (This is the same William Lynn with whom I coauthored the feral-cat conservation article discussed in chapter 2.) This trio writes about the urgent need to *preserve nature*. "Well, of course!" might be an understandable first reaction to such a statement, yet a critical distinction explains their use of this phrase. Too often the language of conservation science focuses, they say, on *conserving natural resources* instead of *preserving nature*. A focus on resources is often embedded in an anthropocentric and instrumental view of nature—one that asks first and foremost how nature can be managed for the benefit of humans, to the exclusion of asking about the interests of other animals. Let's think yet again of Tahlequah and the orca population of which she is a part. Treves, Santiago-Avila, and Lynn discuss in a paper in *Biological Conservation* how US and Canadian wildlife agencies determine maximum sustainable yield for extracting salmon from the water. The calculations are human focused and ignore other consumers of salmon like orcas, seals, and grizzly bears whose well-being may be integrally tied up with salmon.

What if the needs of Tahlequah and her pod mates were figured into the equation when fishing quotas are decided upon?

This kind of approach invites further reframing of ethics issues. How should we think about the salmon themselves? How does their desire to live (whether based in instinct or in consciousness) factor in? In the human realm, what about the difference between feasting on salmon as a luxury food and eating salmon because it is part of one's subsistence basis? Should the clamor for salmon among people whose foodways are not traditionally salmon-based be distinguished from the foraging ways of indigenous people?

Santiago-Avila, Lynn, and Treves specialize in asking mind-expanding questions, and they do it again when they write about the management of gray wolves in Wisconsin. Their framework rests on the explicit inclusion of predators like wolves in the moral community, defined as the community of beings whose lives should become our moral concern. This inclusion, the ecologists say, would break the world of carnivore management out of its sticky bind: trapped between one focus on human needs and another on species or ecosystems (but not individual animals). What's desirable is a goal to extend "moral considerability to both individuals and ecological communities, recognizing that both have a well-being that needs to be explicitly considered at the same time."

But how to do this? Here we find ourselves right back in the realm of ethics as they pertain to hunting. For Santiago-Avila et al., ethics should explicitly be incorporated into carnivore management policies in such a way that lethal management isn't the initial go-to response across the board. During the 2012–14 period of federal "delisting" from endangered status, gray wolves in Wisconsin became fair game for "sustainable hunts." Hunters were allowed to take wolves with firearms, bows and arrows, steel-jawed foothold traps, and tracking dogs. Kills across the three years were 117, 257, and 154 wolves respectively. Rhetoric around the hunt centered on conserving wolves by keeping the wolf population at target levels. In fact, as the authors' documentary analysis shows, the nine federal and state documents governing Wisconsin wolf management focused almost exclusively on human interests, such as human enjoyment of wildlife inclusive of hunting opportunities. There was no strong push toward nonlethal management methods, and concern for individual animals went only so far as keeping their suffering to a minimum once shot with a gun or arrow or caught in a trap. In the authors' words, "the vital interest of wolves in living is subordinated" in every way to human recreational interests. As is true in many states, wolves themselves are nearly demonized as causes of livestock kills and diminished ecosystem diversity, when in fact the numbers for Wisconsin show low predation on cattle. Wolf presence there is even linked to *increased* ecosystem diversity.

Carnivore management is complex, and I've been able only to hint at some of the issues here. Importantly, it should be recognized that some of these "fresh" questions are fresh only in a modern Western context of wildlife management. We would do well, in the words of animal-law scholar Maneesha Deckha, to "imagine relations with animals anew" by looking to non-Western and indigenous cultures and their traditions for "better, harmonious, and nonviolent ways of living with animals." Although taking up this view goes beyond the scope of my subject here, I once again recommend a reading of Deckha's work on this theme.

Next I move away from wild lands to explore what happens when wildness is no longer allowed an animal. What does zoo or aquarium living mean for animals? How may compassionate action for these animals be expressed?

4
Animals in Zoos

For an octopus groupie like me, the moment was surreal: Professor (full name Professor Ludwig Von Drake), a male giant Pacific octopus at Boston's New England Aquarium, approached the side of his tank where I stood. On a gorgeous September day, I had been invited behind the public area into the aquarists' work space. Now I was instructed to stand on a short movable staircase in front of one of the two octopus tanks. Next to me offering a snack of fish to the Professor stood Wilson Menashi, a longtime volunteer caretaker of the aquarium's octopuses and supervisor of my encounter. With sure and forceful movements, one of the Professor's eight arms climbed the tank wall and embraced my own arm. I had no fish to offer; I was being greeted simply for the curiosity of it. As the bright-white suckers studding the Professor's arm tasted my skin, I flashed on the amazing thought that in that moment I was wrapped in a smart creature's brain.

More correctly, in part of his brain. Octopus neurons are distributed throughout the animal's arms, a challenging pattern for mammals like us to imagine. It's often said that meeting an octopus is like meeting an alien, but I didn't feel that; instead I felt in the presence of a gorgeous and formidably smart creature. The suckers are complex organs in their own right. As Sy Montgomery puts it in *The Soul of an Octopus*, "Each sucker is operated by individual nerves that the octopus controls voluntarily and independently. And each sucker is fantastically strong." I felt that strength and was both enraptured by it and grateful for Wilson's presence, because he peeled the suckers off my arm when the Professor became overenthused about encircling me.

It was Montgomery who had arranged for me to meet Wilson (the name Mr. Menashi went by; he died in 2019) and the Professor. Wilson fervently believed this kind of interaction—because it is entirely up to the octopus whether he chooses to participate—is good enrichment for the animals. Aquarium residents don't choose their own captivity of course; both the Professor and the female octopus Freya in the adjoining tank were wild caught in Pacific waters. For this reason, any notion of "choice" by aquarium animals needs to be understood as quite limited.

As the Professor and I interacted, Freya spread out her magnificent mantle and arms across the clear window that separated her own tank from the Professor's. "She's jealous," we joked. No one was seriously suggesting that humans can detect a state of jealousy in an invertebrate mollusk, if mollusks are even capable of such a state in the first place. We *were* recognizing, though, that the two octopuses are highly attuned to their environment and that in some way they were thinking about events going on around them. After leaving the Professor for an aquarium tour and some lunch, we returned and spent some time with Freya, who at about forty pounds outweighed the Professor by fifteen. I was immediately struck by the difference in her manner from the Professor's. Despite her larger size, the movement of her body and limbs occurred in a lower key than the Professor's excitable one. It was as if an intense rocking piece by Springsteen and the E Street band (think "Badlands") had modulated into a calmer, more reflective, but still sharply provocative melody (think "The River"). I was flattered when she tasted my skin even in the absence of any fish snack from Wilson; her encircling motions were far gentler. I was able to see her gaze quite clearly as one of her eyes fixed in my direction. When we parted, no red raised "bath-mat pattern" circles were inscribed on my skin as had been the case once the Professor withdrew his arm from mine.

Cephalopods like octopuses light up many animal lovers because they live by their wits in ways we never suspected, until quite recently, that they could. For a few years now I've been fairly obsessed with cephalopod science, so that one way my family and friends express fondness for me is by embracing my octopus stories. Here's a good one that illustrates the kind of thinking-in-the-moment of which octopus brains are capable.

An octopus in waters off the South African coast is in trouble. Caught on camera by a dive team filming underwater for the *Blue Planet II* television documentary narrated by Sir David Attenborough, she has been seized by a pyjama shark. (For convenience, I'm picking a pronoun for the octopus with a 50% chance of being right.) Just as it looks as if the octopus is doomed to become fish meal, she jams some of her arms straight into the shark's gills, rendering the shark unable to breathe. After a struggle, the fish is forced to let go. The scene shifts and again a shark attacks. This time (watch for yourself via the URL I offer at the back of the book) the octopus deploys her arms to collect and drape herself with shells from the sea environment. Before us materializes a scalloped wedding cake or a fussily decorated hat—certainly no octopus is visible! The shark noses around some, no doubt scenting the octopus, but—where is she? Suddenly the octopus jets away, having saved herself through an act of cognitive reasoning. Her emotions we can't guess, but octopuses in captivity do flash their moods on their skin through the chromatophore cells present there.

These celebrities of the sea are at once familiar—we smart mammals do recognize a brainy attitude when we see one—and otherworldly. There's no face to gaze upon as we do with an elephant or a chimpanzee, a dog or a cat. I had to study a diagram just to find the octopus brain, located above the arms near the funnel, although as I have noted most neurons are distributed across the arms. (*Arms* is the accurate term; *tentacles* is not.) The other organs are found inside the mantle, that bulging area I originally assumed housed the brain. Can we readily feel compassion for a creature whose working parts we can't resolve into the form of a familiar sentient being?

At the Virginia Aquarium in Virginia Beach in 2015, I spent some time watching a common octopus, whose natural habitat is the Atlantic Ocean. An enrichment puzzle, an oval hamster tube stuffed with shrimp and tiny toys, was floated by the aquarist into the octopus's tank. The animal—unnamed, probably a female about three years old—moved her arms in a coordinated way as she worked out how to unpack the edible prize inside. For thirty minutes the octopus was occupied with this puzzle, a period during which her chromatophores darkened from red to dark red, almost surely a sign of her engagement and excitement. Watch an octopus for a while as I did in Virginia Beach and Boston, and you catch the cephalopod rhythm, different from ours but notably cerebral.

Is it acceptable to keep a clever octopus enclosed and on public display, deciding that she should be an "ambassador" for her species? The "ambassador" concept is ubiquitous in the zoo and aquarium world. Individual animals give up their freedom because zoo and aquarium scientists hope that up-close viewing of them creates in visitors a greater appreciation for the species in question and, more broadly, the pressing need to preserve the natural world. Of course there's no consent form issued to the confined animals. They have no effective way to resist becoming ambassadors. For that reason I think the term is slightly shady and certainly self-serving. (The "self" in this case is the zoo-aquarium world.)

In *The Soul of an Octopus*, Montgomery captures perfectly the delicate dance of octopus captivity. About the keeping of Octavia, an aging giant Pacific octopus who lived at the New England Aquarium in years prior to the Professor's and Freya's tenure, Montgomery wrote this:

> Because of human intervention, Octavia never got to meet a male to fertilize her eggs. Despite her assiduous care, she would never see her eggs hatch. But we had fed her and protected her; we had provided her with marine neighbors, interesting views, and entertaining interactions with people and puzzles. We had kept her from hunger, fear, and pain. In the wild, virtually every hour of every day would have brought the risk that a predator would bite off part of her body, or that she would be torn limb from limb and eaten alive.

Montgomery's passage is apt because the totting up of costs and benefits to captive animals is meaningless if the alternative—the wild—is made out to be a pristine place of unfettered freedom. As we have seen (chapter 3), it isn't for almost any animal. The aquarists who care for octopuses at the best captive facilities respect their charges and feel genuine affection for them, as I saw for myself in Boston and Virginia Beach. This care may prolong the animals' lives, compared to life in the ocean. At the same time, there is something jarring about what happens when an octopus ages out of public display. When one octopus stops eating, thins, or ails, Montgomery explains, the aquarist "orders a new one." The new animal often shows up via Federal Express, as we might order a new toaster or a new pair of running shoes.

Would I want to be kept in captivity as protection from all the harms of my human life of freedom, ranging from car crashes to infectious disease? Would I want to be confined with puzzles to amuse me, individuals of another species to interact with, and most of my choices made for me? By grappling with these thoughts, I mean to point us toward another set of questions: Isn't something greatly amiss about a system in which one species controls every aspect of other animals' lives primarily for that species' own entertainment? Do other animals (some might wish to stipulate sentient animals) have an inviolable right not to be kept captive by humans? This issue is pressing in the twenty-first century. Should animals be in zoos at all? Which animals, and which zoos? How should we think about zoos, and how might we practice compassionate action when we visit them?

*   *   *

Scimitar-horned oryx are elegant mammals, adapted exquisitely to life in their natural home, the deserts of North Africa. Their name reveals one of their most striking features: horns that curve back from their head in a glorious arc. The pale color of the oryx's body and face—a paleness that helps cool them in the hot temperatures of their homeland—is interrupted by a red swath around the neck. The face is slashed by black markings. Shaped over time by the forces of evolution for a furnacelike climate are hooves adapted for walking on the sand, and eyelashes and eyelids that protect against sand whipping against the face. These antelopes can cope perfectly well with heat, reaching at times an internal temperature of 116 degrees Fahrenheit. Plants they favor, ranging from grasses and roots to melons, yield water when consumed. When necessary, oryx can survive for months without drinking at a source of standing water.

Given this set of adaptations, it's easy to picture a herd of oryx making its way across the Sahara or the Sahel, leaving tracks in the sands of Morocco, Tunisia, Algeria, Libya, Egypt, Mauritania, Mali, Niger, Chad, or Sudan. These days that image is a mere wish; in 2000, the species was declared extinct in the wild. No individual had been sighted in its native region since 1988. The eons of evolution that prepared the oryx to thrive in scorching desert could not equip it to withstand the incursion of humans into their homelands. Although no single cause is responsible for the oryx's extinction, several pressures cluster under an "anthropogenic" umbrella: people hunted the animals for meat; people poached their coat and their horns; people reduced oryx land and resources as they farmed and grazed livestock.

Scimitar-horned oryx do reside in zoos, where, I suspect, people may walk right by their enclosures without a second glance on their way to the so-called charismatic zoo dwellers: the big cats, great apes, elephants, or pandas. Antelopes? Pretty enough for a moment's glance, but hardly stars at the zoo.

Yet in another way scimitar-horned oryx are zoo luminaries, because the hope that exists for these beautiful animals to retake their natural habitat is zoo centered. Zoos around the world have collaborated with wildlife agencies centered in Abu Dhabi and Chad in order to keep the scimitar-horned oryx breeding in captivity and to work toward reintroduction efforts in the wild. In the United States, oryx have been bred at the Smithsonian Conservation Biology Institute in Front Royal, Virginia, an arm of the National Zoological Park. The Front Royal oryx became test subjects, along with oryx at the Fossil Rim Wildlife Center in Glenrose, Texas, for GPS collars to be worn by animals reintroduced in North Africa. Conservation biologists studied any behavioral or hormonal changes to the oryx wearing the collars, then shared the data with the manufacturers, who worked to improve the collar's fit.

A great leap forward in the reintroduction occurred in 2016 when a herd of around twenty-five oryx was established in Ouadi Rimé-Ouadi Achim Faunal Reserve in Chad, a protected area the size of Scotland. Later that same year, following an oryx mom's gestation period nearly the length of humans', conservation scientists celebrated the first birth of a scimitar-horned oryx baby in the wild in at least two decades. There's nothing like a wild newborn of an "extinct" species to fire up scientific commitment! More releases followed, and reports in late 2019 indicate a total of 202 oryx roaming freely in the reserve.

Successful conservation projects like this one, a large-scale cooperative effort aimed at restoring an animal to its homeland, focus on benefits to the animals themselves. They stand in sharp contrast to the "entertainment-first" perspective that most zoos adopt. The harsh realities of life for many animals in captivity are coming into increasingly sharp relief as investigative journalists, photojournalists, and animal activists peel back the curtain to reveal shoddy conditions and practices at many of the world's zoos. As my concern for zoo animals has deepened, I have become convinced that it's time for a change in outlook toward the notion of ambassador animals.

In June 2016 I listened to Dennis Kelly, then director of the National Zoological Park, describe the oryx project in glowing terms as we sat next to each other in the Washington, DC, studio of the Diane Rehm radio show. Kelly and I were speaking on air with host Tom Gjelten sitting in for Diane, with *New York Times* blogger Andrew Revkin Skyping in as the third guest. The three of us were asked to grapple with this question, do zoos have a place in the modern world? My job, as I saw it, was to mount the most cogent argument for rethinking the zoo system as it now exists. Naturally enough for a zoo director, Kelly spoke from a different perspective.

The immediate impetus for the show was the death of the silverback gorilla Harambe at the Cincinnati Zoo the previous month. A toddler had fallen into the zoo's gorilla enclosure, and when powerful Harambe began to drag the child through the water of the moat, zoo employees shot him. In my on-air remarks I suggested that "blame mode" was not very helpful. Social media had exploded in the wake of Harambe's death—indeed Harambe was to become a worldwide-popular meme, with his image photoshopped into all sorts of bizarre scenes. His photo appeared online, for instance, alongside those of celebrities who had died that same year, including Muhammad Ali, Prince, and David Bowie. Too much online animus was, I thought, directed (by one set of outraged persons) at the zoo employees who shot Harambe or (by a competing set of outraged persons) at the parents in charge of this little boy who wandered away on his own toward the gorilla enclosure. Didn't zoo employees do the best they could to protect a young child in a moment of sudden crisis? As for the parents, having been the mom of a fast-moving and headstrong toddler, I could never criticize them; what happened to the boy's parents could happen to any parent in a flash.

On the air we mostly discussed not Harambe's death but instead the larger situation with zoos (see a full transcript at a link provided at the back of this book). How can zoos build enclosures to prevent this sort of catastrophe from unfolding? More broadly, should gorillas be in zoos in the first place? Should tens of millions of dollars be spent on new zoo enclosures for elephants? Should orcas be made to perform at SeaWorld, a facility that is accredited by the AZA, the Association of Zoos and Aquariums?

Learning about the oryx project from Director Kelly's remarks was a highlight of the hour's conversation for me. I was struck also by something else that Kelly said: "We continue to be the favorite place in our area, in Washington, for families with children. It's a magical experience; 2.6 million people come." This emphasis on human entertainment led me to ask him, how often is the zoo a magical experience for the animals kept there?

For an animal lover who got her start in zoos as a graduate student, voicing this question to the top administrator of one of the most famous zoos in the world was the product of a long journey. Without a doubt, the zoo world, including the very zoo that Kelly led, helped me to grow professionally. The first fellowship I landed as a graduate student to conduct original research on primates involved observing two adult orangutans named Les Tunka and Toba housed at the Oklahoma City Zoo. I arranged for a device to be manufactured that acted as a food puzzle for them, so that they could retrieve items to eat from it using a ladle tool, then observed their exploration of the apparatus. During the fellowship period I was housed in the basement of a building on zoo grounds, the upper floor of which was devoted to animal necropsies. If I was at home when an animal was brought in for dissection, a pungent sensory experience followed, most acutely, if memory serves me, with an ostrich. I continued as an avid student of orangutan behavior the following summer, this time with a fellowship at the National Zoological Park—the same zoo where I would, years later as an anthropology professor, bring students to assist me in observing and filming the gestures of a family of gorillas. And of course, the same zoo whose director I would debate on public radio thirty-four summers later.

At the National Zoo, staff are knowledgeable about and devoted to their charges. New Year's Eve 1999 sticks in my mind because zoo employees arranged a sleepover at the zoo, not because they enjoyed spending a holiday night away from their loved ones but because (as amusing as it may seem now) wild worries existed about Y2K ("year 2K," or the year 2000). What would happen to all our technology at the moment our clocks ticked over into a new century? Would computers and other machines fail to function or somehow go haywire? (The answers turned out to be nothing and no, respectively.)

More routinely, at team meetings, staff reviewed not only basic care plans of food, exercise, and enrichment for the animals but also the latest animal-behavior articles in science journals. They discussed and debated when it was safe to allow animals to resolve their own conflicts and when human intervention was required. Let's say an adolescent male gorilla begins to challenge the group's stronger silverback, and fights between the two males increase in frequency and intensity. When should the group be left to work out the changing dynamics on its own, and when should a transfer for one of the males be arranged, mimicking what often happens in the wild when subadult males depart their natal group to establish a new group of their own? Might the subadult be a good candidate for transfer under the Species Survival Plan, when animals and their genes are moved around across states? Zoo-to-zoo animal transfer unfolds in consultation with the keeper of what's called the International Gorilla Studbook, to ensure genetic diversity in zoo breeding, or "ensure" insofar as the animals matched up choose to follow the plan. Management of captive animals isn't just about distribution of bananas and cleaning of cages. It regularly involves choreographing the lives of animals, some from endangered species and pretty much all with distinct personalities and preferences.

How often at zoos do the resident animals enjoy positive experiences? This question is central to figuring out how, when, and where to put compassionate action for zoo animals into action. Yet I know of no direct way to answer this question. Millions of animals are confined at the world's zoos. In the United States alone, 230 zoos and zoolike facilities are currently AZA accredited. (Other countries or continents have their own accrediting organizations. Around 370 facilities are accredited by the equivalent body in Europe, the EAZA, for example.) When David Grazian published his book *American Zoo* in 2014, the US number was 228: 138 conventional zoos, 43 aquariums, 10 hybrid zoo/aquariums, 18 safari and theme parks, 15 science and nature centers, 2 aviaries, and 2 butterfly houses. A total of 6,000 species, made up of 751,931 individual animals, were housed in these places. What picture do we have of their lives?

Writing in *Zoo Biology* in an article titled "In Pursuit of Peak Animal Welfare: The Need to Prioritize the Meaningful over the Measurable," Jake S. Veasey makes a nuanced argument that captivity isn't *necessarily* tied to negative animal welfare. Traditionally, physical welfare has been prioritized over psychological well-being in assessing how well animals do in zoos, and this should change, according to Veasey. Many zoos in North America, for instance, feed processed chow to large carnivores. This diet may work well for the animals in the physical sense, or it may not; Veasey points to health risks related to muscle changes and oral health. What almost certainly goes missing, though, in a zoo's evaluation process are the psychological consequences of this diet to animals who evolved to hunt. The answer, Veasey suggests, is to make the emotional well-being of zoo residents the primary indicator of animal welfare.

In this focus on welfare, Veasey points us in a good direction, because as I'm about to outline in some detail, zoos all too often fail animals. Keep one point in mind, though: in centering animal welfare, Veasey embraces a starting point divergent from one rooted instead in animal rights. As an ethics guide on the BBC website puts it, "Animal rights advocates are campaigning for no cages, while animal welfarists are campaigning for bigger cages." No matter how well-treated zoo residents may be, on a rights perspective their well-being is violated by the very fact of their captivity.

Zoos are run by and primarily for humans. Even when zoo personnel are committed to good animal welfare, they are only human, and humans make mistakes. It's a generous impulse to forgive human error, and at the same time, it's the animals who pay. Gorilla youngster Kabibe was a favorite among the staff and visitors at the San Francisco Zoo. After having been first rejected by her mother Nneka and then hand raised by the zoo for six months, she enjoyed a close relationship with her grandmother Bawang. One day in 2014, when Kabibe was fifteen months old, the gorillas were being moved from their outdoor to their indoor enclosure. Kabibe darted in an unanticipated direction and was crushed to death under a hydraulic door. There was no time for a zookeeper to deploy the door's "instant stop" switch mechanism intended to prevent such accidents. In the wake of this death of a highly endangered primate, the zoo paid a fine of $1,750.

San Francisco Zoo workers, especially those who cared for the gorillas, must have been devastated at the tragedy that ensued. There's no use in pointing blameful fingers at an individual, any more than there is in accusing Cincinnati Zoo staff for wrongdoing in the death of gorilla Harambe. In Kabibe's case even more than Harambe's, though, this was an accident waiting to happen. Five zookeepers told the *San Francisco Chronicle* newspaper in the wake of the youngster's death that "safety in the 30-year-old gorilla enclosure was compromised by a flawed layout, problems with the doors and inadequate staffing." To the zoo's credit, administrators then hired an expert in captive great apes, Terry Maple, to assess the enclosure. His report was alarming, according to the *San Francisco Chronicle*: "A person using the control panel with the emergency button would not have a clear, unimpeded view of all of the doors—or of the enclosures behind them. And the doors aren't designed to stop when they hit something, like garage or elevator doors."

The San Francisco Zoo is not the only institution at which this kind of accident has occurred. In 2005 a lion cub at the Niabi Zoo in Illinois was killed when an eighty-pound pulley on a door in his enclosure failed; the door fell on him, severing his spinal cord. That same year a monkey was killed by an electric door at the National Zoo, as a capybara was four years later at the Calgary Zoo.

Nor is it just doors that cause harm. Let's look at a single accredited zoo, the National Zoo, in a single year, 2013. Earlier I praised my experiences with professional staff at this zoo. Yet that professionalism could not prevent a sad litany of events that year: A lesser kudu died from a broken neck after becoming startled and running into a wall of the antelope enclosure. A gazelle died after crashing into a wall on the same day that a zebra, housed in an adjoining enclosure, attacked a zoo employee who hadn't properly secured the animal before cleaning the area. A four-month-old Przewalski's horse colt living at the conservation center of the zoo, the same facility I noted in discussing scimitar-horned oryx, charged a fence and died. A red panda named Rusty escaped from the zoo and wandered the DC neighborhood of Adams Morgan before being caught in a net and safely returned.

Are the incidents that year at the National Zoo representative of what happens in zoos more broadly? While that would not be an accurate claim, I could easily write a book chapter devoted entirely to zoo tragedies. Escapes don't always end as benignly as red panda Rusty's did. When a Siberian tiger named Tatiana escaped from her enclosure at the San Francisco Zoo on Christmas Day 2007, she killed a seventeen-year-old boy and injured two other teenagers. Tiger expert Laurie Gage suggested that it was highly likely, though not certain, that Tatiana had been provoked: why else would she have jumped from the bottom of a dry moat to the top of a wall, then hauled herself over the top, leaving behind claw marks? The father of one of the injured teenagers in fact told police that his son reported he had been drunk that day and had yelled and waved at the tiger.

Tatiana died in what the *Los Angeles Times* reported to be "a hail of police gunfire." To hark back once more to Harambe's death, my problem isn't with that decision, as tragic as it was. Options are limited when lives are at stake in an unfolding crisis. Tranquilizer darts fired at large, highly aroused mammals, like gorillas and big cats, may fail to take effect in time. What's notable is that once again—in a pattern running through many zoo incidents—the enclosure was found to be inadequate: the wall of the tiger enclosure was lower than federal standards require. In this case the fine was $1,875.

Just as with the accounts of accidents documented in zoos, accounts of escapes are multiplied many times over. Some get a lot of press attention in the way that Tatiana's escape did—as with the gorilla Jabari, who was killed after escaping from the Dallas Zoo in 2004, or the three chimpanzees killed after escaping from a small zoo in Nebraska the following year. Yet I haven't succeeded in finding a database that would furnish statistics about the frequencies of escapes.

To consider fully the ethics of zoo captivity, we need to broaden our gaze. In Europe, zoo animals die in yet another way that is unnatural. In a practice not found (or at the very least not routine) in the US, healthy animals are culled as "surplus" beings for whom the zoo no longer has room. The killing of a healthy young giraffe named Marius at Denmark's Copenhagen Zoo in 2014 ignited furious discussion worldwide and opened my eyes to this practice. In the sorrowful pantheon of animals who become celebrities only in death, Marius is right up there with Harambe—except that Marius had done nothing remotely worrisome. He was born, lived his life, and at age two was killed by an intentional bolt-gun strike to the head. Marius's body was publicly dissected, then fed to zoo lions. Copenhagen Zoo officials refused to send him to another zoo that might, they explained, be "substandard," so they killed him instead.

In 2015, also in Denmark, Odense Zoo staff killed a healthy nine-month-old lion they marked as "surplus." As an educational endeavor, the lion was then dissected in front of school-children. The BBC reports that upwards of three thousand healthy animals, perhaps as many as five thousand healthy animals, are killed in European zoos every year. That number stunned me when I first learned it, and it stuns me still. When zoos breed animals, they should, I believe, take on responsibility for the physical and emotional well-being of the babies born. As an anthropologist, I work to understand different cultural practices. The Danish cultural value of introducing young children to animal dissections is not a practice to be dismissed in a knee-jerk fashion. Whether it's a moment ripe for learning or instead for emotional distress experienced by children who see (and from news accounts, smell) a young lion being cut up in front of their eyes, I don't know. When it comes to killing healthy animals because they no longer fit in with a zoo's scheme to entertain its visitors, for me any notion of cultural relativism is overtaken by empathy for healthy young animals with years left to live. Is a short-term solution really so elusive? Giving birth-control pharmaceuticals to breeding females is a routine practice in US zoos, one that directly addresses the specter of "surplus" animals.

Looking beyond accidents, escapes, and culling, we come to the conditions in which zoo animals live their everyday lives. The news here isn't good. *National Geographic* opened one of its online articles in 2019 with this eye-catching paragraph: "In a new report, an animal welfare group has flagged hundreds of zoos affiliated with the World Association of Zoos and Aquariums (WAZA) for mistreating animals, including making big cats perform in gladiator-style shows, elephants play basketball, and diapered chimpanzees ride scooters." The animal welfare group in question is called World Animal Protection, and another of its stunning conclusions is that 75 percent of WAZA's 1,241 affiliates allow at least one animal–human interaction to occur.

These up-close encounters range from petting cheetahs in an enclosed yard to swimming with dolphins. Dolphin encounters, for instance, occur at SeaWorld in the United States, a member of AZA, and other AZA-accredited institutions allow hand feeding of animals or close-up selfies with them. The San Diego Zoo, widely considered to be a top global zoo, offers on its website (I looked on February 25, 2020) this opportunity for $99 and up: "See exotic cats climb and jump and much more! Bring your camera to this fun and interactive experience, as we bring the animals out to you for an up-close view. Our expert trainers will also take you behind the scenes to feed, touch, or help train some of our animal ambassadors. You will hear amazing stories about each animal you meet, and find out how the San Diego Zoo is helping to save species here and around the world. Some animals are unique to this experience and can only be viewed by attending Animals In Action! Reserve your spot today!"

At the Columbus Zoo, staff members remove cheetahs from their enclosures, drive them to locations around Ohio, and exhibit them for money, in the name of conservation. At the zoo's website (I looked on February 25, 2020), underneath a photograph of four zoo employees surrounding a collared cheetah lying on a table, this question is posed: "Have you ever wanted to see a cheetah up close?" For a one-hour presentation, the text explains, the cost is $600 to bring the cheetah to adult "community groups and college/university students" within two nearby Ohio counties, and $800 within the state but outside those two counties. In this case, any stress associated with up-close encounters with humans is surely magnified for the animals by up to hundreds of miles of transport outside the zoo.

At both San Diego and Columbus Zoos—more examples in the United States alone could be cited as well—the message of "up close, personal and with selfies" goes against conservationists' recommendation for keeping our distance from wild animals (chapter 3). In privately owned roadside zoos in the US, those not accredited by the AZA, problems are sometimes much more severe; the quality of care is often questionable and sometimes downright horrifying. These places are often licensed and inspected by the USDA, the Department of Agriculture. Grazian reports 2,764 licenses given by the USDA to "animal exhibitors ranging from roadside attractions to high-tech breeding centers." The plight of bears who aren't given adequate pools of water in which to cool down in summer's heat (chapter 1) only hints at the scope of the problem. Even when no headline-grabbing deaths occur, the grinding daily misery brought about by bleak old-style concrete cages with iron bars or dirty glass windows leads to a wearing away of the spirit for untold numbers of animals.

Images taken by photojournalist Jo-Anne McArthur of the organization We Animals reveal the conditions under which zoo animals are too often forced to live even in accredited zoos. McArthur visited numerous zoos around the world from Canada to Croatia, Germany to Australia and Poland to the United States, identifying them in her book *Captive* by country. No city or zoo name is specified. As I lingered over the photographs, I thought maybe most of the zoos, depicted in page after page with sterile living quarters for animals, were nonaccredited. I was wrong. "I specifically visited some of the best zoos in the world, to show that it's the same there [as in nonaccredited zoos]," McArthur told me. "As a rough estimate, I'd say that 75 percent of the zoos represented in *Captive* are accredited." By the phrase "it's the same there," McArthur explained, she meant not things like cage sizes or quality of care but that "the animals experienced similar boredom and lack of autonomy."

For three days I sat with *Captive*, taking in the images as fully as I could, proceeding a little at a time. An Asian elephant confined in a Slovenian zoo stands alone and indoors on dirty concrete. The elephant leans up against a green-painted wall in a bleak room adorned with steel bars, feces on the floor, and a bare piece of wood that resembles a thin tree trunk. A mandrill monkey lies on a ledge in a German zoo. Out of focus in the background is a zoo wall and, again, some kind of tree trunk. In focus are the monkey's eyes, gazing right at the photographer and as empty as his or her enclosure. Or are they? Is the monkey's gaze perhaps a knowing, resigned one? The gaze of a lion photographed by McArthur, surrounded by cage mesh and bars at a German zoo, is equally memorable. Caught in midstride, the maned male has the eyes of a contemplative.

Surprising to me in *Captive* is how often McArthur includes zoo visitors in her photographic frame and the extent to which their presence adds poignancy. The image I return to most often shows a Baltic gray seal sitting alone in a small pool of greenish water at a Lithuanian zoo. The seal rests on a white platform in the water; the pool's foundation is concrete or some other hard white material. To the railings around the pool's perimeter are affixed multiple white balloons, and there stand dozens of staring spectators. Surrounded by life, the seal looks utterly alone.

Typically a zoo visit, McArthur notes, lasts between one and three hours. To all of us McArthur issues a challenge: "Use all of the zoo's opening hours to stay and be with the animals. Spend an hour at the bear enclosure, memorizing her every move. Count the seconds it takes her to pace from one end of the fence to the other. . . . I challenge you to stay with that animal all day and not leave sensitized to the depravity of captivity."

One morning in 2019 at Disney's Animal Kingdom in Orlando, Florida, I experienced the power in McArthur's challenge and the difficulty in meeting it. In the "Oasis" section of the park, my attention was caught by a mammal in the swine

family called a babirusa, native to Indonesia. A male with formidable tusks—or accurately, upper canines that, as with all
babirusa males, had pushed through the skin to curve back in a
spectacular arc over the face—paced through part of his enclosure. Back and forth he went, across the dirt, past plants and
trees. His path did not vary. I realized that I was witnessing a
stereotypy: the persistent repetition of an action that has no
function. In zoo animals, stereotypies usually indicate abnormal behavior that points to stress.

I didn't have the heart to stand there watching the babirusa
cover the same patch of ground over and over, not even for one
hour, and thus I failed McArthur's challenge. I left him, as he
could not possibly leave his captivity. As I toured other animal
enclosures and enjoyed lunch with my family, however, that
pacing pig did not leave my mind. Four or five hours later I made
my way back to the babirusa enclosure. Now it was midafter-
noon, and a tuskless female was present in the enclosure instead
of the male. She paced also. Her path was slightly different, but
the nature of her movement was the same. I filmed her briefly,
as I had done with the male, then spotted a zookeeper at work
one enclosure over. Approaching her, I considered how to pose
questions that conveyed my concern in a tone of collegiality. Deciding not to mention my own work with animals, I remarked
on the animals' pacing. The keeper told me that the babirusa
"walk, dig, and forage" in their enclosure. What I had seen was
pacing, not walking, I told her. From that point the conversation
did not go well. The keeper said that she had worked with the
pigs for ten years, emphasizing that they don't pace all day and
that they are "adored" at Animal Kingdom.

Trying again, I asked what Animal Kingdom thought about
the pacing and what could possibly be done. Enrichment does
occur, the keeper responded, such as distributing special items
that take time for the animals to forage. When I ventured to

say that the babirusa don't seem happy in their enclosure, she laughed in a not-nice way. Even as I uttered it, I knew that the word *happy* represented a risk, a word easy to dismiss as mere anthropomorphism: yet animals do have better days and worse days, better lives and worse lives, and they frequently express emotions. This we know.

Once back home, I mailed a letter to Animal Kingdom, expressing my concerns about the babirusas' pacing and about the keeper's response to me. Thus I spoke up twice about my worries for the animals and their care: once in the moment on site, then again by mail. A few weeks later, a detailed reply arrived in my email inbox from Scott Terrell, who identified himself to me as a veterinarian and the director of Animal and Science Operations of Walt Disney Parks and Resorts. The letter was very welcome in its specific addressing of both my concerns. Most importantly, Terrell wrote this about the babirusa:

> I have asked my science and welfare team to review this case and let me know if any action is required. I agree 100% with you on your statement about emotional states and looking at the animal from an output-based perspective. I believe we can infer a lot from observing the behavior of our animals to assess their affective or emotional states. In fact, we are doing a lot of work at DAK to drive this focus across the zoo community through proactive welfare assessments. I do know that our babirusa team is very focused on reproduction now and I wonder if this animal may have been exhibiting some anticipatory behavior.

A challenge endemic to speaking up at zoos and aquariums is the rarity with which outcomes can be known. I may never know what, if anything, happened regarding either the babirusa's pacing or the keeper's method of communication with the public after Terrell wrote his email to me. On the other hand, I might; Terrell and I have exchanged further cordial emails; his animal-behavior expertise combined with his openness in communicating is impressive (and I'll have more positive things to say about Animal Kingdom shortly). I do know that my speaking up was a small act of compassionate action. If others have spoken up or will speak up too, the resulting cumulative record of park visitors' concerns may strengthen a chance of closer staff attunement to these animals' pacing, and to the nature of keepers' interaction with genuinely concerned members of the public.

With an exception here and there, I have constructed a fairly dismal picture of zoos. Might that position be contested? Might the "zoo ambassadors" meme carry kernels of truth after all? Are the costs to individual animals of captivity, in all but the most egregious cases, offset by a large gain to the viewing public in a way that loops back around to help animals in the long run? Perhaps zoo patrons come away from a day at the zoo with increased knowledge about animals and about the importance of conservation measures. If this were true, the zoos-as-entertainment concept would be too simple, and expressions of compassion for zoo animals too simple as well.

The data on this issue are mixed at best. The first longitudinal study to track whether visitors retain what they learn about biodiversity in the wake of their zoo visit appeared in *Zoo Biology* in 2017. Senior author Eric A. Jensen and his colleagues contacted 1,640 people, a subsample of 5,661 respondents who had participated about two years before in a previsit and postvisit assessment survey. That earlier survey had been administered at twenty-six accredited zoos in nineteen countries around the world. How did Jensen's team arrive at the number 1,640? That was the number of people who had offered their email addresses when they answered the original survey two years before and thus could be contacted with follow-up queries. When the new survey was made available online in eight languages, 161 people (out of the 1,640) responded. Researchers thus ended up with a data set from 161 people who had answered an identical set of questions three times: at zoo entry, at zoo departure, and at two years following the zoo visit.

In an attempt to measure an understanding of biodiversity, the researchers asked these respondents "to list anything that came to mind when they thought of biodiversity," with space for up to five answers. To measure knowledge of actions to help biodiversity, they asked people "to think of an action they could take to help save animal species," with up space for up to two responses. Using a content-analysis methodology and a quantitative analysis, Jensen et al. reported the results: two years after the zoo visit, the level of biodiversity understanding among respondents held constant, and the level of knowledge of actions to help protect biodiversity had significantly increased.

The interpretations offered by the researchers make for the most intriguing part of the paper. To their credit, Jensen et al. note that only 10 percent of the people who had provided their email addresses responded to the follow-up survey. They might also have noted that a final sample of 161 people represents 2.84 percent of the original sample of 5,661. Could it be that people more attuned to biodiversity issues are more likely to complete the follow-up survey, meaning that the zoo visit might not have played much of a role in the increased knowledge? The authors acknowledge that possibility. Their thrust, however, is to suggest that the immediate positive effects of a zoo visit— positive effects already established in the original survey—"may be long lasting and even help lay the groundwork for further improvements over an extended period of time following the visit."

Maybe. Or maybe not. What had happened in the lives of the 161 respondents since the zoo visit about two years earlier can neither be known nor measured. Some of these folks might have taken college courses about biodiversity, read books about biodiversity, or visited museums with exhibits about biodiversity in the period of time that had elapsed since their zoo visit. Nor was it known what the other 97.16 percent of original respondents might have said in response to the follow-up questions. Their answers might have greatly strengthened the researchers' suggestions about the value of the zoo visit, or instead demolished it. We simply don't know.

Curious, I sought out in *Conservation Biology* the paper that had emerged from the original survey, the one with the pre- and immediate postvisit data points of all 5,661 people. To say that the results surprised me would be an understatement. Borrowing from the paper's abstract, I'll let the words of Moss et al. tell the story:

> There was an increase from previsit (69.8%) to postvisit (75.1%) in respondents demonstrating at least some positive evidence of biodiversity understanding. Similarly, there was an increase from previsit (50.5%) to postvisit (58.8%) in respondents who could identify actions to help protect biodiversity that could be achieved at an individual level. Our results are the most compelling evidence to date that zoo and aquarium visits contribute to increasing the number of people who understand biodiversity and know actions they can take to help protect biodiversity.

Without question, the study does demonstrate that a zoo visit increases some people's understanding of biodiversity issues. The quantitative tests undertaken show that the differences reported reach statistical significance. Moss et al. too are to be credited with transparency, because they acknowledge that an increase in knowledge is not the same thing as an change in behavior: in other words, the information gained during a zoo or aquarium visit may not translate into direct action for animals or the environment in any way. Fair enough. An aspect of the results remains unaddressed, though: shouldn't the magnitude of the positive change reported be assessed against the cost to the animals of living in confinement? That is, where is the multispecies context for assessing the fact that knowledge went up by 5.3 percent on one measure and by 8 percent on the other? Is this gain—indeed "the most compelling evidence" so far in the entire zoo and aquarium world—sufficient to make the animal-ambassador concept a worthy one? Is the celebratory tone of the paper—look, we're not just entertainment institutions, we really are educational too—appropriate given how often knowledge did *not* increase after a zoo visit?

Jo-Anne McArthur addresses the cost-benefit argument in two ways in *Captive*. At one point she writes that "no arguments for conservation or education are worth [the] sacrifice" that zoo animals are forced to make. At the same time, she showcases an innovative approach at the Detroit Zoo that gives me hope for a fresh vision of the future for captive animals, one that stops short of complete zoo abolition. The Detroit Zoo's CEO, Ron Kagan, endorses a model for zoos that in McArthur's words centers on "housing only rescued animals and providing an experience for both humans and non-human animals in which both benefit." While the zoo isn't there yet—Kagan's statement invokes aspiration rather than the present-day reality—a look at its Polk Penguin Conservation Center, opened in 2016, underscores its commitment to doing things a better way.

King, macaroni, rockhopper, and gentoo penguins live in the center, which was designed specifically to increase the penguins' opportunities to make decisions about their own behavior and thus to behave more naturally. The Detroit Zoo says it is the largest penguin center anywhere in the world. "A major increase in land space, significantly deeper and greater water space and more variety of substrates are available to the penguins in their new home," the zoo's website declares. Comparing the penguins' behavior in their previous enclosure at the zoo and in the new penguin center revealed that the king penguins increased the amount of time they swam "more than four-fold, with peaks reaching up to 10 times more water-related behaviors." The penguin center has not gone without its troubles, though. Faulty waterproofing was discovered in 2019. Groundwater seeping under the building's foundation forced relocation of the penguins and a need to close the center for months of repairs, currently scheduled to finish in summer 2020.

That zoo penguins swim more naturally in some environments than others doesn't mean that zoo life is the best life for penguins. We come up hard here against the animal welfare versus animal rights distinction: Is it enough to make captivity better for animals by increasing their welfare little by little as they are kept in zoos for us to view? Or is it better to advocate for no captivity at all for animals who are healthy and capable of living in the wild? Is it an intrinsic violation of animals' right to freedom to keep them captive? One way out of accepting a binary set of options—either captivity is acceptable for animals in accredited zoos that attend to their well-being or zoos should be entirely abolished—is to circle back to Kagan's vision, an advocacy for zoos as places where rescued animals, unable to live in the wild, take over the "ambassador" slots, benefiting *them* as well as *us*.

Lori Gruen in *The Ethics of Captivity* writes that "understanding the particularities of captivity is necessary for determining whether or not a particular form of captivity is ever defensible." Here is a key starting place for each of us as we contemplate whether or how to visit zoos. Broad-brush words of praise or condemnation aimed at "zoos" simply don't work well across the board, because zoos vary so much.

Many zoos publish their email address and phone numbers online, and on site docent volunteers often interact with visitors at strategic points at the animal enclosures; there's always a way to ask questions. Exactly how big are the enclosures? Do the animals have access to grassy areas (or whatever landscape is appropriate for their species, including climbing or swimming areas) every clement day? Are they housed in ways socially appropriate to their natural behaviors? To what degree are the animals given choices about how, with whom, and where they spend their time? Do some animals whom we cannot see reside "off exhibit"? If so, why are they there, and under what conditions do they live? Of the animals we do see, who are they—that is, what are their ages and family relationships (if posted signage doesn't inform us)? What enrichment items or activities do keepers make available to the zoo residents, and how often? What percentage of the animals were rescued? Does the zoo envision moving toward a rescued-animal sanctuary model in the future?

In a 2019 research paper written for a class at Lehigh University, graduate student Angie Rizzo pulls no punches in arguing that zoos not only "fabricate a representation of the natural world" but also invest too often in commerce over conservation. "Whether marketing plastic toys in their gift shops, highlighting their 'corporate sponsorships' with the fossil fuel industry, or selling alligator tacos at the food vendor (which, yes, I did see firsthand) zoos in many ways are curtailing true conservation efforts," she writes. Hold in mind Rizzo's point the next time you wander into a zoo restaurant, kiosk, or gift shop. Zoos must generate revenue, but *how* they do this vis-à-vis principles of conservation becomes another opportunity for our close attention. Given that most zoos serve fast-food burgers, chicken nuggets, and other meat from domestic animals who may be exhibited for children to touch in a petting-zoo section, I would add that their messages of loving care for animals tend to be broadly confused at best.

The entertainment-to-education ratio available at zoos is malleable; to some degree, it's up to us. Assessing the physical and emotional health of zoo animals is not a casual job. To be done fairly, it requires multiple visits and listening (at least at accredited zoos) to what on-site professionals have to say. Yet this need for a serious, sustained approach shouldn't be a deterrent to engagement. Health-care workers urge patients to enter doctors' offices armed with informed questions, take notes once there, and follow up with more questions as needed, enabling a full participation in their own health care. Veterinarians may do the same when it comes to pets at home. That model can be adapted to a communitywide engagement aimed at looking out for the physical and emotional health of zoo animals. (When it's best to take this engaged "eyes on" approach at a zoo or instead withdraw all support by no longer visiting is a decision to be made on a case-by-case basis.)

A visit to the zoo needn't be all about carrying a notebook to list problems and harboring a readiness to hate everything we see. It's not the animals' fault, after all, that they're caught up in the zoo system. Getting to know individual orangutans and red pandas, raptors and turtles, in our own local zoo, and to follow their life histories, may be thoroughly enjoyable, a process that does not preclude a skeptical approach to the overall zoo system. There's a reason so many animal lovers fell into a romantic crush on the hippopotamus baby Fiona after her birth, two months premature and very much under normal weight, at the Cincinnati Zoo in January 2017. A superstar, engaging and photogenic, Fiona was and is beloved: she triumphed over uncertain odds of survival and behaves in utterly cute ways. I would have gone to see her had distance easily allowed. Families who take their children to zoos shouldn't be judged negatively, as if they somehow are enacting a failure of compassion or worse, an act of hostility against the animals. The trick is in where and how we visit. We may seek out animals beyond the camera-ready superstars; take a version of McArthur's challenge and stay on one patch of ground awhile to *really look* at what an animal experiences; ask the questions I've mentioned, shared with our children if they are old enough to grapple with ethical issues; and speak up where the animals need us to advocate for them.

For roadside zoos, though, the calculus is different. A refusal to pay entrance admission to these facilities that spring up or worse, endure for years, is a tool of protest along a path toward closing them down entirely. Grazian takes up this point as he concludes *American Zoo*: "We ought to start by gradually ridding ourselves of all roadside animal attractions, circuses, and non-AZA-accredited zoos that exhibit animals more exotic than domesticated farm animals. [The USDA] already regulates these cavalier zoos. It has the authority to dramatically raise its quality standards to meet or even exceed those of the AZA, and over time shutter those zoos that fail to achieve those benchmarks." No reason exists to exclude farm or petting-zoo animals from these basic protections; otherwise Grazian's goal is reasonable, but it does lead to more questions.

Where would residents of shuttered zoos go? Could they ever be reintroduced to the wild? Through a focus on apes and monkeys, our closest living relatives, we may think through this question. Any idealistic notion of reintroducing nonhuman primates to their home forests in Africa, Asia, or South America needs a quick reality check. The John Aspinall Foundation, run now by British businessman Damian Aspinall and named after his father, who raised gorillas at Howletts in Kent, England, reports that "an impressive number of animals" born at Howletts and a sister park nearby have returned to their natural habitats. In addition to western lowland gorillas, these include, according to the foundation, black rhino, Javan langurs and gibbons, European bison and clouded leopards. Damian has become a vocal opponent of zoos, telling *CBS 60 Minutes'* Lesley Stahl in 2015, "If I could extinguish all zoos over the next thirty years, including my own, I would. I wouldn't hesitate."

Yet zoo-raised animals lack the experience to keep themselves safe in a dynamically changing environment. Have you ever boarded a plane to seek beauty and quiet in a faraway place, then upon disembarking found yourself feeling like a stranger in a strange land? The chatter of voices in conversations that seem to be unspooling at high speed, the slightly unfamiliar mannerisms and customs you find yourself observing, the new habitats to navigate using a map—all may bring a thrill accompanied by a dizzying disorientation. Let's push the analogy and in this thought experiment send you from the city into the bush, where you set up camp with a few friends and make a first meal, with some false starts and stress along the way. Wild animals who might be hanging about and weighing you up as a snack worry you considerably. In the end, though, it's no great hardship to figure out how to eat, sleep, and explore the area with a reasonable margin of safety, having prepared ahead of time.

Next, try out a few moments of cross-species perspective taking. In this nonhuman scenario, the plane lands and after some hours of overland transport during which you dozed thanks to a sedative meant to keep you calm, you are released from a crate into a vast forest. The vista of an alien world looms before you, many times larger than the enclosure in which you were born and lived for years. You smell animal danger in the air and have little idea of what is safe to eat or where is safe to sleep; why you are suddenly where you are is a confounding mystery. This mental exercise tells us that a gorilla reintroduced to the wild must be a very confused gorilla. As the president of Dian Fossey Gorilla Fund, primatologist Tara Stoinski, put it to Stahl on *60 Minutes*: "I think that humans have a very romantic notion of what the wild is like, and the wild is not a place where it is safe and animals get to roam free and make choices. They have to find food, they have to avoid predators, they have to find mates. And then you add on top of that all of the challenges that humans are imposing, whether it be hunting, habitat loss, disease." While Aspinall means well, and while his efforts may make him feel virtuous, his reintroduction efforts don't really amount to conservation at all, according to Stoinski.

When Aspinall sent a family of eleven lowland gorillas to an island in Gabon, West Africa, the result was five dead gorillas, including four adult females and one five-year-old juvenile. The cause of these deaths was never definitely determined, but multiple deaths point to some unfolding crisis during the animals' adjustment process. "Back to the wild" enrichment programs may school individual animals ahead of time in what to expect when they arrive back "home" ("home" only in an ancestral sense, of course). On site, humans may help them transition to the novel conditions by offering food. Sometimes this measure may be enough, but often risks remain.

Conservation biologist Benjamin Beck analyzed details of 24,212 reintroduced primates—prosimians, monkeys, and apes—from 234 reintroduction programs, adding weight and heft to individual case studies. Of that total number, 95.9 percent of the animals were wild born and 4.1 percent were captive born. One of Beck's goals was to evaluate success of this type of operation, a tricky thing to measure. He used two criteria for success. The first, Beck writes, "is a lower bar (survival of some of the released individuals for at least one year, and integration with wild conspecifics or post-release reproduction, and ability to survive without provisioning or human support). The second is a higher bar (contributed to the establishment of a self-sustaining wild population)." Beck reports that 43.2 percent of the programs rate as successful using the lower-bar criterion. Of these, 14 percent also met the more stringent criterion.

Looked at one way, this analysis is heartening: nearly half of the reintroductions met with some measure of success. From another perspective though, the results aren't so rosy. Non-human primates, especially monkeys and apes, are long-lived animals; survival of just some released individuals for "at least a year" may be no cause for celebration from the point of view of the released animals themselves. Beck concludes that "reintroduction, even when well planned and executed, is rarely beneficial for the wellbeing of an individual primate. Hunger, aggression, pain and suffering, or at least discomfort, and conflict with humans are common after reintroduction. Freedom comes at a price."

Beck, who had a distinguished career as a zoo scientist including at the National Zoo, goes on to conclude that "life in a supportive, well managed, captive environment is preferable to life in the wild" for many orphaned, rescued, or long-term captive primates. I don't disagree, but as I imagine Beck knows better than most, well-managed captive environments are comparatively rare.

Maybe sending animals to sanctuaries is a more realistic answer, instead of aiming for reintroduction to the wild or actively maintaining the zoo system? Sanctuaries still mean confinement for the animals, but in the best ones the goal shifts from entertainment, and even from education, to prioritizing needs of the animals themselves. The scenes with which I opened this book, set in a cow barn at Farm Sanctuary in Upstate New York as I visited animals in the company of shelter director Susie Coston, attest to this. For his chapter "Sanctuary" in the

volume *Critical Terms for Animal Studies*, Timothy Pachirat—
who was on that same barn tour with me—interviews Coston
and notes her laser-beam focus on the "wants, desires, and
aversions" of specific residents. "When I asked Coston an abstract question about how Farm Sanctuary navigates the tension
between the animals' safety and their autonomy, for example,"
Pachirat writes, "Coston replied by talking about how the sanctuary is constantly adjusting the social groupings of its pigs in
order to accommodate the pigs' desires about whom they want
to spend time with and the tendency for certain pigs to become
the subject of harassment by other pigs. She also told me about
how when a sheep needs to go to the hospital [on sanctuary prop-
erty] for veterinary care, her entire family group travels with
her in order to keep all of them feeling secure."

This passage zeroes in on precisely how top-flight sanctuaries differ from accredited zoos: constant flexibility in management of the animals, aimed at increasing individuals' chances
to thrive. At both sets of institutions, social groupings may be
adjusted for the animals' well-being and good medical care may
be offered. At the best sanctuaries, though, the individual animal's well-being faces no competition with a need for animals
to be "on exhibit" for people to see, a strong constraint in zoos
because it affects whom among the animal residents can be
moved where and when.

Some years ago I visited the Center for Great Apes in Wau-
chula, Florida, a sanctuary dedicated to taking in and caring
for orangutans and chimpanzees rescued from various bleak
situations such as the forced training and cruelty animals
may face in the TV and movie industry. There apes live off exhibit and away from exploitation, including the chimpanzee
Bubbles, who had become pop star Michael Jackson's pet, and
orangutan Bam-Bam, who had played Nurse Precious for three
seasons on the televised soap opera *Passions*. Through a series

of arboreal covered walkways, apes moved around the facility with a good deal of personal choice. No longer did these apes need to live as status symbols or performers for our pleasure.

A network of sanctuaries across the country and much of the world carry out this work in large part through donations of time or money from concerned animal lovers. If roadside zoos were to be shuttered, many thousands of animals would nevertheless lack places to go; to achieve the excellence of Farm Sanctuary or the Center for Great Apes is a lengthy and expensive project. We don't have enough good sanctuaries even for all the monkeys and apes who are in the process of being retired from biomedical facilities or who will soon be in that pipeline, much less all the other animals. (See chapter 5.)

Given the abundant need for rescue of animals, one risk is a rush to set up so-called sanctuaries that don't deserve the name because they neglect or exploit their charges. A network of these places exists, too, sadly. Doesn't the name Zoological Wildlife Foundation sound impressive? Consult Trip Advisor online about this facility in Miami, and you will find accolades about what a great place it is for the animals and what a fun day can be spent there with one's family. Digging just a little deeper reveals bad news, however. On the ZWF's own website, a young boy is pictured holding a gibbon, a small ape from Asia. The text reads: "Meet many of our exotic animal stars the way you've always wanted to: UP CLOSE & PERSONAL! Book now!" Clicking on that "Book now!" button on the day I explored the site (November 13, 2018) leads to another photograph, this time of a baby chimpanzee hoisted onto the shoulders of a paying tourist. Potential visitors learn about what is on offer: "This 1-hour guided tour offers a zoo experience like no other including hands-on interactions with reptiles, primates, small mammals and birds of prey. $85.00 (Ages 18+) $45.00 (Ages 4–17) Free for ages 3 & under."

Here is nothing short of a recipe for disaster, exactly the kind of opportunity with animals that should not be embraced. The risks are many: disease transmission from people to animals; bites or bruises during interactions with wildlife, perhaps especially concerning when young children may be the victims; and people coming away with the impression that it's just fine to approach wildlife for close encounters and selfies. Up-close encounters sometimes result in injury (and even death) to humans and could end up killing the animal too; as we have seen, when an encounter goes wrong and wildlife managers must intervene in a hurry, lethal force is often the first line of defense. This so-called foundation in Miami is in reality an exploitative business.

What, if anything, would be lost, given these systemic problems across all varieties of zoos, were zoos to close? Could a concerted program of gradual attrition be put into place? Adult animals would be cared for until their deaths, without any breeding or exhibiting of new generations of babies. In the "loss" column, those elegant oryx come back to mind, reintroduced to their desert homelands. In 2016, AZA-accredited zoos and aquariums contributed over $216 million to wildlife conservation, the first year in which the donations total surpassed $200 million.

The sweeping work of the Wildlife Conservation Society based at New York's Bronx Zoo is notable in this regard. On the WCS website the photographic galleries of global and regional "flagship species" ranging from snow leopards to skates and rays conveys this organization's scope. Assigned by NPR to review Alex Dehgan's book *The Snow Leopard Project: And Other Adventures in Warzone Conservation*, I was entranced to learn about the WCS's on-the-ground ecosystem preservation in the mountains and on the plains of Afghanistan. In areas considered remote by Westerners, some still teeming with land mines from three decades of wars, are vital ecosystems with resident

Marco Polo sheep, markhor or spiral-horned wild goats, and carnivores including snow leopards and lynx. Thanks to determined labor by local and international conservationists, two new Afghan national parks, one at Band-e-Amir and the other at Wakhan, now protect these animals within their borders. Yet one question strikes me as key: why are traditional zoos necessary for that kind of conservation work to go on?

David Grazian suggests a model reminiscent of the Detroit Zoo director's that is, I think, realistic and attainable going forward: Accredited zoos could reduce the variety of animals they represent "on exhibit." They could venture beyond an obsession with the cuddly and cute species that pull in visitors who flock to on-site gift stores stocked with stuffed-toy replicas. Accredited zoos could highlight fauna from fruit bats to spiders, species that are more amenable to living in generous-sized enclosures. Compelling tales with a focus on biology, behavior, and evolution could be conveyed to visitors, using interactive signage, videos, and virtual-reality experiences. Roadside zoos would be dismantled gradually through attrition and a cessation of reproductive breeding.

Imagine an outing with your family to a zoo that contained no elephants, gorillas, pandas, or seals. Rescued animals, each unable to safely live in the wild, would be the stars of this experience. Would you be excited to spend an afternoon in such a place? I would. Adults and children alike could celebrate encounters with fascinating animals, buoyed by the knowledge that the animals themselves were being helped and that no healthy, free-ranging individuals were taken into confinement for the sake of our afternoon's fun.

This kind of outlook requires an adjustment in thinking, because for so long zoos that feature exotic wildlife have been celebrated as entertainment. My own turning point came about through my practice of arranging field trips to zoos. For many years it felt natural for me to take my William & Mary students to the National Zoo, my old orangutan-watching home. I knew the nonhuman primates there and respected the staff. The students and I observed gorilla youngsters in tumbling play and listened to the duetting songs of male and female gibbons; these activities brought to three-dimensional life the science articles, photographs, and video clips I used in the classroom. Structured on-site assignments offered my students a chance to practice data-collection sampling protocols, like the focal-animal sampling I had used in Kenya, a method in which a researcher focuses on the behaviors and interactions of one animal at a time for a prescribed number of minutes. As I saw it then, my responsibility as an educator was to explain primate patterns of play, aggression, and mother–infant bonding as they unfolded before our eyes and how those patterns might be reliably recorded for analysis. I just wasn't thinking much about the ethics of captivity.

Then I switched our destination to the Metro Richmond Zoo in Moseley, Virginia. Closeness to the college, allowing reduced travel time, was welcome, but the dozen chimpanzees at MRZ were the main lure. Owned by James Andelin and unaccredited by the AZA, this zoo and its way of housing chimpanzees became my own critical lesson, a case of the instructor learning more than her students.

Each day at MRZ, about half of the chimpanzees were allowed out of a low building located on an island to move about a grassy area that featured a single climbing structure. The others remained indoors. For apes who had evolved to range over forest or savannah by splitting up into ever-changing small parties, and to explore every aspect of their environment sometimes through making and using tools, the island must have felt incredibly confining. I saw no ropes or hammocks, straw, toys, or tubs made available for the apes to manipulate or play with.

As a class we still collected data, but soon enough I began to discuss ethics of captivity with the students in a way I had never done before. We had plenty of reason to do this: not far from the chimpanzee island was a small glass-fronted hut where baby chimpanzees or orangutans were raised apart from their mothers, and not far from it were rows of small mesh cages for a variety of monkeys.

During this time, one of my undergraduate students became especially concerned about the chimpanzees' lives. Brittany Fallon had come to William & Mary with volunteer experience at Save the Chimps sanctuary in Florida, and after graduating she went on to observe and publish on the behavior of free-ranging chimpanzees in Uganda for her doctoral degree. At MRZ, Fallon volunteered to make and present to the chimpanzees various enrichment objects, little puzzles and food treats to occupy their formidable minds at least for a time. I asked her in 2018 to reflect back on that period. In an email message, she wrote this: "You may remember that their chimp colony was *way* too big for the space they had, and the two groups got rotating time outdoors on that pathetic little island. They remain some of the more stressed chimps I have seen, lots of hair plucking, bloody skin from plucking and rocking."

According to a 2011 paper by Lucy Birkett and Nicholas Newton-Fisher, stress among zoo chimpanzees is common. These researchers' data on "abnormal behavior," defined as behaviors atypical of wild-living individuals, come from forty chimpanzees living in six accredited zoological institutions. In all six groups, six abnormal behaviors were found: eat feces, rock, groom stereotypically, pat genitals, regurgitate, and fumble nipple; two more, pluck hair and hit self, were present in five of the six groups. It's not that the chimpanzees were constantly distressed; Birkett and Newton-Fisher take care to note that the apes performed some abnormal behaviors only briefly or rarely. Yet the data give cause for concern. "From the perspective of human psychiatry, some of the behavioural abnormalities demonstrated by chimpanzees might be seen as symptoms of compromised mental health, i.e. mental illness, if they were observed in human primates," the pair concludes. The possibility of compromised mental health in the chimpanzees at MRZ struck me very strongly.

On-site discussions with my students about zoo ethics no longer felt like enough. I expressed my concerns about the chimpanzees to zoo management and reported the chimpanzees' condition to the USDA. Next I decided to stop altogether the zoo visits with my students. It felt wrong to support with our dollars a zoo that allowed its chimpanzees to live as I saw those chimpanzees living.

Over two thousand animals ranging from chimpanzee to Bengal tiger and snow leopard to kangaroo live at the zoo now, which also operates a cheetah breeding facility. To the long-standing sky ride and safari-train ride, a zipline course has been added. The zoo remains unaccredited by the AZA. It's easy enough to verify that last fact by checking AZA's own list of accredited zoos, which is regularly updated. To be extra sure, I sent a message to MRZ in fall 2018 asking for confirmation and an update about the chimpanzees who reside there now. From the zoo's social media team I learned that a second island has been built, allowing nine chimpanzees to utilize one and two elderly chimpanzees the other. On the accreditation question, the response included this comment: "We have chosen to not be AZA accredited and instead are ZAA (Zoological Association of America) accredited; however, we work with both organizations in their animal programs." When I pressed a bit, back came this reply: "ZAA and AZA are both trade organizations with strict accrediting standards. Some people like to drive Fords, some Chevrolet. At this time, MRZ has chosen to be accredited by ZAA."

On the surface this may sound reasonable enough. No doubt the fact of this accreditation reassures potential and actual MRZ visitors, who might conclude that a privately owned zoo's practices are supervised by an organization with "strict" standards. But there's a major problem: the ZAA is a sham according to reputable animal advocacy organizations. Founded in 2005, it exists to circumvent the AZA's much more stringent set of standards. Here's a pithy summary offered by HSUS (Humane Society of the United States): "The deceptively-named Zoological Association of America (ZAA) has weak standards, accredits poorly run roadside zoos and private menageries, and promotes the private ownership of exotic pets and the commercialization of wildlife."

Support for this assessment comes from HSUS's side-by-side comparison of policies of the AZA and the ZAA. Whereas the AZA explicitly acknowledges that wild animals do not make good pets, the ZAA defends private ownership of exotic animals; ZAA-accredited facilities may breed and sell a variety of wild animals to the public. The AZA forbids prosimians, monkeys, and apes to be sold, traded, or given to individuals or to animal dealers known to place primates with individuals. ZAA institutions, by contrast, may sell primates to pet dealers. Caging requirements also differ greatly between the two bodies: For chimpanzees the AZA requires 2,000 square feet of indoor and outdoor space, with vertical heights of over 20 feet. The ZAA requires 240 square feet and 8 vertical feet.

In short, it's no ethical prize to be accredited by the ZAA. I expressed my dismay about this situation to my correspondent at MRZ, specifically about the zoo's "some people prefer Fords, others Chevrolets" comment. The ethical dilemma regarding the MRZ is not a simple one. Where would the zoo's two thousand animal residents go should the zoo be shut down? Could a gradual cessation of breeding be a first step toward eventual phasing out of the zoo? Concern for MRZ animals collides with the reality that MRZ is first and foremost a business. Richmond-area residents do flock to its gates, and the resident exotic animals remain part of its appeal.

Sometimes successful interventions can be carried out. In a five-year period (2012–17), PETA rescued sixty-five bears from roadside zoos (and recall the rescued bear Dillon from chapter 1). A roadside zoo in Georgia, the Yellow River Game Ranch in Lilburn, was shuttered entirely in December 2017, in part because it kept bears in concrete pits. Some of that zoo's six hundred animals went to a nature center in Jackson, Georgia, and others, according to the Mother Nature Network, would find homes with the help of the Georgia Department of Natural Resources. Then came a twist to the story: A local couple decided to take over the zoo and turn it into an animal sanctuary. By this point, only a few dozen animals hadn't already been placed elsewhere; these included four bears, still living on concrete. The new co-owner, Jonathan Ordway, told the *Atlanta Journal-Constitution* in July 2018 that the bears would soon live on more than two acres with a pond and waterfall. That's compassionate action close to home in a big way. Indeed, the Yellow River Wildlife Sanctuary opened in May 2020 with newly rescued animals ranging from lemurs to lynxes joining the former ranch residents. It remains to be seen whether this place is truly up to the job of providing sanctuary that effectively centers the animals' well-being.

Even closer to home for me than the MRZ chimpanzees are the animals kept at Busch Gardens theme park in Williamsburg. Thankfully, the monkeys who years ago were housed in tiny, iron-bar cages are no longer there. Nor is the small petting zoo, where cute baby animals would show up every spring, gone by the next year to make room for a fresh crop of youngsters. That's progress; evolving standards or public pressure or both no doubt helped bring it about. Nowadays at Busch Gardens I see some positive aspects for its animal residents, enough to have adopted this park as my place to practice an "eyes open, speak up" compassion.

My favorite area to visit is a valley nestled between Ireland and France, two of the seven "countries" into which Busch Gardens is organized. It features an enclosed aviary called Lorikeet Glen through which people may walk and observe a variety of birds up close, and two large cordoned-off outdoor enclosures called Eagle Ridge and Wolf Haven. At Eagle Ridge four bald eagles reside, all of whom suffered severe injuries that prevent them from flying. Housed together, they walk (or fly at low altitude for short distances) around the enclosure, sitting in companionable pairs or breaking the silence with an occasional screech vocalization. The eagles are Penny, whose wing was amputated after he was shot illegally in Virginia over twenty-five years ago; Abigail, who for reasons unknown suffered a fracture in her clavicle that left her unable to fly; Roosevelt, whose wing feathers were badly damaged when he was struck by a vehicle in Florida; and Taft, who was twice as unlucky as the others. Injured as a baby when his nest was blown out of a tree during a Florida storm, Taft was released back into the wild once his fractured bone, also a clavicle, was repaired and had healed. Three years later he suffered another fracture, this time of the wing and too severe for him to fly free.

Beyond these facts, I wanted to know more about the eagles' social relationships. Yet from periods of casual observation, I couldn't work out on my own anything about friendships or rivalries among these birds. Did they just tolerate each other's presence, or were their lives enriched by each other's company? Correspondence with Busch Garden's zoological coordinator, Timothy J. Smith, helped me out. Roosevelt and Taft, the two eagles from Florida, arrived at the park in December 2016 and were introduced to Penny and Abigail the following spring. The newcomers, Smith told me, "assumed subordinate roles to the other two and all fell into the pecking order quite quickly. [The four eagles] have continued to grow closer since then. They have occasional disagreements, but overall there is good energy on the habitat." All four, Smith explained, "do move around quite a bit, and you will see them crossing paths and sharing spaces often. Penny is our elder of the group, and it seems like he is getting more activity now that the young boys are here. We look at that as a good thing for him, as it doesn't allow him to be sedentary on the habitat."

Careful planning at the park enhances the daily social lives of this quartet of eagles, each of whom is benefited as a rescued flightless bird now living in a safe environment. Each has been trained to go into his or her own enclosure; often the door to the inside is left open so that the eagles, as Smith says, "are able to get some individual time if they need it." This last fact is heartening, because anything that increases the animals' ability to make their own choices, and to avoid human noise and gaze when they wish, is a positive factor for their well-being.

Adjacent to the eagles is Wolf Haven, where at any given time two of the park's five gray wolves may be visible in the grass or playing in the water. Kaya and Beo are sister and brother. Kitchi and Maska were raised together but are unrelated. Captive bred, these four are healthy animals brought at a young age to the park under the "ambassador model" of keeping animals on display for educational purposes. Boise, the fifth wolf, is, like the eagles but unlike the other wolves, a rescue animal. Found wandering in Boise, Idaho, he was at first thought to be a lost domestic puppy. "Upon further review," as Smith dryly puts it, "it was discovered he was a lost wolf pup." No success came from attempts to locate his wolf pack, and he ended up at Busch Gardens. Originally Boise lived with the siblings Kaya and Beo, but this didn't turn out to be a good fit for him, and he was placed instead with Kitchi and Maska. "That relationship went very well for a number of years," Smith told me, and then disagreements broke out as to who was the pack's alpha. Boise can now be paired with Maska but not with Kitchi. The wolves, like the eagles, make their social preferences known within the constraints of captivity, and these may shift over time.

Visitors to Busch Gardens in my experience do linger—some of them, anyway—at the relatively spacious outdoor enclosures for the eagles and the wolves. Watching closely when the animals are active, families and friend groups may listen to the recorded speech that plays at Eagle Ridge about the birds and conservation issues, or attend a show that features the wolves' behavior and conservation messages.

Day-to-day experiences of the animals kept at Busch Gardens may be affected quite a bit by the park's methods of entertaining its human visitors. In the "country" of Scotland, speakers are mounted along the fence of the enclosure where the blackface sheep are kept, an area used also by the Clydesdale horses. From these speakers blares music. Whether the animals habituate to this loud sound, plus the ambient noise of thousands of people passing by every day, I can't know. I do wish the park would prioritize the animals' sensory comfort: surely park visitors can walk a few hundred yards without a need to hear loud music. Thinking back to the noise-induced stress of the Pacific Northwest orcas, I imagine the sheep and horses' relief when they rotate off display to quieter back pastures, when the park shutters for around twelve hours each night, and when during some winter months it doesn't open at all.

As the music example indicates, human entertainment is a priority at Busch Gardens. During one summer visit, I noticed that an employee stationed at Wolf Haven spoke in an agitated way into her walkie-talkie. Soon I spotted the reason: one of the wolves' muzzles gleamed with blood. A small mammal, maybe some kind of rodent, had slipped into the enclosure—and didn't make it out. The wolf had acted toward that small animal in precisely the way that wolves have evolved to act. Busch Gardens didn't wish to upset the public, however; it's better public relations (from the park's point of view) if wolves are described as predators but never observed in the act of predation. The small carcass therefore needed to be removed quickly, and the park employee was on her walkie-talkie arranging this.

Does this whitewashing of wolf behavior fit well with a conservation message about wolves, or with a claim that zoos educate the public about the lives of animals? I don't think so. A world in which zoos make public displays of releasing live animals into predators' enclosures, constructing a chaotic and cruel mini Roman Colosseum tableau of death, is an unwanted world to be sure. It is not necessary, however, to scrub the zoo of animals' natural behavior. To communicate to zoos that we aren't afraid to see natural behaviors unfold before our eyes is to express an understanding of who animals really are.

At Busch Gardens I speak up about concerns, including the loud music, the scrubbing of animal predation from visitors' gaze, and occasionally caging issues, for example when a large python was kept in a glass-fronted enclosure that seemed too small. The park's ownership by SeaWorld Entertainment causes me to feel some guilt about my annual season's pass; at SeaWorld theme parks in Orlando, San Antonio, and San Diego, dolphins and whales are held in unconscionably small tanks, and I don't visit those parks. At Disney's Animal Kingdom (DAK), where I observed the pacing babirusa, some animals face similar noise and crowd pressures as those at Busch Gardens. At DAK, though, I also see genuine attempts to offer many animals choice in their movements, and a notable commitment to presenting a set of messages about environmental conservation.

The conservation messages that visitors to DAK encounter are wrapped up in a fully "themed" experience meant to rouse positive emotions, to bind a person to the landscape in which she finds herself (that is, DAK and no other place), and to reflect lessons about humans' evolutionary trajectory. At DAK, visitors "walk inside a story," experiencing the unexpected; animals are not predictable at DAK, nor are visitors' encounters with them. This explanation comes from Walt Disney Engineering's Joe Rohde, whose formal title is executive designer and vice president, Creative, and whose online talks are compelling. Three sets of values inform DAK, Rohde says: the intrinsic value of nature; the adventure experience as developmental, so that parkgoers don't always know what will happen around them; and a personal call to action regarding animals and the environment. Everything comes together in *narrative* at DAK, which gets us back to the notion of "theming"; the human brain has evolved over millennia to make sense of our experiences through storytelling.

At DAK (five visits so far), I do see Rohde's vision at work. Across the 110-acre Harambe Wildlife Reserve, giraffe, wildebeest, zebra, and varieties of antelope roam, with enclosed areas set aside for hippo, rhino, mandrill monkeys, and other African wildlife. On the Kilimanjaro Safari ride, vehicles carry visitors through the reserve; on either side, animals may move closer or farther way to various degrees. Vehicle drivers double as "safari" guides who think quickly to provide riders with accurate animal-behavior information as unpredictable scenes unfold with animals of first one species and then another, and who are scripted to urge attention to conservation values at the ride's end. The positive emotions of which Rohde speaks—urged by creative theming and ripe to increase a visitor's compassionate action for animals—is highly visible among both adult and child riders, who often call out in excitement when animals are spotted nearby or engaged in social behavior.

Disembarking from the "safari" ride, visitors encounter a path that opens up toward two side-by-side enclosures featuring grass and water, where the gorillas live. At any given moment, adult gorillas, including several silverback males, may stay within or move out of the public's gaze; juveniles may tumble in play on grassy slopes or with objects they manipulate. No bars or boredom of the type Jo-Anne McArthur records with her camera in *Captive* are readily visible here.

My claim isn't that DAK represents a model of animal well-being: captivity is still captivity, after all. DAK isn't a landscape rooted in animal rights, a point underscored by my discussion of the pacing babirusas and supported also by concerns about high noise levels and the nature of the gift and food shops that sell plastic toys and animal meat, respectively. No assessment has been attempted, as far as I know, of DAK visitors' investment in compassionate action once their stay is concluded.

Like DAK, many zoos and animal parks are a patchwork of smaller cages, larger enclosures, and open expansive acreage. In a single zoo, some areas make at least a minimally acceptable home for animals, whereas others are dismal. I understand that no zoo captivity is acceptable for some animal lovers; I find it helpful to make distinctions along a continuum, working toward a fresh vision for what zoos can be.

In late winter 2019 I visited the Virginia Zoo in Norfolk. Three white rhinoceroses huddled together on a patch of dirt in a moderately large and extremely barren outdoor enclosure, two female cheetahs rested in an outdoor area in which they couldn't possibly get up to speed in a full run, and orangutans behind glass in a small room full of "enrichment objects" (like barrels and burlap) were subject to relentless human gaze. By contrast, at the large, open-plain area of the zoo's "Okavango Delta," animals moved about with vitality. Across this spacious landscape with its large pond roamed Masai giraffes, yellow-backed duikers, ostriches, southern ground hornbills with their brilliant red coloring, screeching geese, and big-horned Ankole cattle. With the single exception of a female duiker recovering from a wound on her back, who chose to stay alone along the perimeter fence, these animals appeared to be engaged with their companions and their environment. Individuals chose where to walk and with whom to spend time; the cattle at one point ran about in a way I interpreted as playful or at least indicative of high spirits.

Some enclosures at some zoos provide spacious, intriguing surroundings for their animal residents. This fact deserves acknowledgment. It doesn't let zoos off the hook, though. Taken as a whole, the zoo system is broken, for all the reasons this chapter makes clear. Working toward the achievement of these three goals is a beautiful path for compassion action: closure of roadside zoos; uncoupling of conservation work (like the project for scimitar-horned oryx) from traditional zoo design and from goals of breeding of exotic animals in order to increase revenue; and reform of accredited zoos in ways that encourage rescued animals' natural behavior as much as possible through good care and housing. Reform along these lines would be achieved in tandem with reducing the overall number of zoos and the numbers of animals held in them.

Roadside zoos may find themselves soon at the end of their viability *if we help bring that about*. An ethics-based evolution of accredited zoos may happen *if we press for it to happen*. When we lock eyes with animals at a zoo, it can be with a pledge to take notice of the realities of their lives, to ask questions about how those lives go day by day, and to care more about their well-being than about a few hours of our own entertainment.

5

Animals on Our Plates

Rising sea levels, extreme weather ranging from mega-hurricanes to raging fires, people around the world forced from their homes as they flee climate catastrophes: in addition to emerging viruses such as SARS-CoV-2, these are among the most profound concerns of this young decade. A large cadre of scientists says that the most effective response each of us can make is to eat less meat and less dairy, because the animal-agriculture industry contributes heavily to the greenhouse gas emissions that in turn cause unprecedented levels of human-caused climate change.

About that science I will say more shortly. For now, I want to point out how compassionate action for animals can align effectively with care for our warming planet. By eating fewer animals and animal products, or none at all, we exercise kindness to all living beings. Making that choice will be relatively easy for some people but for others, whether for reasons of economy, family or cultural tradition, or even ingrained taste preferences, much harder. Writer Jonathan Safran Foer spoke about reducing meat, seafood, dairy, and egg consumption in a conference keynote talk in 2019. Don't measure the distance of what you are doing from perfection, he told us. Instead measure the distance between what you are doing and doing nothing at all. Keep trying, even when it's hard.

In this chapter I aim to construct a space in which to explore questions around animals and food in ways that embrace people all along the continuum from meat-and-cheese lovers to folks who wouldn't dream of eating any meat or cheese, ever. If you are not yet ready, or able, to become vegan or vegetarian, how can you make a meaningful contribution? What can the activism of long-term vegans teach us about how to move forward to repair our food system? How can an invitation for rethinking what (and who) we eat acknowledge the fact that for many people, food rituals are tangled with the traditions of culture and family? By now it won't surprise you to learn that my "way in" to these questions is to begin with a story.

*   *   *

"Rabbit will be brought to the table tonight as an appetizer, as well as gourmet organ meats including duck kidneys." Hearing these words in the breakfast room of an inn in rural Vermont one summer morning, I tumbled into a state of acute discomfort. To the innkeeper who had brought this news, the expression on my face must have looked peculiar. I had not eaten meat in years. Just three months before, my book on the science of how farmed animals think and feel had been published. I didn't want anything to do with bunny appetizers or organ meats!

Rabbits I had never once eaten. I flashed back to play sessions with our two pet rabbits from earlier years, long-haired male Caramel, whom we adopted from Sarah's Montessori classroom cage, and later short-haired female Oreo, whom we brought home from our local shelter. Both rabbits sought our attention and captivated us with their daily bunny routines. Now, at the inn, those images were crowded out by one of a plated rabbit, a chunk of sauced meat, something I'd never consume. The duck kidneys? Those I made a concerted effort not to imagine.

The innkeeper noticed that none of the four of us at the table, Charlie and I and our friends Marsha and Pat Autilio, had ordered bacon or sausage to go with our eggs, toast, yogurt, and oatmeal. This observation led to her question: would we find the rabbit and kidneys at dinner that night acceptable, or did we wish to eat elsewhere instead?

What followed was a delicate choreography, both verbal and nonverbal, among the five of us. Each of us lived with animals. The innkeeper had the evening before shown us photographs of her two beloved whippets. It was rescued raptors at the nearby Vermont Institute of Natural Science in Quechee that had brought us all together in the first place; Marsha and Pat's daughter Anna Morris is VINS's lead environmental educator. Thanks to her, Charlie and I had spent the previous afternoon among magnificent Harris hawks, bald eagles, and other resident birds. At home Marsha and Pat kept a parakeet as a companion, just as we kept cats.

At the inn, the main course is customized for each guest by way of made-ahead reservations. Charlie and I had specified a vegetarian main meal ahead of time, but we hadn't given a thought to the appetizers. *Were* we all okay with the rabbit and the duck kidneys coming to the table? Neither Charlie nor I needed to consume them, after all, even if they were put before us. For a few moments the potential for an easygoing, amicable answer shimmered in the air. I could even sense the words gathering in my throat: "Sure, no problem." There the words lodged; I couldn't utter them.

Marsha spoke instead. "Let's cancel the dinner and rebook elsewhere," she suggested. She thanked the innkeeper, then added, "We had a pet rabbit for many years. I'm not comfortable with it either."

I felt a rush of gratitude to her, my close friend since sixth grade, for the grace with which she handled the situation. I also felt relief, because the discomfort that was obvious in my face and body posture had been at war with a desire not to singlehandedly derail a special evening. In the end, the four of us together with Anna and her then-fiancé, now husband, Rhys, dined together at another inn nearby. There we each selected on the spot from a varied menu: vegetarian dishes for two of us, lamb for two more, and lobster for two more. It was a fine night laced with lively conversation, even though an irony dwelled at the table with us. No rabbits or duck parts were consumed, but lambs and lobsters, yes.

I don't mean to suggest that Charlie and I were the virtuous ones because we ate vegetarian dinners. Pat, to take but one example, had cut back on beef and pork because of his concerns about the human rights violations in animal slaughterhouses, where work conditions are dangerous and emotionally taxing. Foremost among the issues on his mind, Pat told me, were "the terrible labor practices the meat packing industry employs due to long-standing government neglect. Immigrants legal and illegal bear the brunt of these abuses. Workers are frequently seriously injured on the job, receive little assistance, are cast out, often disabled and simply replaced by another willing or desperate worker." (See the book *Every Twelve Seconds: Industrialized Slaughter and the Politics of Sight* by Timothy Pachirat.)

Further, that night I ate animal products. The bread that accompanied my pasta almost certainly included milk and eggs, and I spread butter on it.

Even amid tangled ethics like the ones at play at that dining table, understanding the lives of animals may become a compelling starting point for compassion when it comes to whom we eat—or refuse to eat. Cultural anthropologist and domestic-rabbit rescuer Margo DeMello, who has provided a home sanctuary for as many as sixty-five spayed and neutered rabbits at a time, describes "the richness of rabbit-rabbit relationships." In the large group she housed in an indoor shelter that spilled over into an outdoor courtyard, "the rabbits spend their days foraging for food in the courtyard, chewing on cardboard, lounging on their hammocks, and spending endless hours communing with each other—grooming, nuzzling, playing, 'gossiping,' or just hanging out." Only one species, the European rabbit or *Oryctolagus cuniculus*, has been widely domesticated. Whether your pet is a delicate plush lop three-pounder or a Flemish giant weighing three times as much as a newborn human, the origin species is one and the same: all that glorious variation bloomed from the European rabbit. Family-member bunnies, then, like my Caramel and Oreo, can be better understood when we grasp something of "the social nature of European rabbits," as Louis DiVincenti and Angelika N. Rehrig title their paper on the topic.

When European rabbits live freely in the wild, they form stable social groups centered on the warren, a burrow that features multiple entrances. In one common configuration of the group, a dominant male shares a territory with several females and subordinate males. The dominance hierarchy is highly influential, to the extent that the alpha male may request an obeisance akin to that afforded to a small emperor by his underlings: "The dominant buck routinely patrols a territory," DiVincenti and Rehrig write, "and as often as daily, requires a submissive act from all other rabbits, both male and female, sharing the same space." This submission from the lower-ranking rabbits may be something as simple as a retreat, a ceding of a path to the dominant.

One male rabbit is in strict command, then? No, as it turns out, rabbit social interactions are more flexibly structured than that. Male territories do overlap, and females, who are called does, may stop cold any unwanted advances from males through bursts of aggression. Some ethologists suggest that rabbits don't so much *want* to be social as they merely tolerate nearby social companions when resources are limited, such as areas suitable for warren construction. In one study, rabbits joined up together when safe cover from predators was limited but dispersed when that cover was plentiful. Still, wild male and female rabbits may form pair bonds that in some cases persist for upwards of one year, and I know from my research into animal grief that pet rabbits may fall into crushing sadness when a mate or social partner dies. Some of that wild sociality, then, remains inherent in our pets, at least when house rabbits are given opportunities for companionship with other rabbits.

Like other animals, rabbits thrive when their needs are met and undue stress is avoided. They revel in the times when something wonderful happens to engage their senses. Best Friends Sanctuary in Kanab, Utah, posts an online guide to "basic house rabbit behavior and bunny body language." Bunny dancing, it notes, signals pure happiness and may include "leaping, doing a binky (jumping straight up and spinning in the air) and racing around." Rabbits, whether with companions or on their own, signal their moods, ranging from contentment (a bunny flopping on his or her side) to alarm (thumping vigorously in rhythm at some distressing disturbance or noise), as I saw and heard with Caramel and Oreo. During sudden bouts of leg-thumping from the bigger, bulkier Caramel, my human family of three would jump up in an attempt to suss out the source of his alarm. Each rabbit, naturally, expressed a distinct personality. Caramel enjoyed lapping up yogurt from a spoon and scarfing raisins from my hand. I have no scientific proof to offer, but I came to believe that he liked the opening musical notes that accompanied the HBO *Sopranos* shows on Sunday nights back in the day. Week after week he would hop from his cage onto his "viewing rug" in the den with us precisely as the music poured from our television. Oreo exhibited no musical or viewing preferences but at times of her choosing barreled on short legs into the same den at high speed, hurling her small self onto the couch to sit next to me.

To know that rabbits would prefer not to be eaten is to feel compassion for the rabbit on the plate. My experience with affectionate house rabbits plays a role again here. As Marsha put it when we talked about food at the Vermont inn, the "emotional resonance of food choices" plays a big part in how most people eat, both in what we *won't* eat and in what we *will*. Once a year at Passover, Marsha prepares a leg of lamb, a meal that for her is about much more than flavor because it brings alive family love and memories. "Brisket smells and tastes like home to me," she adds; "it feeds the soul as well as the body."

That desire to join in and perpetuate a family or cultural tradition may become a strong force that coexists with, and at times overrides, the concern we feel for animals. Only in my fifties did I stop eating turkey at Thanksgiving, surrounded by extended family members doing just that, or cease pining for chicken pot pie as my go-to comfort food. Talking with loved ones with whom we share meals can become an opportunity to teach children what *our* family values, what *our* culture values. "What is ethical eating for *us*?" is a terrific conversation starter, at least if everyone present is able to listen without immediately squaring off in judgment and recrimination. For some people, the answer differs from the one in my house: they may hunt as a way to avoid factory-farm food (chapter 3), or seek animals for meat who were raised and slaughtered on small family farms, or embrace veganism 100 percent with no meat or dairy consumed under any circumstances at home or outside the home. As I think through these divergent choices, I keep coming back to a question: don't all animals express a drive to live, whether a conscious preference for robust well-being or an instinct for self-preservation? Living with this question is what has led me along a path from my chicken-pot-pie-loving days to where I am now, nestled right up against one pole of the reducetarian spectrum.

Reducetarian Aims

Overwhelmingly often, I choose vegetarian and vegan foods to eat. Yet the term *reducetarian* remains an accurate descriptor for me. Brian Kateman and Tyler Alterman coined this term in an embrace of every person who is committed to eliminating or cutting down on meat, seafood, dairy, and other animal products in their diet. At the third annual reducetarian conference organized by Kateman in 2019—the same conference at which Jonathan Safran Foer urged us not to be too hard on ourselves if our diets aren't always perfectly plant based—Kateman reviewed the four central tenets of the reducetarian perspective.

It's not all or nothing. The choices aren't only to continue to eat as you always have, if you were raised as an omnivore, or instead to "go vegan." It is not a binary. To embrace veganism is a wonderful option, and at the same time, other choices are available too for reducing animal foods from your daily intake.

Incremental change is worth celebrating. When a loved one gives up eating chickens, let's say, or switches from dairy milk and cheese to nondairy products at half her meals, she is making a positive contribution. It should be recognized as such rather than called out as not good enough.

All motivations matter. Maybe you eat fewer animal foods because you're primarily concerned about your own risks for heart disease or other ailments. Perhaps the climate crisis is your main motivator. Or it could be that animal well-being matters most to you. There's no hierarchy, no "best reason" for embracing a change in eating habits.

We're all on the same team. Vegans, vegetarians, and redu-cetarians share a good deal in common. Recognizing that and uniting in a common goal, for example to greatly reduce or end factory farming, is a good thing.

Skeptics may ask, okay, if a person is content with only meat-less Mondays and eating meat the other six days, or decides to consume only fewer chickens but relishes pork and bacon, how does that even count as compassionate action for animals? Can that person *really* be on the same team with a vegan who is wholeheartedly committed to exposing the harms of animal slaughter wherever they occur, on small family farms as well as in factory farms? Why not just urge that everyone go vegan or at least vegetarian, anyway? I'm asked questions like these fre-quently, sometimes by people who are puzzling out where on the food spectrum they want to be, at other times by people who cast doubt (sometimes in a pretty hostile way) on my "street cred" in speaking up for animals because I am not purely vegan.

One set of answers comes in Foer's *We Are the Weather: Saving the Planet Begins at Breakfast*: "We cannot keep the kinds of meals we have known and also keep the planet we have known," Foer declares, and he's right. He also notes, though, that "the best way to excuse oneself from a challenging idea is to pretend there are only two options." This means, as I see it, that compas-sion for animals anchored in a discourse of exclusion—"genuine animal lovers eat *this* type of food, never *that* type of food"—isn't as powerful as it could be. It's not even as compassionate as it could be! With our world in environmental crisis, limiting the notion of who "the helpers" are—with a nod here to Mister Rogers's counsel to "find the helpers" when trouble comes—is shortsighted. Animals raised for meat or dairy, or animals meant to become seafood, are suffering, and our entire Earth is suffering in ways that animal agriculture contributes to dis-proportionately. I want to spell out why I think that adjusting what foods we eat is the single biggest opportunity we have to help animals—and along the way, to help ourselves.

Vegetarian and vegan diets, thoughtfully assembled, are nutritious and healthy for most people. The American Dietetic Association's statement sums up the views of numerous national and international health organizations: "Appropriately planned vegetarian diets, including total vegetarian or vegan diets, are healthful, nutritionally adequate, and may provide health benefits in the prevention and treatment of certain diseases. Well-planned vegetarian diets are appropriate for individuals during all stages of the life cycle, including pregnancy, lactation, infancy, childhood, and adolescence, and for athletes." The phrase about "health benefits" of vegetarian or vegans diets hints at a large literature that documents the ways in which these diets may reduce the likelihood for cholesterol-related and heart troubles, and the risks of some cancers. It's abundantly clear that people, including elite athletes, thrive on eating vegan foods.

Vegan activist Julia Feliz Brueck, writing in *Veganism in an Oppressive World: A Vegans of Color Community Project*, warns that using the terms *vegan* and *plant-based* interchangeably is misguided. Veganism, she asserts, is not a diet. That statement may sound odd to some nonvegans, but it is an important one to take on board. Most vegans aspire to enact compassion not only for so-called food animals but also for animals used in (for example) entertainment, product and medical testing, and the fashion industry. Brueck is no fan of reducetarian goals that fall short of veganism, and I understand her sense of urgency.

At the same time, consuming vegetarian or vegan foods exclusively may result in physical distress for some people. In 2017 the BBC spoke to a few people, each of whom had been highly committed to veganism, whose bodies just didn't cope well over the long term. One couple had been vegan for 26 years. Both partners suffered from bodily ills ranging from irritable bowel syndrome (IBS) to slow thyroid and high cholesterol; in their case, adding some meat into their meals aided their health. (Skeptics may insist they could have coped by managing their vegan intake better, a point I'll return to later.) As someone who lives in and with a fractious body, I sympathize with this plight, although my own situation is a bit different.

I do fine without eating any cows, chickens, turkeys, lambs, goats, ducks, pigs, octopuses, crabs, lobsters, and almost all fish, and with consuming few dairy and egg products. The array of nondairy cheeses, milks, and ice creams available now thrills me both because I love their taste and because, like millions of others with my ancestral history, I get nasty lactose-intolerance symptoms when I consume dairy foods. Yet some aspects of plant-based eating cause symptoms just as unpleasant. Let's just say, without sacrificing my privacy to the details that no one wants to hear, that many vegetables and lentils cause me severe gastric distress. Any dish with red or green peppers in it curses all my working bodily organs (or so it feels upon any accidental ingestion). Mostly I find workarounds for these issues. Through continual experimentation, I learn what works: quinoa is a friendly food, for instance, and the occasional half of a black-bean burger is fine. Vegan pizzas light up my life, as do many varieties of "bowl" dishes and casseroles. Still, I can't comfortably eat a lot of the staples that grace vegetarian and vegan menus.

Sometimes I anticipate a new vegan food, only to experience bodily rebellion. In spring 2018 Charlie and I went out for a special dinner to mark the five-year anniversary of my cancer surgery. Half a decade after that torturous night when in my hospital bed I felt that I was a bear, we celebrated my new status as "cured of cancer" according to medical standards. For weeks we had planned our outing around ordering our first-ever

Impossible Burgers. Unveiled to great fanfare in 2016 by the company Impossible Foods, these plant-based patties feature heme, the molecule that gives meat (and our own circulating blood) its red color. In Impossible Burgers, the type of heme used is soy-based and called legheme. Originally Impossible Burgers were pricey and available in relatively few urban locations, but by 2018 they were more affordable, featured on many restaurant menus, and advertised as tasting enough like meat to appeal even to hamburger lovers. We didn't crave meat, but we did want to check out the heme effect and took ourselves to the Trellis restaurant near Williamsburg's historic district to do it.

The burgers were brought to our table draped in vegan cheese and accompanied by fries and a tiny side dish of vegan mayonnaise. The reddish tinge of the heme was highly visible. The first bites pleased my palate greatly; Charlie felt the same. Excited by a new addition to our no-meat lineup of foods, we talked happily on about this and that, anticipating what delicious dessert we would finish up with. About one third of the way through eating the burger, I began to feel peculiarly full. By the halfway point, the stuffed-full sensation had grown into a wretched feeling. I soon stopped eating altogether; we boxed up two unfinished Impossible Burgers and left for home without any thought of dessert. What a disappointment on a night meant to celebrate good health! I had swallowed a basketball, or so it seemed. Back home, moaning just slightly while surfing the internet, I discovered that some people react with great sensitivity to soy. No more Impossible Burgers for me. That conclusion was strengthened for me when I finally sampled a Beyond Burger, from the company Beyond Meat, made of plant products like pea protein with no soy and, for me, no distressing aftereffects.

A friend of mine who lives in North Carolina, a kind person and voracious reader who understands the links between meat eating and problems for our planet and for animals, explained to me why it's impossible for her to adopt a vegetarian or vegan diet. I will call her Mary. When Mary was growing up, her mother was intensely afraid of dogs and cats. The family's meals were meat-based. These two circumstances strongly influenced Mary's early experiences of animals and food. At the home of her father and stepmother, the situation was different: Mary was *ordered* to eat vegetables. This policy resulted in battles at the dinner table, some lasting for hours. "I found vegetables (and the force and threat of the pressuring behavior) so repellent that I won as often as I lost," she told me.

Mary was able to break free of these childhood strictures: she came to deeply love cats, and her diet did expand. However, she continued to have a bad relationship with vegetables, even though, in her words, "it's not rocket science to realize that being vegetarian is a more compassionate, evolved way to live." Mary experimented with different combinations of foods. "I do have severe (once crippling) stomach issues," she noted. "The first thing a gastroenterologist tells you is to cut vegetables out of your diet during a flare-up. When I hit my thirties, my life was one long flare-up. So being a vegetarian was never an option even if I had liked vegetables. For years I could barely leave my apartment, my IBS was so severe." For a year Mary ate no red meat, but later she folded it back into her diet. "I always ate chicken and some fish, though," she explained. "And there's no way I could ever stop eating cheese, so being a vegan is not an option for me, nor would it be. I don't see an ethical problem with milk products for myself."

When it comes to dairy foods, Mary and I diverge, as I will explain shortly. The point for now is this: Mary is far from alone in disliking the experience of being shamed for what she does and does not eat. In his book *The End of Animal Farming*, Jacy Reese reports that in a 2017 census-based poll of US adults, 97 percent agreed with the statement "Whether to eat animals or be vegetarian is a personal choice, and nobody has the right to tell me which one they think I should do." Intense resistance to changing how we eat, Reese notes, is a fact of human psychology, and compassion-based discussions need to take it into account. This isn't to say that I *agree* that eating meat and dairy is accurately described as a personal choice, not when billions of animals are terribly affected, as is our whole planet. The question remains this: can productive dialogue emerge if one conversational partner doesn't even try to grasp the other's experiences and feelings?

Mary surprised me by adding a comment about this very issue—the ways in which food choices are discussed—even though I hadn't asked her about it. "Your complete lack of trying to make me feel guilty and your affirmative style," Mary offered, "made a huge difference (remember my childhood stubbornness when it comes to being pressured or forced into anything). Since then, I do have at least one day a week when I eat no meat/chicken/fish."

Three choices exist, as I see it, when a person opens up about her family history and food choices as Mary has done. One option is to inform Mary politely but firmly that she needs to try harder. After all, plant-based foods fulfill our protein needs without meat or any other additions except for sources of vitamin B-12. Delicious vegan cheeses increasingly grace grocers' shelves (replacing some of those early, noxiously rubbery ones I still recall). With this stance, concern for animals crowds out compassion for Mary. Mary herself clues us in to what might happen thereafter: she would shut off, or maybe even double down on her food choices. I also would ask, who are *we* to instruct Mary on what *her* body can tolerate? I'm the best judge of what my body can handle, and recognize as valid that same knowledge in others.

Path number two tacks in the polar-opposite direction. Here we listen to Mary and affirm that she has the right to eat whatever she pleases. We offer nothing substantive to the conversation beyond this, adopting a stance of complete nonconfrontation. This choice bows to an ethic of "to each her own" and amounts to an opportunity lost when it comes to animal empathy.

Choice three seizes opportunity. It aims to create back-and-forth dialogue in which the aim is for both conversational partners to learn something. Dialogue is in fact what transpired between Mary and me. I can no longer turn away from knowledge that cows on dairy farms are separated from their offspring within days of giving birth, allowing them to be kept near-continuously pregnant in order to produce large quantities of milk. Routinely the male calves are killed for veal, and the dairy cows, once "spent," are sold to slaughterhouses at cull auctions. I told Mary these things, especially vivid to me after reading Kathryn Gillespie's *The Cow with Ear Tag #1389*.

As part of her ethnographic research into the dairy industry, Gillespie attends a cull auction and watches as "severely worn-out cows" are brought forward for sale. Most, she writes, are only five or six years old, "though their bodies looked ancient." At first it's hard for her to focus on any one individual, given the scale of the suffering on view. Gillespie begins to gaze into each cow's face. Then a limping Holstein cow with ear tag #1389 is brought forward. Her body had been wrecked by dairy production: her udders showed unmistakable signs of mastitis, her hide was covered in abrasions, her ribs and hip bones stuck out. No one bid on her, not even when the auctioneer called out a price of $5 per hundred pounds (or $35), down from the initial price of $20 per hundred pounds. Right as she was being led away unsold, cow #1389 collapsed in the auction ring. "Several cows were brought in one at a time," Gillespie writes, "turned in circles, were sold and exited while the cow lay on the floor, her mouth foaming with saliva and her breathing labored." The next morning, cow #1389 was found dead in her pen at the auction house.

The physical and emotional pain of pigs, chickens, cows and other animals raised and killed for meat is conveyed in Jonathan Safran Foer's *Eating Animals*, my own *Personalities on the Plate*, Isa Leshko's book of stunning photographs and prose *Allowed to Grow Old: Portraits of Elderly Animals from Farm Sanctuaries*, and many other books. Documentary films including *Food, Inc.* and *Speciesism* take up this material as well. When I embrace this material, it is emotionally challenging for me, even at times excruciating, as it is for many others. I have come to think hard about the necessity of not turning away from animals' pain. Philosopher and animal-studies scholar Kathie Jenni, in a paper titled "Bearing Witness for the Animal Dead," puts it in a way that arrested my attention: "Remembering and bearing witness to animal suffering is not simply or primarily an act of compassion, nor is its importance exhausted by beneficial consequences. It is something that we owe to the animal dead as an affirmation of respect and a practice of justice." Even toward animals whom we can no longer help, animals who are beyond our compassionate action, we still have a duty. "It helps us to avoid collusion with perpetrators," Jenni writes, "and rescues the animal dead from oblivion."

Even with increased attention to bearing witness for animals in our culture, in my experience the plight of dairy cows remains dimly understood outside vegan-vegetarian-reducetarian circles. This may be in part because milk, cheese, and ice cream still seem so completely innocuous to many of us raised on consuming them. Animals like cow #1389 remain invisible to us when we select milk from the dairy counter, a wedge of fine cheese, or an ice-cream cone on a summer's day. I shared some of this perspective with Mary, and in exchange I learned from Mary about real-life obstacles to the adoption of a plant-based diet. It's fair to say that Mary and I inhabit different ends of the reducetarian spectrum. On my end, I aspire to make less harmful choices as best I can, and Mary experiments too.

Disabled vegan Michele Kaplan gently chides omnivores who assert they could never give up cheese purely because they love it. "They just choose not to," Kaplan writes, "which is different from the disabled person who due to their disability / chronic illness, may not have the choice." Maybe, though, a disabled person just isn't trying hard enough to find the right balance of plant foods? Could the claimed disability even be an excuse to allow the person a free pass to eat whatever they want? Kaplan will have none of that, and I am glad. This suspicious way of thinking, she writes, "is incredibly harmful and triggering and so as a disabled vegan, I say: believe them every single damn time. I would rather let that one hypothetical person, that 1 out of 10,000 (assuming they even exist) 'off the hook,' then give the remaining 9,999 people yet more crap to deal with. Disabled people often experience social and systemic ableism on a daily basis. The last thing the community needs is further discrimination."

In her book *Beasts of Burden: Animal and Disability Liberation*, artist and disability activist Sunaura Taylor describes ableist roots in animal advocacy that privilege aspects of cognition and rationality in animals. She sees grave danger in this: caring for and about animals shouldn't be predicated on animals' thinking abilities any more than caring for and about humans should be. Taylor notes another way in which ableism creeps into animal activism: assuming that vegan diets work for everyone. For some disabled people, eating a vegan diet is personally "too extraordinarily difficult" due to "extreme health issues." Specific physical conditions may be the cause of the difficulty, or the constraints inherent in a need to rely on other people to prepare one's food. In envisioning the links between animal rights and disability rights, Taylor's book balances a respectful awareness of others' political, economic, and health struggles with an insistence that these obstacles not become an excuse for contentment with the status quo. Greater access to healthy plant foods for abled and disabled bodies, she says, is the way forward toward positive change.

Acute reactivity to certain drugs is commonplace for some of us. Given a megadose "boost" of potassium by an emergency-room doctor when I was dealing with acute pain, I vomited it up within hours even though most folks tolerate it just fine. Individuals respond variably to foods as well. I can't even smell a green pepper without feeling anxious, no doubt a psychological reaction after becoming physically ill upon ingesting green peppers; most of my friends adore them. It's just not possible to will one's body to feel healthy when eating foods that make that body sick.

Moving from the individual to the population level, it's clear that nearly eight billion people on our planet need food to live. In a decade or so, that number will reach nine billion. Plants provide the necessary amounts of protein and other nutrients for good health as long as B-12 supplements are added. As Josh Balk points out in *The Reducetarian Solution*, more than 90 percent of the world's plants are yet to be explored as food sources. Yet as it stands now, immense global inequalities mean that without meat sources of protein, untold numbers of families would be thrown into new levels of food insecurity were they to adopt a plant diet. Think, for instance, of how many millions are fed by chickens and pigs or fish at present.

An idea unfortunately gaining in popularity is to ramp up intensive farming of sea creatures. In Hawaii, vacationers to the Big Island find themselves now with a surprising option in addition to the traditional pursuits of relaxing on beaches, hiking around volcanoes, and joining boat tours in search of whales and dolphins: they may tour the Kanaloa Octopus Farm. The farm is actually a laboratory found on the Hawaii Ocean Science and Technology Park's research campus, where visitors walk down aisles lined with small white tubs and may touch, feed, and play with the octopuses housed in them.

These close encounters may sound reminiscent of my own excited touch session with the Professor, the giant Pacific octopus at the New England Aquarium (chapter 4). At the farm, though, the octopus are grown in service of a very different vision from those of any aquarist wishing an enrichment session for his or her charge: the consumption of more and more of these exquisitely intelligent cephalopods around the world.

Without question, the demand for octopus is on the rise. "People are now eating more octopus than ever: annual global production has more than doubled since 1980, from roughly 180,000 tons to about 370,000 tons," reports Tik Root for *Time* magazine in 2019. Root zeroes in on the environmental damage that this taste for octopus is causing: "Overfishing has already caused the collapse of multiple wild-octopus fisheries around the world, and current populations likely face similar threats." In these threats aquaculture entrepreneurs see an opportunity: if we don't want to wipe out wild octopus populations, the thinking goes, why not raise the animals under intensive farming conditions that can be branded as sustainable?

A growing number of scientists wish to answer that "why not" statement in blunt terms: because octopus are carnivorous animals, the ecological impact of aquaculture is not correctly described as sustainable. In a hard-hitting 2019 essay, a team of scientists led by Jennifer Jacquet concluded this: "Octopus farming would increase, not alleviate, pressure on wild aquatic animals. Octopuses have a food conversion rate of at least 3:1, meaning that the weight of feed necessary to sustain them is about three times the weight of the animal. Given the depleted state of global fisheries and the challenges of providing adequate nutrition to a growing human population, increased farming of carnivorous species such as octopus will act counter to the goal of improving global food security."

Even if this sustainability problem somehow weren't the case, the four authors add, octopus farming with its highly impoverished habitats is still unethical, as it would be for any sentient animal. Lori Marino and I have arrived at the same conclusion, writing that same year that the "unnatural and sterile" conditions of intensive octopus farming replicate terrible conditions found at factory farms. Intensive rearing of fish under similar conditions deserves scrutiny as well. In sum, excited advertisements for the benefits of aquaculture too often underplay substantive concerns regarding sustainability and animal well-being.

Might entomophagy help the global food security situation while incurring fewer negative ecological consequences? Large-scale eating of insects is endorsed by the Food and Agriculture Organization of the UN, which states that food security will be enhanced when insect consumption is taken seriously. Small packets of creeping or flying protein are already beloved foods in many parts of the world. As biological anthropologist Julie Lesnik notes in her book *Edible Insects and Human Evolution*, our evolutionary trajectory was shaped by insect eating as well as meat eating. That some human populations today avoid insects as food is a deviation from long-term normal foraging practices for our species.

Yet insects are animals, and if eating pigs, chickens, and cows raises ethical questions, should the eating of crickets raise some too? Feeding the world through extra tons of protein derived from crickets, ants, termites, and caterpillars might reduce the ills of factory farming and thus align with compassion for many animals, but what about costs borne by the insects themselves? Insects are far from the simple creatures they are often made out to be, as both insect science and stories like the one about Bee's friendship with the woman who rescued her (chapter 3) convey. It's a pretty obvious ethical trap to express disgust at some people in Asia who eat dogs while many Americans stud everything from burgers to chocolate bars with bacon. Is it a similar trap to rage at factory farming of pigs but not at large-scale farming of insects? A vegan is likely to answer this question differently than an omnivore would. *Are* the two examples meaningfully different, because pig consciousness is vastly more developed than insect consciousness? To what degree do insects feel pain? I think these issues deserve exploration, given that entomophagy is touted as a solution to food insecurity.

People who forage at subsistence level, struggle in poverty, or just face a hard time making health-care payments may not be able to make choices that consistently benefit other animals. It's not just a matter of money; many financial analyses in fact suggest that eating a healthy vegetarian or vegan diet is less expensive than eating a meat-centered one, both in short-term savings on food costs and in long-term savings on medical bills. Yet the point stands: it takes time and effort to reshape how a family is fed and how family members eat, and not everyone may have those resources available. This point is reminiscent of Sunaura Taylor's when she brought up broad political and economic challenges to veganism, and it resonates too with the writing of Garrett Broad in *More Than Just Food: Food Justice and Community Change*. Alternative food movements remain overwhelmingly white, Broad notes; in his view, the most powerful vision for social change is one that goes beyond a focus on food alone to take aim at equality in economic development and access to health care.

I wish to underscore one conclusion that becomes increasingly clear month by month: it is a matter of urgency that people move toward plant-based eating in large numbers. Jane Goodall, a cherished voice of environmentalism and the world's foremost expert on behavior and conservation of wild chimpanzees, says as much in an essay written in 2018 for the *Guardian*. Goodall identifies three damaging factors of animal agriculture, in addition to cruelty to animals: destruction of wild lands because crops must be grown for animal feed; fossil fuels used in large quantities to transport grain to animals, animals to slaughter, and meat to tables; and pollution of our soil, rivers, and seas from animal waste together with agricultural runoff.

Eating a plant-based diet to the maximum degree manageable, then, is taking compassionate action for entire world. The lead paragraph of another 2018 article in the *Guardian* puts it plainly: "Avoiding meat and dairy products is the single biggest way to reduce your environmental impact on the planet, according to the scientists behind the most comprehensive analysis to date of the damage farming does to the planet." That comprehensive analysis, or more precisely a meta-analysis that aggregated data on 38,700 farms in 199 countries around the world producing forty different agricultural goods, was published in *Science* by J. Poore and T. Nemecek. It's a fascinating article full of purple, turquoise, and green bar graphs that codify startling statistics.

Meat and dairy production eats up 83 percent of the world's farmland and produces a whopping 56 percent of agriculture's greenhouse gas emissions, but provides only 37 percent of protein and 18 percent of calories. Let's linger for a moment over this protein statistic: all the meat and dairy produced by global farming ends up giving to the world's population only a little over one third of our protein. Of course that 37 percent represents a critical resource, but it comes lashed to a set of severe costs to our environment. Even the lowest-impact animal products and aquaculture systems, Poore and Nemecek report, exceed average impacts of substitute vegetable proteins when it comes to greenhouse gas emissions.

These two researchers show us yet again how an unfolding crisis situation reveals opportunities for change. In describing the "transformative potential" of shifting to a diet that excludes animal products, they zero in on the US. Here in my country, where per capita meat consumption exceeds the global average by a factor of three, dietary change on that scale would have a much greater effect than in many other countries, reducing food's harmful emissions somewhere between 61 and 73 percent. This fact is tantalizing in its vision, and it may tempt us toward a passionate and personal activism. I fall prey to a certain fierceness myself when I watch people consume steaks and barbecue and fried chicken and milkshakes day after day. I want to gently shake them, family members and friends as well as strangers, and ask them, *How can you* still *eat all that meat and dairy? Don't you know the facts?*

Yet sometimes "the facts" elude me too, longer than they should. Only in 2020, through reading Alex Blanchette's book *Porkopolis: American Animality, Standardized Life, and the Factory Farm*, did I fully grasp just how ubiquitous in American life is "the corporate pig," to take just one animal example. I knew already that pig parts are turned not just into pork chops, bacon, and sausage but also into gelatin used in marshmallows, gummies, and Jell-O. But Blanchette's list of pig-derived gelatin products goes further: "photographic prints, makeup and other cosmetics, gel-based medical pills, sandpaper, waterproofed fabrics, some wines, simulated mammal tissues for ammunition testing, material for culturing cells in laboratories, paper money," and possibly the pages of his book, and this one (as a binder). "Radically disassembled" pigs are found not only in the food consumed by millions of dogs and cats but also (already now or coming soon) in asphalt on American highways. Blanchette's conclusion expands the message I've offered here about compassionate action: "Rather than simply refusing to eat meat, a basic demand should be the right to remain autonomous from the factory farm—not to be forced to subsidize these operations within our mundane actions."

Many vegans have said things along these lines for years, and it's on me that I wasn't able to hear them fully until recently. A popular stereotype about vegans renders them as punishingly judgmental about nonvegans' consumer choices and thus about the moral compass of nonvegan folks generally. In my experience, this vegan stereotype is wrong far more often than it is right. Repeatedly I have heard vegan colleagues and friends say that a life based in compassion means *comprehensive* compassion.

In "Vegan," their chapter for the *Critical Terms in Animal Studies* volume, New Zealand animal studies scholars Annie Potts and Philip Armstrong contrast identity veganism with aspirational veganism. Identity veganism, they write, "is associated with a sense of ethical 'purity,' since people subscribing to this version tend to believe their lifestyle is morally advanced with respect to nonvegan lifestyles." Potts and Armstrong use the term *vegan police* to mean people who take the view that veganism is the only way to fight back against institutionalized violence to animals. Aspirational veganism, by contrast, is more a "practice or process" than a lifestyle, aimed at "eliminating or minimizing exploitation of, violence against, and the killing of others." This aspiration, as I have noted, goes beyond not eating meat, dairy, and eggs to encompass an ethic that fights against the abuse of animals in all realms. The goals of veganism "are not helped by being judgmental of the paths followed by others in the direction of more compassionate living," Potts and

Armstrong write. Aspirational vegans know large-scale harvesting of plants too may result in harm to animals. This knowledge is part and parcel of the *aspiration*—to know that it is nearly impossible to eat without causing some negative impact, yet to strive to live in ways that minimize that impact.

Harsh judgments by vegans directly to and about nonvegans do occur (as do insults flowing in the opposite direction). On May 8, 2018, someone associated with a group called Farmgirl Photography posted to Facebook a picture of a pregnant woman next to a pregnant cow, with the caption "Both feeling a 'little pregnant.'" The comment was meant as humor. A group of vegan activists exploded online in anger and hostility. (I archived comments from the page of a vegan activist who shared the post by Farmgirl Photography, which was taken down at some point, making it impossible to see the comments at the original post.) The calmest remarks ran along the lines of this one: "So sad, even as a mother to be, she still can't make the connection." Others went further. "Twisted and demented," wrote one person. Another wrote, "They are all subhuman," with "they" referring to dairy farmers. Others threw around the terms "sociopath" and "psychopath," again referring to farmers. One stated, "Fuck her and her unborn child." Which of these comments did the pregnant woman herself see? That I can't know, yet it's clear that the attacking remarks were intended to be seen by her. The comments I archived were authored by people who celebrated leaving rude responses on the original post, urged others in the group to "flood" the woman with comments, or acknowledged being blocked immediately for commenting at the Farmgirl Photography page.

This fury emerged because the supposedly humorous comparison isn't funny at all: in reality, the mom human will raise her baby whereas the mom cow will not be allowed to do so. As I have described, separation of mother dairy cows from their babies happens right after birth; the cow may grieve for her lost offspring, showing agitation and distress through altered body language and unusual vocalizations. Yet I cannot imagine that the farmers on the receiving end of the awful comments took in anything but the shock of such hate. How can being told you are "subhuman," or receiving an obscenity directed at your unborn child, lead to a willingness to reassess anything or to meaningful dialogue? How does vengeful raging fit with a worldview based in compassion? How could such outbursts amount to effective advocacy for cows?

I posed these queries to the vegan activist on whose Facebook page I had first seen the pregnancy photograph and subsequent comments. Ryan Phillips of Williamsburg, Virginia, carries out "in the street" animal activism, at times accompanied by one or more well-loved pigs: Pumpkin; Charlotte, who is Pumpkin's daughter; and Millie. Almost certainly, none of these three would be alive had they resided on a farm, because pig slaughter occurs at age six months. Now they live with Phillips and other animals, including two cows, at the small Life With Pigs Farm Animal Sanctuary. Whether at the sanctuary, out walking in the historic district of Colonial Williamsburg, or visiting college campuses across the country, Phillips invites people to experience the beauty and playfulness of farm animals by way of affectionate encounters.

Here's what Phillips had to say in reply to my query about the kerfuffle surrounding the photograph.

My goal in creating posts that engage (and sometimes enrage) other vegans is to inspire them to get active for animals. Ideally, activists will not let their frustration and anger turn into blind rage and personal attacks towards those seen exploiting animals. When comments devolve into attacks of a personal nature unrelated to the animal abuse being addressed in a post, it can be counterproductive and lead people looking on to question the sincerity of animal activists promoting compassion for animals while being so derogatory towards non-vegans in ways unrelated to the abuse being targeted.

I believe we can still powerfully attack the actions of an animal abuser without making personal attacks. In the case of the pregnant woman posing next to the pregnant dairy cow, this was a hugely popular post on that woman's Facebook page. And the overwhelming response previously showed a complete lack of compassion for the cow and awareness of the hypocrisy involved. [The original poster's] goal was to portray dairy farming in this idyllic and endearing manner. But, because activists were so inspired by the comment I showed pointing out the reality of what happens to dairy cows and their babies, we were able to get this misleading post removed and hopefully make this person rethink exploiting the suffering of cows for her memes.

The nasty comments made about the pregnant woman represent a practice of identity rather than aspirational veganism. Phillips's own activist philosophy has elements of both, I think. He firmly asserts that there's a place for guilt in the kind of intense vegan activism to which he's dedicated his life: guilt, he says, plays "a vital role in the reasons behind people choosing to reconsider what they think of as food." Recalling my conversation with Mary, who reacts negatively to guilt, I wonder about how often "guilt discourse" works. Is there hard evidence either way?

Vegan activist Tobias Leenaert takes up that question in *How to Create a Vegan World* even as he adopts an approach different from Phillips's. Leenaert's book title at first may appear at odds with a theme I'm developing here, that not everyone will be able (or willing) to go vegan. Leenaert's writings, though, have inspired me because of their balance of firm advocacy and abundant kindness. *How to Create a Vegan World* is laced with statements like this one: "Vegans are too few in number for our collective indignation to have a substantial impact. . . . Right now we should be careful with our anger." In a set-apart feature of the text called "How to Be a Nonjudgmental Vegan," he declares that "most people who feel judged will be less likely to listen and change." Following this are bulleted tips that urge vegans to "catch yourself when you're being judgmental," "realize that you don't know people or their situation," "remember that everyone is different," and "comprehend that people may be doing great deeds, which you aren't."

The history of civil rights and other major movements for social justice tells, Leenaert says, that pushing consistently for gradual change works better than insisting on radical change all at once. From this perspective, reducetarians are central to achieving greater justice for farm animals. After all, "as a group, meat reducers save more animals than vegetarians and vegans," Leenaert notes. He supports reducetarian strategies, not because as a vegan he thinks reducetarian efforts go far enough but rather because he believes a more inclusive message will galvanize more people. Sometimes behavior changes first in small steps, and attitude shifts follow.

In *I Feel You: The Surprising Power of Extreme Empathy*, journalist Chris Beam writes that "a most radical and propitious empathy" comes from a model where "we can expose violations while caring for the violators, especially when we see that the violator is also inside of us." Beam is not talking specifically about people who eat meat, and were I to adopt the word *violator* for omnivores I would not be inviting much dialogue! But Beam's central point, as I take it, does relate to the approach I'm discussing here. None of us avoids causing some degree of suffering to *someone*, and at times many someones, when we eat. Frugivory is possible, for instance, only because of other beings' forced sacrifices: animals' land is taken for the growing of fruit, and migrant workers toil in the heat to pick the fruit with low wages and no health-care benefits. As Gillespie writes in *The Cow with Ear Tag #1389*, eating plant-based foods "does not ensure the fair treatment of the farmworkers producing fruits and vegetables or the distant laborers living in conditions of slavery or otherwise harmful conditions to produce nondairy chocolate, coffee, sugar, or bananas."

Here are three mantras I find helpful to repeat: We are all in it together. Any choice of food imposes costs on other beings. Each of us may strive to bring our food choices in alignment with our compassion for animals and for people. My friend Diane Brandt Wilkes put it this way in a 2018 Facebook post from which I have permission to quote: "Our life purpose is to keep doing those hard things. Examining our beliefs and behaviors, analyzing them for congruence. Changing them as necessary to be in alignment with our inner compass. It's very hard work. It never ends. The process is our purpose. There's no finish line."

It's a tricky enterprise to assess the overall positive impact for animals of the excitement around vegan, vegetarian, and reducetarian eating. Meat consumption is on the rise globally. As Bill McKibben writes in *The Reducetarian Solution*, people in developing countries who have barely contributed to the global-warming crisis can now afford meat, and many like the taste exceedingly well. Nearly half (49%) of all factory-farmed animals now live in China. At the same time, in his 2019 TED talk Bruce Friedrich notes that in 2018, the average North American person ate two hundred pounds of meat. Two hundred pounds! Injecting some humor into his talk, Friedrich notes since *he* personally didn't eat any meat at all that year, someone out there in North America ate four hundred pounds of it.

Mostly though, Friedrich doesn't joke about meat eating, and it's easy to see why. When floodwaters hit the industrialized farms of North Carolina in the aftermath of Hurricane Florence in fall 2018, animals were abandoned to drown. I can only imagine the terror of the confined 3.4 million chickens and fifty-five hundred pigs who died as the waters rose. Storm by storm, the toll taken on farm animals in North Carolina over the years has been enormous, including the twenty thousand pigs who died there during Hurricane Floyd in 1999. People are harmed immensely as well, and not only during hurricane season. As I wrote for National Public Radio after Hurricane Florence, the lagoons full of pig waste and bacteria at hog farms are infamous: "Hog farm neighbors say the stench is intolerable; the pork-processing giant Smithfield Foods has so far lost three lawsuits filed by North Carolinians over the environmental harms of pig waste."

This is once again painful stuff, news we would rather not hear. As I write this paragraph in summer 2020, concern about the negative effects of meat consumption are on the rise because of the COVID-19 pandemic. It's too early to distinguish short- from long-term consumer trends at this stage, but signs indicate that more people are gravitating toward plant-based meat substitutes, sales of which rose 35 percent nationally during a four-week period in April-May 2020 according to the *New York Times*. Perhaps the global transmission of the SARS-CoV-2 virus brought home to these new customers the risks not only of capturing and confining wildlife (like bats) in Chinese wet markets but also of crowding thousands of pigs and chickens row by row in American factory farms. These practices increase the risk of viruses jumping across species and causing illness, death, and economic calamity; many of us will recall the swine flu H1N1 outbreak in 2009–2010 as one recent example. Or maybe the customers' motivation was simpler, though as sad: the high level of COVID-19 illness among meat-processing workers. For some people newly attracted to plant-based meat, perhaps both factors played a role. It's nonetheless clear that most people in the US still can't imagine life without meat: the *Times* also reports that meat sales continue to rise.

Over the years I have come to realize how much emotional pain may result when vegan and vegetarian eaters, and to some extent reducetarians as well, spend time with others who seem to eat animals with no second thought. Thanksgiving feasts, Fourth of July barbecues, and other holidays religious and secular that call for big feasts often revolve around meat. During these celebrations, turkeys, cows, pigs, chickens, and other animals are, in Carol Adams's term, "the absent referents" behind the flesh on the plate. It's not being dramatic or difficult to feel (or to express) great distress about that fact, and sometimes it's not always healthy to continue trying to enter into meaningful dialogue with others who tune out animal suffering.

In fall 2019 I was invited to attend a gathering of scientists, farmers, media people, and others in Carthage, Tennessee, at the family farm of former vice president Al Gore. Renowned for his sounding of the climate-crisis alarm bell in the 2006 film *An Inconvenient Truth*, Gore had set up this small conference at Caney Creek Farm to discuss agricultural sustainability, carbon sequestration, and soil and food quality. I wanted very much to go, so I RSVPed with a yes and a request that I be served no meat at any meals; made hotel and driving arrangements; and began to prepare by reading about the farm's work. Given that lambs and pigs are raised for slaughter on Caney Creek Farm, I accepted from the start that I would find myself among people with a variety of perspectives on food, animals, and animal rights. My thinking at this stage was twofold: I would learn from others joined in common cause against factory farms, and perhaps I could share some of my knowledge about cognition and emotion in farm animals, and why that knowledge matters for how we eat.

As part of my preparation, I signed up for Caney Creek Farm's newsletter. Less than a week before the start of the conference, my first issue arrived by email, and all my plans came crashing down. "You're invited to our Fall Lamb Roast!!!," I read, regarding an event scheduled for *after* the conference. The newsletter writer explained that every year the farm puts on a potluck-style event to thank customers and others in the local community. "This is a whole animal roast," the person wrote, "and we invite you to be a part of the entire butchering and cooking process. If you feel like it's time to witness this side of your meat eating habits, this is a great way to do it. Come as early as 10:00am to help prep, kill, butcher, and enjoy the day with us! We have yard games, live music (bring your instruments!), and the Caney Fork River to keep us entertained while the lamb is roasting."

Whether the farm truly allows untrained locals to participate in the killing and butchering steps or the invitation is for visitors to observe up close as farm staff carries out those steps, I don't know. Either way, the image of families urged to attend a slaughter for entertainment, while children nearby cavort in play, violated a key expectation I had held. Wouldn't a farm devoted to compassionate care of the environment treat the slaughter process with respect? Even though the lamb roast would occur only after I had departed the farm, I knew I couldn't attend the conference in good conscience. When I said as much to the conference organizers and to the farm itself, I cited language on the farm's website that pledges care for animals to the highest standards. The lamb roast, I wrote, dishonors an animal's life and his or her sentience, and is inconsistent with care and community as I understand those terms. At no point did I hear back from anyone.

I do see a growing awareness of the cruelty of animal slaughter, at least as it is practiced in industrial slaughterhouses. Undercover exposés, like those in Blanchette's and Pachirat's books and in virtual reality films, alert a whole new generation to what goes on behind closed doors. My first jolt of VR came when I strapped on a headset at the Sundance Film Festival in Park City, Utah, in 2015. The short film *iAnimal* features undercover footage from a Mexican slaughterhouse. Jointly created by the international animal-rights organization Animal Equality and the company Condition One, it brought me to tears. In VR you are right there with the pigs who endure a metal bolt to the head that does not immediately kill them. When the twelve-minute film concluded, Animal Equality leaders Sharon Núñez and Jose Valle had to comfort me—an embarrassing circumstance, but they were very kind and I have followed their work ever since.

While conversations about feral cats, hunting, and animals kept in zoos may run hot, in my experience nothing cuts as close to the bone as discussing what or who we eat or refuse to eat. Sunaura Taylor in *Beasts of Burden* rightly says that we shouldn't care only about animals whose actions we recognize as intelligent. Even so, I see the same thing happen over and over: fascination flares when people learn about tool-using octopuses or personality-plus pigs—or clever bees. For me, that's a superb path to dialogue because talking about animal thinking and feeling offers a way in to issues around animals and food. Often people tell me that they cut out or cut down on eating pigs (or chickens or octopuses) because they learned from a scientist about the inner lives of those animals.

Lori Marino, the scientist with whom I cowrote an essay about octopus ethics, reminds us in a 2017 review paper in *Animal Cognition* that chickens are birds. What a startling way to begin a scientific paper! The need to cite that basic fact is real, though. Chickens are typically "categorized as a commodity, devoid of authenticity as a real animal," as Marino says. Drawing on the work of psychologist Rosa Rugani, Marino explains that chickens grasp something about numbers. Picture a group of tiny chicks, only days old, who were reared to imprint on small balls. (Yes, chicks will imprint on almost anything or anyone.) The chicks were shown one set of three balls and a second set of only two. Each set was then made to disappear behind an opaque screen. In this free-choice test, the chicks chose to in-spect the screen that blocked the larger set of balls. The coolest part comes next: after the balls were made to vanish behind the screens, some were transferred from one screen to another, one by one and in plain sight of the watching chicks. Chicks again chose the screen hiding the larger number. This is quite a feat because it requires "computation of a series of subsequent additions or subtractions of elements that appeared and disap-peared," as Marino explains.

Marino concludes, after reviewing numerous scientific papers, that chickens reason, make logical references, are "behaviorally sophisticated" in their social interactions with others they recognize as individuals, and may show empathy for others. In an email exchange I had with her, Marino em-phasized that most people really don't view chickens as birds. Our brains tend to exclude *this* animal, most familiar to us from chicken-wing Superbowl celebrations and baked-chicken reci-pes, from the stars of the bird world: jewel-like hummingbirds who visit our nectar feeders or brainy crows and ravens whose tool-using feats stud the science headlines. "We are psycholog-ically invested in making sure we protect ourselves against the reality of who chickens are," Marino told me, "because if we eat them then it makes us uncomfortable to acknowledge their sen-tience, their awareness, their emotions. It becomes a circular reality—an inconvenient truth."

Chickens, at least many of them (grumps and outright misanthropes can be found in most any species), respond positively to human kindness. Other farm animals do too. Writing in *Applied Animal Behaviour Science* in 2018, animal scientist Munira Shahin shows that when people stroked the neck of cows who reside on a commercial dairy farm for five minutes a day for fifteen days, the cows relaxed around humans. Even the cows judged to have a more highly reactive personality did this. Kindness is perceived by many creatures, and it matters to them. I saw this for myself when I met Bonnie at Farm Sanctuary (chapter 1) and the young calves on whom she kept her protective eye.

Rosamund Young in *The Secret Life of Cows* recounts stories of dairy calves at Kite's Nest farm in Worcestershire, England, who thrive when given the chance to remain with their mothers as long as they choose. Even grown females residing in another area of the farm may seek out their mothers for solace during difficult life events. The cow Dolly II did this at Kite's Nest after she gave birth to a dead calf and required veterinary care for a displaced womb. Traversing three fields, she arrived at the side of her mother, who licked and comforted her. Six days later, Dolly II left her mother and resumed her normal routine.

Stories about the behavior and inner lives of animals—from wild rabbits and octopuses to domesticated chickens and cows—invite us to think before we eat. Yet, reminiscent of responses to the plight of bears held captive on bile farms (chapter 1), people may turn away from these stories. That happened when I spoke during a series of fundraiser teas on behalf of the Heritage Humane Society animal shelter in Williamsburg. The idea was this: people would pay to eat good food at a café and listen to my science-based stories about animals who think and feel, and the money would go to the shelter. This central idea worked beautifully. For nonprofit animal organizations, I waive my speaking fee, and sell and sign my books on site. Three times I went through the speak-then-sign-books sequence, and each time I met with the same result at the book-selling table: people who care deeply about rescue of cats and dogs looked over copies of *How Animals Grieve* but averted their eyes away from *Personalities on the Plate* with its subtitle *The Lives and Minds of Animals We Eat*.

Only minutes before, after all, most if not all attendees had eaten chickens or pigs. (A vegetarian meal had been prepared for me, so I don't know what specific meats were given to my audience.) A few folks seemed to conclude, though standing mere feet away from me, that their remarks somehow wouldn't reach my ears. One woman looked at *Personalities* and remarked into the surrounding air, "Oh no, not this one. Is she trying to make everyone vegetarian?," then carried on muttering about the book. I don't take such responses personally. It can be genuinely challenging to hear that the food on your plate once had good days and bad days, smart thoughts and deep feelings.

A future is coming with a more empathetic relationship between animals and the food on our plates, of that I feel sure.

*   *   *

The science-fiction television show *The Orville*, brainchild of writer and actor Seth MacFarlane, set four hundred years in the future, debuted in 2017 and I fell for it hard. Like the beloved original *Star Trek* series to which it's an homage, *The Orville* takes on serious issues centering on social justice and the lifeways of other cultures. Beings from various worlds (even one who has been described as "a sentient green glob") work and socialize together. *The Orville*, though, throws in its own special touches, its own brand of campy humor.

In almost every episode, officers of interstellar spaceship the USS *Orville* order up from a small countertop "replicator" machine whatever food or drink strikes their fancy. Immediately and out of thin air, that item materializes (as it did also on shows like *Star Trek: The Next Generation*). Super-strong and alien-browed chief of security Alara Kitan, from the planet Xelaya, orders up Xelayan tequila to calm her nerves at a rough moment. Earth human first officer Kelly Grayson selects a thick slice of chocolate cake when she's in a romantic funk. All foods are replicated perfectly and to the desired specifications.

First Officer Grayson's food choice resonates with me. Twenty years on, I still reminisce about a piece of chocolate cake I ordered in a Paris restaurant, because it sent me into orbit without benefit of space travel. Given access to an *Orville*-style food-synthesizer machine, I'd select chocolate cake too, along with the chicken pot pie I haven't eaten in nearly a decade. That is, I'd order it as long as the chicken was "clean meat" and the milk and eggs in the cake were equally clean.

Here on Earth in the present day, food-technology companies are making enormous strides toward clean foods that will ease animal cruelty in a big way. (But see Benjamin Aldes Wurgaft's *Meat Planet: Artificial Flesh and the Future of Food* for an incisive exploration of the view that complex societal problems are solvable with technology.) Within my own lifetime if my mother's and maternal grandmother's longevity genes hold, foods made from meat, cheese, and milk synthesized from starter cells extracted from living farm animals will be widely available. They are termed "clean" products because they are made in bioreactors with no need for animal slaughter. That term is a bit clinical, an ironic thing because the products it describes are born of compassionate action for animals and the Earth, including for people who crave meat. Clean meat foods are *built* by way of muscle-specific stem cells taken from individual animals, so unlike the Impossible Burger or the Beyond Burger, clean-meat burgers are *of animals*. Combined with plant-based foods, might clean meat revolutionize what we eat once and for all? Might the hellish conditions of factory farms and the so-called humane slaughter of farmed animals killed at just a few months or years old be drastically reduced? The potential for change is staggering. In some types of clean meat, not even muscle biopsies are needed for starter cells, because the product can be brewed from yeast or other microbes.

The technical details and descriptions of the food items soon coming our way are outlined in Paul Shapiro's *Clean Meat: How Growing Meat without Animals Will Revolutionize Dinner and the World*, Jacy Reese's *The End of Animal Farming*, and Benjamin Aldes Wurgaft's *Meat Planet*. Hamburgers and chicken nuggets, favorite foods of millions, are on the horizon in animal-free form (animal free except for those starter cells, that is), as is seafood. Shapiro acknowledges that some folks spit out an "ugh" at the prospect of "laboratory meat." Don't we instead want to fill our bodies with natural foods? Asking that question overlooks a fact now established by multiple studies: meat from slaughtered animals is riddled with growth hormones and dangerous bacteria. Clean meat is free of these substances and at the same time circumvents the heavy toll that traditional animal agriculture takes on the environment.

Expanding the future of food to include more plant-based *and* clean-meat eating aligns with compassionate action for animals. True, some vegans and vegetarians may reject clean meat altogether because it's constructed from those starter animal cells, and because fetal bovine serum is frequently still used in its preparation (at least at the time of this writing). I understand that choice. When visiting Disney World in winters 2019 and 2020, I was delighted both times to sit outdoors with my family at the Rose and Crown English Pub at EPCOT and enjoy either vegan bangers and mash or vegan fish and chips. These plant-based meals were so satisfying that I had no yearning for "real" meat or fish, or for a clean meat or fish product either. All hands on deck are needed in a global project to eat less meat, though, and this includes omnivores who may prefer clean meat to plant-based foods.

In all these emerging foods, taste matters to consumers. When we took Sarah, who is vegetarian, to Food for Thought restaurant in Williamsburg, they ordered the Gardein chicken, a plant-based selection. After a few bites they looked uncomfortable and then blurted out, "I don't think this is vegan!" The taste was nearly identical to the traditionally prepared chicken that they used to eat, and they worried that some mix-up had occurred in the kitchen. We flagged down the server, who laughed kindly at our question. People *often* ask that, he told us; one diner had even become combative in his skepticism, fearing he was being forced to eat "real" chicken! But yes, the chicken served to Sarah (and earlier to the excitable diner) was indeed vegan. As Bee Wilson puts it in *The Reducetarian Solution*, the whole idea is to create meatless meals that deliver deliciousness: "It is not a case of making do with less but of realizing that, actually, everything doesn't taste better with bacon."

With so much concern for animals, what about compassion for plants? Plants are wild beings too, connected to their surroundings and capable of evoking feelings of connection in us. Standing among the towering trees in Prairie Creek Redwoods State Park near Klamath in extreme northern California in autumn 2018, I felt as blissful as when the bison herd flowed close to me in Yellowstone National Park (chapter 3): the breath caught in my throat, and tears blurred in my eyes. Truly massive, these trees' height rivals that of skyscrapers, with a girth as great as 27 feet. Charlie and I had hiked part of the park's Ossagon Trail into the forest, away from the road: the only humans around, we heard no sounds other than birdsong. Bright-green ferns and other plants I couldn't name made up a thriving forest floor, and I knew that small animals must be nestled in natural cubbies all around us. I thought of the indigenous Yoruk peoples who had so often walked this trail, heading for their village along the Pacific coast. Now and again I pressed my palm lightly against a redwood's trunk, wondering about that tree's age. Some coastal redwoods are two thousand years old. I couldn't shake the idea that I was standing amid wisdom to which I had no direct access.

From information published by the Save the Redwoods League, I learned that coastal redwoods today are found only along a 450-mile strip in California and a tiny part of southern Oregon. Owing to modern-day pressures ranging from global warming to tree poaching, this swath represents only 5 percent of the redwoods' original territory. The two of us were lucky to be among them sharing moments of beauty and calm.

Trees of many varieties may astonish us. In an afterword to Peter Wohlleben's best-selling nonfiction book *The Hidden Life of Trees*, the forest ecologist Suzanne Simard describes how when radioactive isotopes were introduced into the "busy, cooperative internet" between paper birches and Douglas firs, she discovered that carbon was transmitted back and forth between the trees. "The birches, as it turns out," she writes, "were spurring the growth of the firs, like carers in human social networks"—and later on, the firs reciprocated. Research like this on tree interconnectivity became the basis for one of Richard Powers's most compelling novels, *The Overstory*, in which a set of central characters intensely bond with each other—and with the trees that they understand function in the world as socially interconnected beings.

It's not just trees either. Plants may recognize their kin and choose to respond differently to them than to nonkin, according to a 2019 review article by Elizabeth Pennisi in *Science* magazine. Plant ecologist Susan Dudley grew American searocket in pots under two experimental conditions: with relatives or with plants that were nonkin but from the same population. Surrounded by relatives, the searocket constrained its root growth, apparently so that kin could readily share in limited resources like nutrients and water. Housed with nonrelatives, by contrast, it was no holds barred: the root system expanded. Another team led by Rubén Torices carried out a similar experiment with a Spanish herb, growing it in pots alone or, Pennisi writes, "with three or six neighbors of varying relatedness." The herb put out flowers in greater abundance when kin were present, "making them more alluring to pollinators."

To be sure, not all plant scientists agree on how robustly these experiments support the notion of true kin recognition in plants. Though admittedly I'm a novice at interpreting plant science, I can't help but think how cool is it that mustard plants shift the way they arrange their leaves to reduce shading of neighbor relatives but not neighbor nonrelatives. Plant ecologist Jorge Casal found, Pennisi says, that because of this shift the mustard kin "cumulatively grow more vigorously and produce more seeds." Turning to a different plant species, Casal discovered that when near kin, sunflowers that were planted closely together send their shoots off to the side to grow in directions away from their relatives. The "leaning away" sunflowers produced more oil than those experimentally constrained from doing so. Bright-yellow sunflowers are my favorite flora. Will I ever admire them again without pausing and wondering, is this sunflower communicating with nearby kin?

As plants come alive for us in new ways, questions about how we should treat them have gained traction. Certainly any drawing of hard boundaries between plants and animals is problematic. The genus of organism called *Euglena* exhibits some characteristics of plants, like making its food through photosynthesis. Yet when light is not available for photosynthesis to take place, it can also capture food from the external world as animals do. Additionally, it moves by means of a tail-like flagellum as some animals do. We can go further, though, and consider not only basic biology but also concern for all life: excluding plants from our care means we have missed the very point of endeavoring to live with compassion.

Gardening and other forms of caring for plants connect us to the natural world; healthy plant life creates refuges for insects, birds, and other small animals. My friend Stephen Wood, who lives in northern Virginia, spends hours of his nonworking time to help trees, carrying with him a set of tools and lots of patience. "I've been clearing English ivy, Virginia creeper, and poison ivy vines off trees primarily on park and state land about one or two times a month for about three to four hours per session," he told me in 2018. These vines otherwise would strangle the trees, causing loss of tree life and of animal habitat as well. "I'd say I've cleared around seventy-five trees over the last year or so," Wood estimated, and he continues doggedly on. Here is an innovative way to take direct action on behalf of the living world.

Are plants conscious, able to experience the world subjectively in the way that octopuses, chickens, cows, and other animals do? The scientific consensus here is no. Plants learn, respond, and network in ways not akin to the learning, responding, and networking of animals. This fact doesn't mean that plants are inferior to animals, any more than neurologically simpler spiders are inferior to spider monkeys. Each living species of plant or animal is adapted to be what or who it is and to function well in its own niche (at least if humans don't destroy that niche). It does mean that plants' experience of the world is not a conscious experience.

I like tremendously what Mark Hawthorne has to say in his book *Striking at the Roots: A Practical Guide to Animal Activism*. Hawthorne focuses specifically on people's worry that plants might feel pain. First, he notes that without a central nervous system, plants aren't able to experience pain. That's indeed the consensus of most scientists. Let's say you are still skeptical about this, based on the view that if plants are capable of recognizing kin and acting accordingly, we haven't yet probed the limits of their experience. Hawthorne's next sentence, then, speaks directly to you: "If you really want to believe that plants feel pain, you should be aware that 70 percent of crops go to feed farmed animals, so if you truly care about plants, not eating animals is the best way to ensure their safety."

Plant-based eating, in contrast to eating meat, seafood, and dairy, reduces harm to our planet and its living creatures in concrete (if imperfect) ways. That's what aspiring to compassionate action is all about: weighing the alternative choices thoughtfully and doing the best we can.

6
Animals in Research Labs

One Sunday summer morning I took a drive with a friend through the campus of the University of Illinois at Urbana-Champaign. I had flown in from Virginia the day before, and that evening I would deliver a talk on animal emotion to the 2018 summer institute on animal–human relationships. Jointly sponsored by the Animals and Society Institute and this branch of the University of Illinois, the weeklong gathering brought together early-career scholars from seven countries to a series of talks, workshops, and artistic events. Before the whole thing began, I had a few free hours. What better way to spend them than hanging out with some local animals?

Driving down a rough road, we arrived at the university's horse farm. We got out and stood by its fence to take in the view. Foals snuggled up to their mothers; juvenile males kicked up their heels in playful mock fighting. The sun glinted off the horses' chestnut-colored coats. All in all, the picture was one of joyful movement and relaxed socializing. Here was exactly the "animal high" that I had sought—indeed that I routinely seek. If I'm at a party, I look for the dog or cat. If I'm traveling, I seek a good spot to encounter local wildlife. Now my friend and I had found a few moments of equine bliss.

Driving farther along into the agriculture school section

of campus, we came upon a sign marking the Dairy Cattle Research Area. My eye caught sight of a cow, but my brain couldn't immediately make sense of the image before me because a large, clear, ring-shaped window was embedded in the cow's side. The ring looked like an ocean liner's porthole, transparent and able to be pulled open by a person. Down the cow's flank seeped a kind of liquid discharge. Placidly the cow chewed her food as she stood next to a "normal" cow with no portal. Under a blue July sky, no other humans within sight or sound, the scene took on an eerie feel. Who was this cow? To what use in dairy research was she put? At that point my mind was stuffed with thoughts of animal joy and grief—the subject of my talk in just a few hours. I couldn't help but wonder, what did this cow experience when people reached through the portal into the very depths of her body?

Coming upon the cow with the portal shifted our mood instantly. Gone was the lightness I had felt watching the horses, replaced by puzzlement and a slightly sick feeling. What invasive procedures had been carried out on this cow? She wasn't alone in her altered status; among the scores of cows visible as we drove along the road, I spied two more with portals identical to the first. Later I would learn that the first cow's name is Brooke and that she—and other cows with portals, whether on that campus or on any of numerous other agricultural or veterinary campuses in this country and beyond—is a "fistulated cow." The fluid dripping down Brooke's flank emerges from her body when her rumen contracts and causes the fluid layer inside that organ to rise above the level of the fistula.

The rumen, one of the cow's four stomach chambers, is key to understanding what's going on here. A cow's rumen acts as a kind of fermentation vat where microorganisms swarm incoming food and break down the tough, fibrous stuff. During the fistulation process, a veterinary surgeon implants a cannula in the cow, a plastic tube that connects the rumen with the cow's outer skin where the portal sits. After the cow heals, various scientific activities may be carried out: studies on which food items are most nutritious for cattle; transfaunation, or donation of bacterial material from the healthy fistulated cow's rumen into the body of a cow who is fighting off some illness; and teaching of veterinary students who wish to learn about bovine anatomy and digestion.

Seeking to learn online about "Brooke the fistulated cow," I found an article in *Modern Farmer* magazine with the jaunty title "Holey Cow: The Wonderful World of a Fistulated Cow." With that "holey cow" pun, surgery on a healthy cow becomes an occasion for humor and an imagined great life for these cows, who number in the hundreds in the United States alone. "It's no wonder a fistulated cow at a veterinary school is treated like bovine royalty," writes reporter Anna O'Brien.

The University of Illinois student newspaper, in a story about Brooke, quotes veterinary-school professionals referring to her "life of luxury" on campus. The emphasis in this piece is on the good that Brooke does for others. Reporter Rebecca Jacobs interviewed Rachel Griffith, one of Brooke's primary caretakers. "Every time we give rumen from Brooke to a sick cow, every time we give plasma from Brooke to a cow that needs to eat, every time we give a blood transfusion from Brooke to a cow in need, that's a life saved," said Griffith. "She saves lives every day." Students learn how to do injections and physical exams using Brooke. And presumably, judging by the fact that reporter Jacobs was invited to "put her arm inside with a plastic glove to feel around," she's invaded quite regularly by students. Jacobs noted, "It's easy to slide your arm through the different levels of digestion."

Benefits do accrue from the fistulating of healthy cows. For one thing, nitrogen and methane emissions from cows have been reduced through experimental analysis of forage extracted from these cows' rumens. For another, sick cows truly are helped by transfaunation, a kind of direct probiotic treatment. Early in life, every cow—like every person—becomes "transfaunated" naturally. As the title of Ed Yong's book about the microbiome puts it, *I Contain Multitudes*—my body is teeming with microbes, and so is yours and so is each cow's. A calf's rumen becomes transfaunated originally when his or her mother begins licking her baby after birth, and the transfaunation increases with every interaction the calf has with the environment. It's not the presence of a teeming microbiome that's different about a fistulated cow; it's that humans reach in, extract a sample of the microorganisms, and carry it to an ailing animal. (In humans the fecal transplant procedure is based on the same idea. A donor's fecal matter is introduced into the body of a person ailing with a stubborn bacterial infection such as *C. difficile*, and the transfer often brings the infection under control.)

What happens in the lives of fistulated cows is normalized by veterinary researchers, who accept it as routine. The costs to the individual animal are assumed to be low and are kept under wraps while the benefits are tallied and touted publicly. In a 2019 conference presentation, Elizabeth Tavella and Brandon Keim conveyed this contrast poignantly. "Holey cow" portrayals, Tavella and Keim noted, make for a kind of "savior" rhetoric, while "at the same time, the presentation of these cows completely deemphasizes their subjectivity, and they are portrayed as feeling no discomfort, or even feeling nothing at all."

Surely there's an irony at work here, one that relates to all fistulated cows and not just to Brooke: these cows are meant in some sense to be *transparent* animals. Come close enough and you may direct your gaze—and your touch—right into their bodies. But can we ever know how it *feels* to these animals when people enter their bodies? As we saw in the previous chapter, cows relax around humans who stroke them gently. Cows show prowess in problem solving and exhibit signs of distress upon separation from their calves. How probable is it that they feel *nothing* physically or emotionally regarding continued ingress into their bodies by individuals of other species? If they are stroked gently and talked to gently, then might their experi- ence—as a research subject, a transfaunation donor, a recep- tacle for students' searching hands—involve little to no stress? I don't claim to know the answer.

A 1970 journal article outlines the behavior of four fistu- lated steers on a desert grassland near Tucson, Arizona. While no direct comparison of these animals with "intact" steers was made, the authors conclude that the fistulated steers re- sponded in similar fashion to intact animals described in the literature, on measures such as time spent grazing, ruminating, and idling. Let's hypothesize that this finding holds true across the board, so that fistulated cows in general behave similarly to their nonfistulated counterparts. Would that be the end of the story? Let's go further and assume that these cows do become completely acclimated to the fistulas and to humans poking around in their bodies. Is there no more about which we might wonder? Or from a perspective of compassion, might we ask, what is the postoperative period like for these cows? How often do fistulated cows experience pain or complications?

According to six scientists who published an article in the *Canadian Veterinary Journal* in 2014, "post-operative pain management following rumen surgery is not common practice." Nathalie C. Newby and her colleagues explain that the first step in fistulation is a laparoscopic procedure on the animal's left flank that clamps the rumen wall to the skin. Step two occurs some days later, when the clamp is removed and a cannula is inserted. The cannula, as I have described, is the device through which a person gains access to a cow's interior.

Local anesthesia is administered for the laparotomy procedure itself, Newby reports. Post-op pain relief in the form of NSAIDs is provided to cattle by a little more than half (57%) of the veterinarians working in Great Britain, for example, whereas in Canada, pain relief is offered in almost every case (96.8%) but via short-acting agents rather than NSAIDs. No statistics were included for the US. By email, I asked Dennis French, head of veterinary clinical medicine at the University of Illinois's College of Veterinary Medicine, what happens in the United States. Despite the technical language, I quote his answer in full because French is based at the university where I met Brooke. His explanation underscores the degree to which veterinary professionals do think (even if not precisely in the ways I would think) about the cows' pain and the ethics of fistulation:

All of our protocols for rumen cannulas provide both pre-operative and post-operative pain control. Flunixin meglumine is approved for either intravenous or topical administration in cattle and our protocols ensure that it is used for at least 48 hours following surgery as well as being on-board prior to the procedure. We also have provisions for the cattle if the heart rate is greater than 90 beats per minute or bruxism (grinding of the teeth) is noted, treatment with flunixin may be extended or opioid (e.g. morphine at 0.2 mg/kg q 6–12 hrs) analgesics may be administered to augment pain relief. Meloxicam may also be used as an alternative.

Key factors to grasp from French's explanation are the administering of pain medication *for at least forty-eight hours following surgery* and the flexibility inherent in the protocol, allowing veterinary responsiveness according to each animal's post-op progress. Clearly fistulated cows, just like people, may experience different levels of care according to the time and space in which they find themselves.

Having gained a clearer picture of what happened to Brooke before I came upon her that day in Illinois, my mind frequently strays back to her. In my mind's eye, she stands in the sun with her portal dripping discharge. In that image for me she points up the need to look beneath the surface when it comes to how animals are used in research, to seek a transparency that often is hard to come by. The cheery articles about Brooke don't mention her post-op pain or pain relief, for instance; it's a little chilling to think that she is packaged for the public as a sort of continuously carefree donor animal, a bovine Clara Barton to be admired. Neither she nor the hundreds of other fistulated cows in the US ever had a choice in becoming a donor or a teaching tool.

When I visited the Illinois campus, I felt a sense of joy *with* the horses as my friend and I observed their interactions in their herd. I felt empathy *for* Brooke, by contrast. My sensory world isn't the same as that of a horse turned out in a field, yet we were all mammals out under the sun enjoying the morning. The horses were no less confined than Brooke—they are bred by humans and used in teaching too—yet Brooke stood apart: she was not only confined by humans but also bodily invaded by them (by us).

To put compassion into play for animals who dwell in the world of science, we often have to work hard to look beyond the happy images that it serves the users of animals to construct. This point holds true even when the bodily needs of surgically altered animals are met with care, because *the animals' healthy bodies are still altered in the first place.* The construction of Brooke as a fussed-over cow exists on a continuum with stylized drawings of smiling cows who grace signs outside barbecue restaurants. These depictions are created to strengthen the notion that a surface story is true: these animals are okay with what happens to them, and those events occur humanely. Transparency is equally as contested a notion when it comes to the use of animals in science as it is in the confining of animals to factory farms or zoos.

Biomedical Research

Transparency is often hard to come by in laboratories where animals such as monkeys, dogs, cats, mice, and rats are used as models for the development of human diseases and their treatment. Countless animals—animals who remain literally uncounted in the case of the rodents, as I will explain—are made symptomatic of cardiac disease or neurological illness, cancer or drug addiction or anxiety. Subject to trial after trial as researchers give them drugs or carry out other medical or genetic interventions as potential treatments, they remain invisible and unknown to us.

Once in a while, individual animals do become real to us. Before retiring at Fauna Sanctuary in Quebec, Canada, a chimpanzee named Tom endured fifteen years at the Laboratory for Experimental Medicine and Surgery in Primates at New York University and sixteen more at the Alamogordo Primate Facility in New Mexico. The word *endured* I choose with intent, for here is how Andrew Westoll describes in *The Chimps of Fauna Sanctuary* what happened to Tom: "For more than thirty years, he was repeatedly infected with increasingly virulent strains of HIV, went through numerous hepatitis-B studies, and survived at least sixty-three liver, bone marrow, and lymph-node biopsies. Tom has gone through more surgeries than anyone else at Fauna. . . . He was knocked unconscious at least 369 times, but this number is based on incomplete medical records and is certainly an underestimate."

Think then of Tom, who—had he lived instead in a wild chimpanzee community—might have used tools to find termites or crack open hard nuts to eat, hunted monkeys in coordinated fashion with his partners, and joined other males to patrol his community's borders. Tom never got to do any of these things, of course. A thirty-year confinement in biomedical laboratories like his no longer befalls chimpanzees, because we now know that such research on our closest living relatives does not, in fact, aid human health. In 2011 a groundbreaking report from the National Academies of Sciences' Institute of Medicine recommended that chimpanzees no longer be used in biomedical research in the United States. New hope and, in some cases, new life in sanctuaries has been given to these ape veterans of harrowingly invasive procedures. In 2013 the National Institutes of Health (NIH) announced its intention to reduce the use of chimpanzees in agency-supported biomedical research and to confine only fifty chimpanzees for future experiments. By 2015 that goal had changed: the NIH said it would officially retire to sanctuary every single NIH-owned chimpanzee, almost four hundred. For the first time as of 2017, more US captive chimpanzees, held originally at NIH or at other facilities, live in accredited sanctuaries than in laboratories.

Not all the numbers are so heartening. The most recent figures I found show that 257 chimpanzees owned by NIH still await retirement, as do about 200 more housed in other facilities. The United States now has a national chimpanzee sanctuary, Chimp Haven located in Keithville, Louisiana, the place to which all NIH chimpanzees strong enough to make the trip will eventually go. (Who is and isn't healthy enough to withstand transport is at times a contested matter. Researchers often advocate for debilitated or frail chimpanzees to stay in place, whereas sanctuary leaders often say they deserve to be moved unless the risk factors are truly critical.) The good news is that there's forward momentum with chimpanzees now. The subject of "lab chimpanzees" catapulted into the public eye as a result of advocacy by scientists and activists. They saw that chimpanzee Tom's plight was re-created again and again in laboratories across the country, with vanishingly little benefit to humans. An even greater challenge now involves animals who are featured less prominently in the national conversation.

In the US alone, seventy-five thousand monkeys now reside in biomedical laboratories. Headline news brings them to light on occasion. For the first time in 2018, the Food and Drug Administration (FDA) retired—to Florida, no less!—monkeys who had been used in experiments. At the National Center for Toxicological Research in Arkansas, twenty-six squirrel monkeys had been used in FDA nicotine addiction experiments meant to help teens and young adults. Twenty-four of them, according to the *New York Times*, had been taught by researchers that if they pressed a bar, a dose of nicotine would be released. "After they became addicted," Sheila Kaplan reports, "the scientists lowered the doses and observed the effects."

Craving nicotine is a harrowing experience for a primate; just ask any person who finds it difficult to stop smoking. The act of intentionally bringing about addiction in healthy primates, though, wasn't the reason this situation blew up publicly. That happened because four of the monkeys had died during experimental procedures, "three from anesthesia given while catheters were put in, and one from a type of gastric bloat," according to Kaplan. Another monkey stopped breathing under anesthesia but was revived by a veterinarian. The White Coat Waste Project, based in Washington, DC, and dedicated to fighting wasteful taxpayer-funded animal research, mobilized activists on behalf of the monkeys, including Jane Goodall, who spoke out against the research as both cruel and unnecessary. It was big news when the monkeys arrived at Jungle Friends

Sanctuary in Gainesville, Florida. There's little doubt that the FDA suspended its study and released the monkeys because of the compassion expressed—and pressure exerted—by activists and the public.

Public scrutiny of conditions for Harvard Medical School's monkeys, and of the details surrounding several monkey deaths, helped bring about the 2015 closure of the school's New England Primate Research Center in Massachusetts. (The center specified financial difficulties as the reason, but the drumbeat of negative media coverage cannot be discounted.) Retirement for the two thousand monkeys at the center was not considered as an option, however; from the first it was decided that the animals would be shipped to other research facilities. Instance after instance pops up in the mainstream media detailing poor care for primates in federally funded centers like Harvard's. From the *Seattle Times* in 2018: "Research Monkey Strangles to Death at New UW [University of Washington] Animal Lab"; the article reports that this was "the 10th primate to die accidentally at the UW since 2009, when a male macaque starved to death." From the *Oregonian* in 2012: "OHSU (Oregon Health and Sciences University) Fined by USDA For Monkey Deaths and Escapes at Oregon National Primate Research Center in 2009." OHSU "was fined $11,679 for incidents that led to the escape of nine monkeys and deaths of five at its primate research center."

As Erika Fleury of the North American Primate Sanctuary Alliance explains, most monkeys coming to sanctuaries arrive from research laboratories, with the pet trade and roadside zoos as secondary sources. More and more primate laboratories will probably face scrutiny and in some cases shutdown in the future, and if so the situation with monkeys will come to mirror that of chimpanzees. Writing for the *Animal Studies Journal*, Fleury even envisions a coming "mass exodus" of monkeys. "Lab primates" need physical care over a lengthy life span, mental stimulation, and a chance to recover from emotional trauma. It might be tempting to think of sanctuary care as ideal theoretically but too costly in reality. Fleury neatly busts this myth: sanctuaries are the most affordable way of housing retired primates.

The figures cited by Fleury are striking: housing a colony of two hundred chimpanzees in a sanctuary rather than a laboratory results on average in a savings of $3,800 each day and $1.4 million each year. For monkeys, the savings works out on average to $2,644 daily and $965,000 annually.

Why exactly are sanctuaries more cost effective? In correspondence, Fleury pointed out how greatly the culture of a laboratory differs from that of a sanctuary. Some biomedical experiments are designed to require that nonhuman primate individuals be housed alone, which increases the institutional square footage used and the costs associated with maintaining it. Sanctuaries insist on social housing unless an individual animal is simply too traumatized to allow it (or unless an animal comes to them who is solitary by nature). In laboratories, "indirect costs" add up far more quickly, for instance university operating costs that are absent at sanctuaries, where, Fleury noted, "more dollars go directly to programs that enhance primate welfare, with no diversion for funding human-centered interests."

Funds for retired animals must come from somewhere, and public donations are rarely enough. In her article for *Animal Studies Journal*, Fleury urges researchers to include money in their proposed budgets, right from the start, for the eventual retirement costs of the animals they will use. This concrete proposal is realistic. Even as I hope that fewer monkeys will be used in biomedical research in the future, the number is not going to approach zero anytime soon.

As more people express concern for the plight of laboratory-confined monkeys, the biomedical community pushes back. A popular recent campaign crafted by animal researchers in the United States centers on transparency, a claim of honesty and openness in telling all of us how animals are used in their laboratories. Just two weeks before I would meet Brooke the cow in Illinois, *Science* magazine reported on a "transparency tour" held at the Oregon National Primate Research Center in Beaverton, the same location mentioned in the *Oregonian* report about monkey escapes and deaths. During the tour, people may view three thousand macaque monkeys held in outdoor enclosures. Off limits, however, are fifteen hundred monkeys that the Oregon researchers actively use in research. This struck me as a decidedly peculiar use of the term *transparency*. By email I put the question to Diana Gordon, education and outreach coordinator at the research center in Oregon: could she please explain how a tour set up to exclude the subjects of ongoing research can be touted as an example of transparency?

Gordon told me that the monkeys on active duty, so to speak, would be vulnerable both to human sickness and to stress from people coming close to their cages. About these indoor monkeys, Gordon wrote: "They are comfortable with their care staff 'family,' but having strangers enter into their indoor spaces can be quite stressful for them. For both ethical (concern for the well-being of our monkeys) and scientific reasons (potential interference of stress hormones in study parameters) we simply cannot open up these spaces to the general public." And she added: "It is unfortunate that this is occasionally perceived as being less than transparent, but the health and well-being of our monkeys must come first."

Here is a notable use of the word *family*, offered by Gordon in quotes, to describe the care staff of the research center! In it I found echoes of the suggestion that fistulated cows live "wonderful" lives. The staff at the Oregon research center includes people who require the monkeys to participate in experiments set up around—according to a list provided by Gordon—addiction, aging, the immune system, obesity, fertility, and diabetes.

I confessed to Gordon that I still struggled with the notion that a restricted tour of this nature could reasonably constitute transparency *regarding biomedical research*. Sure, the tour reveals information about the on-site housing of animals who mostly are not experimental animals (though some of the outdoor monkeys do participate in ongoing studies). For transparency to be taken seriously, this is not enough. Why not show a live video feed from the inside areas, circumventing stress and disease risks altogether? Gordon didn't take up the video idea in her answer, and I recognize that it carries problems of its own, involving the privacy of the staff. Outdoors, she explained, people stay at least 12 feet away from the monkeys, a distance that isn't possible indoors. "Measles (and TB, as well) is so contagious," Gordon noted, "that the possibility of transmission indoors rises to approximately 90%. Also, the stress of visitors in the outdoor areas is really negligible."

Whatever this tour is about, it is not about transparency in biomedical research. In Virginia, transparency (or more accurately, its lack) became big news in summer 2018 when it was revealed by Richmond television program *8News* that Virginia Commonwealth University had not retired its research monkeys to sanctuary as a faculty member had first claimed. At VCU, rhesus monkeys are strapped into restraint chairs and injected with substances like cocaine, heroin, oxycodone, or fentanyl in attempts to model the processes suffered by people who become addicted to drugs.

The VCU timeline went like this: In April 2018, faculty member Bill Dewey told *8News* that the monkeys would retire to a sanctuary when the VCU experiments concluded, much in the way that Tom the chimpanzee eventually went to sanctuary in

Canada. At the time Dewey sounded a bit fuzzy on the facts, noting that the monkeys go to, "I guess you call it, a monkey farm." Initially he noted the location as "in Louisiana" but then added, "I am not sure what state they are in." I would interject here that wild rhesus monkeys live in intensely social groups in which maternal relatives stay close to each other through their lives. Mothers, grandmothers, daughters, aunts, and nieces form the core matrilines of the group, while young males transfer out at puberty to live and mate elsewhere. Given this natural history, it's a welcome thought that monkeys could be transferred in small social groups to retirement. However, nothing like this ever happened.

Within four months, Dewey's statement about retirement was exposed as an outright falsehood. Animal advocate and attorney Will Lowrey made use of the fact that public universities are required to share public records via the Freedom of Information Act (FOIA). The FOIA documents obtained by Lowrey detail the experiments with the monkeys, mentioning nothing about monkey retirement. In fact, the documents revealed the opposite: when VCU no longer needs the monkeys, the animals are passed on to researchers in other locations. Fleury of North American Primate Sanctuary Alliance, whom I quoted earlier, told this to *8News*: "I have checked with all of the accredited primate sanctuaries in the country and they have not been contacted by VCU." VCU eventually released a statement on the matter: "While sanctuaries are an option, VCU has not transferred any non-human primates to a sanctuary. However, over the past decade, a number of non-human primates have been sent to other research facilities for long-term, non-invasive behavioral studies." Of course transfer to other research institutions does not constitute retirement for the monkeys. Just as with the Oregon primate center, transparency here is notable through its absence.

What do these cases, one in Oregon, the other in Virginia, tell us about animals in biomedical research? Are they exceptions to the rule that snagged the media's attention precisely because they are exceptional? Or are they genuine alarm bells, representative of a broader problem?

In answering these questions, the success rate of animal experimentation becomes a central fact to consider. A 2014 paper published in the *BMJ* by medical sociologist Pandora Pound and epidemiologist Michael B. Bracken sums up the situation this way: "Even the most promising findings from animal research often fail in human trials and are rarely adopted into clinical practice." Stroke research is one such area. When a person suffers a stroke, there's an interruption in the body's ability to get blood to the brain, which may cause cell death and loss of bodily function. In the United States, stroke is the leading cause of disability. After decades of what Pound and Bracken term "immense human, animal, and financial investment," no treatment suitable for humans has emerged from animal models.

On the relatively rare occasions when animal medical studies are critically reviewed, these two scientists explain, the poor quality of much of the science comes to the fore. One report in the UK surveyed 271 animal studies carried out between 1999 and 2005. In only 12 percent of these studies were animal subjects assigned randomly to the treatment condition or the control condition as rigorous research design requires. Where qualitative scoring was the method used, in only 14 percent of the studies were researchers unaware of ("blind to") who was assigned to which condition. In a review paper for the *Cambridge Quarterly of Healthcare Ethics* in 2015, neurologist Aysha Akhtar wrote, "In 2004, the FDA estimated that 92 percent of drugs that pass preclinical tests, including 'pivotal' animal tests, fail to proceed to the market. More recent analysis suggests that, despite efforts to improve the predictability of animal testing, the failure rate has actually increased and is now closer to 96 percent."

Animal experiments often are not well designed in the first place, and even when they are, outcomes overwhelmingly fail to translate well to humans. Yet biomedical researchers insist that animals are desperately needed to advance the fight against human diseases. This is not transparency. Historically, animals certainly have played major roles in significant health advances. In earlier centuries, mouse models were key to the development of penicillin, experimentation with dogs led to success in blood transfusions and the development of insulin, and research with dogs, rodents, and monkeys brought about the polio vaccine. More recently, cancer research using rodents and monkeys has led to breakthroughs in understanding tumor biology and in crafting some oncology treatments, including chemotherapy. As the survivor of an aggressive cancer, I am grateful for these outcomes. Yet the reality remains: the overall rates of failure are terribly high, and in the twenty-first century we have alternatives to animal models that previous times lacked.

I have mentioned rodents a few times. As contrasted with primates, it's impossible to even know the number of mice and rats used in laboratory experiments. These animals are not covered under the US Animal Welfare Act (AWA), an omission that came about precisely because biomedical industry lobbyists worked hard to bring it about. An amendment to AWA excludes from its purview rats (of the genus *Rattus*), mice (of the genus *Mus*), and birds bred for research. A census of rats and mice used in experiments need not even be reported! This last fact seemed so bizarre to me that I repeatedly cross-checked it for accuracy. Ryan Merkley of the Physicians Committee for Responsible Medicine (PCRM) explained that if research is funded by the National Institutes of Health (NIH), the researchers must submit an "average daily inventory" of rodents used. Merkley called this "a very crude estimate," a "far cry" from what is required for animals who are protected by the AWA. For rats and mice used in experiments funded by other sources than the NIH, no inventory whatsoever is required. According to *Science* in 2018, 76,523 "rats, rabbits, and other vertebrates" were used in chemical safety testing in 2017 alone by the Environmental Protection Agency. That number is roughly equal to that of laboratory monkeys in the US. Whatever the precise tallies, the number of rodents used in experiments is staggering.

In the biomedical world, rodents are interchangeable, one individual for another. Yet outside that world, individual rats and mice may be seen as distinct individuals who are beloved. Eva Cross from the Center for Human–Animal Interaction at Virginia Commonwealth University told me about some of the seventeen rats she has lived with over the years. Eli, a variegated Dumbo rat, had big round ears, a white coat with black spots and black hood, and an extraverted personality. "Every morning," Cross recalled, "I would put on the ladder that connects his cage to the floor, so he could come out whenever he was ready. He would wake up and run down the ladder to greet me. He would hop into my lap and cuddle for as long as I could before I needed to leave for class." Rats express happiness, Cross explained, by grinding their teeth, an action called bruxing; if they brux forcefully enough, the muscles involved cause their eyes to flex out and back, or "boggle." "Every morning Eli would sit on my lap and brux and boggle, and share my breakfast with me," Cross said. On the days Eli accompanied Cross to her job at the college fitness center, he perched on the front desk and interacted with students who came there to exercise.

Desmond was Eli's best rat friend, a black Berkshire Dumbo Rex with a curly whiskers, a black curly coat and white belly, and ears as big and round as Eli's. Desmond was super-smart, Cross told me: "He could figure out puzzles in no time, pulling on a rope to lift a box with treats inside and often hopping away with the entire box. He knew how to spin on command, come when called, jump from the floor into my hand, give high fives, and jump through hoops." Hesitant and uncertain how to act at times with other rats, Desmond expressed a personality less outgoing than Eli's. He forged a trusting relationship with Cross, though: "Desmond would greet me every day when I came home from work. He would run up to the door, and as soon as I opened it and put my hand in, he would lean into my hand and close his eyes contentedly while I gently petted his head with my thumb. He enjoyed sitting in my lap and watching movies with me, snuggled in my arms." For Cross, one thing unites all the rats she has known. "They are endlessly sweet and loving," she said. "They spend the vast majority of their time cuddling together and grooming each other."

Wanting to help rats on a larger scale, Cross founded an organization called Second Chance Heroes. Through this nonprofit, and with the cooperation of university laboratories, she places rats once held for behavioral experiments into the homes of animal adopters. (She also rescues rats who come from situations of neglect or hoarding unrelated to laboratories.) The adoption application she has developed includes five pages of questions and statements; prospective adopters must respond adequately before they are allowed to take rescued rats home. I use the plural "rats" here for good reason. One of the application statements reads: "I understand that rats are very social animals and cannot live alone. I agree to keep my rats housed together unless there are moderating factors like behavioral or health issues." Here is a way to see rats for who they are: intensely social mammals who thrive on relationships with others.

Cross's public activism springs not from a vocal antiresearch stance but instead from a wish to help individual animals, a distinction that is meaningful for her success. "Part of the reason why Second Chance Heroes works," she told me, "is because we are very upfront about the fact that we are not here to take a stance on animal research. We just want to be an option so healthy and sweet animals do not have to be euthanized just because they are finished with their job. Labs can't afford to feed and vet large numbers of inactive subjects in their retirement until they die naturally."

When Cross and I last spoke in March 2020, Second Chance Heroes had made great strides since its inception; it is now a 501(c)(3) nonprofit organization, with seventy-seven rats to date placed into adopters' homes, sixteen of whom had formerly been lab animals. The update she sent to me simply shines with news of how one person can help animals too often overlooked: "The labs have been so happy to collaborate, providing dried veggies, sunflower seeds, and nesting materials in enormous quantities to support the rats while they are in my care. I am so grateful for their open-mindedness and willingness to work with me. We have had adopters come from Maryland, West Virginia, North Carolina, and even Ohio! We have volunteers all over the country sewing and donating hammocks, snuggle sacks, beds, blankets, cage liners, you name it, just for the rats. Donors have covered the cost of veterinary care for several who have needed surgeries or medications."

Rodents' experiences in the laboratory include experiments that are invasive, for example in Alzheimer's research. As far too many people know from shattering experience with loved ones, Alzheimer's is a disease of progressive cognitive impairment. It is characterized by accumulated plaque, made up of amyloid protein, in the brain; over time, a person afflicted with Alzheimer's will experience cell death that causes dementia. The disease rips through families, causing sustained suffering because a person's dementia overtakes their ability to recognize others or even to remember their own identity. At a minimum estimate, 50 million people around the world live with this condition now. According to the organization Alzheimer's Disease International, this number will nearly double every twenty years into the future, reaching 75 million in 2030 and 131 million in 2050. The toll is haunting to contemplate, given the degree to which self-awareness and memory enrich our lives. Naturally, researchers want to throw every reasonable resource at this disease in order to achieve breakthroughs in combating it.

Designating mice as the key tool in the resource toolkit isn't working, however. Mice simply do not contract Alzheimer's disease. Researchers have created genetically modified mice who produce the kinds of proteins that accumulate in Alzheimer patients' brains, yet unlike humans, these rodents do not go on to show memory deficits. The mouse model, even with genetic engineering added in, isn't a relevant model at all. Reporting for the journal *Nature* in 2018, Sara Reardon explains that it's not unusual for experimental drugs to work on the mice in the sense of removing their brain plaques, but when tried on people, the drugs make no positive difference—and may even cause harm. "One high-profile stumble," Reardon writes, came in October 2018 when three companies announced that their drugs (termed BACE inhibitors) "failed in large, late-stage clinical trials. Although the drugs successfully blocked the accumulation of amyloid protein in mice, they seemed to worsen cognitive decline and brain shrinkage in people."

Bart de Strooper, a molecular biologist, puts it pithily in Reardon's piece: "The biggest mistake you can make is to think you can ever have a mouse with Alzheimer's disease." Despite this reality, biomedical researchers are doubling down on precisely that goal by inducing a greater variety of genetic mutations in more and more mice. The brains of some wild mice (as distinct from inbred lab mice) in which plaques have been experimentally induced do exhibit memory problems. This result, in the realm of animal models for Alzheimer's, counts as a "success," though its likelihood of helping human Alzheimer's sufferers is low to say the least.

The situation with ALS, amyotrophic lateral sclerosis or Lou

Gehrig's disease, is similar. In ALS patients, muscles atrophy over time, resulting in a progressive paralysis that eventually is fatal. Symptoms of the disease can be induced in mice, but as a group of researchers led by neuroscientist Vincent Picher-Martel notes, "no animal model fully replicates the spectrum of phenotypes [or observable characteristics] in the human disease and it is difficult to assess how a therapeutic effect in disease models can predict efficacy in humans." (These authors do suggest that interventions customized to individual patients' mutations may one day make the use of animal models for ALS productive.) In their *BMJ* review Pandora and Bracken note that more than one hundred drugs were tested in a mouse model of ALS. Some seemed to slow down the disease initially, but with continuing experimentation, every single one failed. Eight of the drugs had been administered in clinical trials to patients in the thousands.

Maybe it would help to invest in research monkeys or chimpanzees who are biologically closer to humans than are mice? For the first time in 2017, signs of amyloid brain plaques like the ones in human Alzheimer's patients were noticed in the brains of elderly deceased chimpanzees studied in the laboratory. Of twenty chimpanzees whose age at death ranged between thirty-seven and sixty-two, the brains of thirteen showed amyloid plaques; four of these also had the twisted protein "tangles" associated with more advanced stages of Alzheimer's in humans. Lead scientist Melissa Edler had no way to know whether this brain pathology had been accompanied by cognitive decline in the apes, because the chimpanzees' behavior had not been studied. For this reason, the finding of chimpanzee brain plaques cannot be readily applied to helping human patients. Adding a behavioral component to studying aged chimpanzees would make for an unwieldy step, to say the least: as the ages of chimpanzees in this study indicate, these apes may live into their sixties in captivity. Long-term studies would need to be paired with the administration of cognitive tasks and neuro-imaging. Even then, the likelihood that such sustained effort would pay off for human patients is low. Monkey models are already used in Alzheimer's research occasionally, but—in line with the overall statistics that I have already reported—no breakthroughs have occurred.

Beginning in spring 2020, invasive testing on monkeys (and other animals including mice, cats, hamsters, and ferrets) ramped up in the quest to create an effective COVID-19 vaccine. Among biomedical scientists quoted in Jon Cohen's April 2020 article for *Science*, "From Mice To Monkeys, Animals Studied for Coronavirus Answers," the language betrays a certain desperation. One commented that "everybody has been thrown into a rush to get an animal model"; another stated that because many people who get very sick from COVID-19 suffer from comorbidities like diabetes and hypertension, it may be necessary to find or create monkeys with similar comorbidities. Past history of animal models, including the failed experiments I have just reviewed, remind us that we should treat such claims with skepticism.

Cohen describes a study in which eight cynomolgus monkeys were inoculated with SARS-CoV-2. None of the monkeys developed symptomatic disease, but half were killed for autopsy examination. Of these four, two showed lung damage. Writing about this same study the following month for *Science*, Seema S. Lakdawala and Vineet D. Menachery first note that the monkeys "shed virus in the upper and lower respiratory tract, but failed to developed severe clinical symptoms"; they immediately add that animal models like this one are important platforms for investigating COVID-19 in humans. My conclusion is different: an unrelenting focus on animal models as a first-line strategy comes at a cost for laboratory animals and for sick humans alike.

I have considered so far only the efficacy of using animal models for disease. Yet efficacy of primate models—or the lack of efficacy—isn't the whole story. As I've said so often throughout this book, animals want to live, and to spend their days without disabling pain or injury. Humans can't always help bring that about; rates of early death and painful injury in nature are high through predation, disease, and other nonanthropogenic causes. In the laboratory though, we *are* the cause. Subjecting healthy animals to tests and procedures that cause pain, injury, or death is a practice ripe for a compassionate response.

A 2019 article in *Science* by neuroscientist Gregory Corder and his colleagues reports on experiments with mice meant to aid scientific comprehension of the nature of pain. The idea was to study affective circuits in the mammalian brain that make the experience of pain a distinctly unpleasant one. Could understanding this circuitry lead to development of therapies for chronic pain in humans? Chronic-pain sufferers may feel gratitude for researchers' efforts to help, and yet reading the fine print regarding the methods used on the mice may cause upset. Miniature microscopes were implanted into their brains so that the activity of mouse neural cells could be observed. As is routine in the scientific literature, the language of the report is clinical: "We screwed three stainless steel screws into the skull right up to dura and then performed a craniotomy using a drill," Corder et al. write. In his book *Voracious Science and Vulnerable Animals*, former laboratory researcher John Gluck notes how thoroughly he once scrubbed the words he used to describe his own procedures on animals: "Newborn monkeys selected to be raised in isolation were 'removed' from their mothers, not torn from their arms shrieking and terrified." How might the craniotomy sentence of Corder et al., I wonder, be written to more closely reflect reality?

Chronic pain was induced in some of these mice by way of

sciatic nerve injury. A graphic drawing accompanying the text brings home for me what the animals experience: A mouse is depicted with a tiny microscope screwed into its skull. One arrow points to the site of "nerve injury," while a second is accompanied by the words "development of chronic pain." Other phases of the work required that the mice be subjected to so-called nonpainful aversive experiences. Repulsive odor, bitter taste, loud tone, facial air puff, and electric shock are all considered to fall into this category. The mice responded by, for example, licking, lifting or guarding a hurt paw and "rearing or jumping away from the noxious stimuli." At the conclusion of the experiment, researchers kill the mice and dissect their brains.

Mark Schnitzer, who is listed as corresponding author on the paper, did not reply to my email messages asking about methodological details and about his vision for how this work might help humans. What stays with me still are those drawings of injured mice adorned with mini-microscopes. How many mice globally are used in experiments that are similarly invasive? My breath caught when I read one answer in Charles Graeber's remarkably lucid account of cancer research, *The Breakthrough: Immunotherapy and the Race to Cure Cancer*, in a section about tumor induction in mice. One breakthrough involved creating the protein interleukin 2 (IL-2) in the laboratory. Graeber cites a researcher who "calculated that the unused drop of recombinant IL-2 wasted at the bottom of a test tube represented the amount of natural IL-2 that would have formerly required the sacrifice of 900 million mice."

Would I wish for every oncology experiment using rodents never to have happened at all? I can't truthfully say that. Alongside the images of suffering rodents in my head come other images: children hooked up to IVs on pediatric oncology wards, and adults undergoing what Graeber calls the "cut, burn, and poison" techniques of cancer treatment (surgery, radiation, and chemotherapy) that I too experienced. Some past experiments were based on what one researcher in *The Breakthrough* refers to as "crummy mouse models" of cancer. Others made a positive difference in the long path toward developing cancer drugs. It's crucial to see how disposable has been the well-being of the experimental animals, whose thoughts and emotions are assumed to be nonexistent or of no concern. Thinking back to Eli and Desmond's loving and playful behavior with Eva Cross, could we envision a different model? Could the thoughts and feelings of rodents and other "lab animals" serve as motivation to seek nonanimal medical models of disease? For many activists and some scientists, the answer is yes, a point I'll return to later in this chapter. For now, the language used by many scientists suggests that animal sentience isn't much on their minds.

About the four baboons who lived in his laboratory in Munich, Germany, researcher Bruno Reichart said this to *Scientific American* in 2018: "They can hop around, eat, drink and they are enjoying life. They watch TV—their favorite is the cartoon with the chipmunk." The baboons, it turns out, did these things after hearts from genetically engineered pigs had been sewn into their chests. All four monkeys were soon killed—one pair at 90 days postsurgery, the second pair at 180 days postsurgery. Reichart's jaunty tone fails to take into account the animals' lived experience, just as sunny news headlines make light of what fistulated cows go through. The baboons' desire to live, and the "donor" pigs' desire not to become vehicles for harvesting organs, endures apart from whether the pigs' hearts ever help humans in need of cardiac transplants.

Don't ethics boards review animal experiments and ensure that the monkeys, pigs, mice, and other animals are free from unnecessary suffering? I'm asked this question with great frequency. Animal lovers may assume that ethical oversight is in place to ensure that laboratory animals' pain is treated, their deaths are held to a minimum, and their housing is designed with their comfort in mind. In answer, I would emphasize *one critical point above all others regarding animals in biomedical research*: the "protection" system for laboratory animals in federally regulated and federally funded facilities, including universities, is weak. The IACUC, or Institutional Animal Care and Use Committee, a system put in place in 1985 by the US Congress and Public Health Service (PHS), is stacked against the animals' interests.

The IACUCs' mandate includes no explicit direction to consider ethical principles. That fact was the single most startling one that I learned when investigating how this system works. Committee members review proposals for animal experiments, but ethical questions may be freely ignored. Nothing prevents the committees from taking up those questions. Yet the reality is, according to Lawrence Arthur Hansen in the *Journal of Medical Ethics*, that IACUCs have "restricted themselves to technical or advisory roles" in suggesting revisions to experimental proposals. The most comprehensive analysis cited by Hansen came up with a 98 percent approval rate for in-house proposals—that is, proposals put forth by one's own colleagues within an institution. When instead, proposal review was carried out "blind" *across* institutions, the very same proposals were judged to be problematic in 61 percent of the cases. The problems noted ranged from lack of comprehensibility to poor research design to unconvincing justifications for the planned experiments with animals.

No doubt it's human nature for people to be gentler with their criticisms when dealing with immediate work colleagues, people with whom they interact every day, than with strangers. The problem is that the makeup of IACUC committees exacerbates this tendency. Working with Justin Goodman and Alka Chandna, Hansen carried out a study of twenty-one of the top twenty-five NIH-funded research institutions' IACUCs. They found that 67 percent of the IACUC members were animal researchers and 15 percent were institutional veterinarians. Non-affiliated individuals (10%) and nonscientists (8%) made up a minority of the membership. Perspectives of people outside the system, who may care deeply about what animals are made to experience in the experiments under consideration, are by fiat swamped by the views of those inside the system. "Because U.S. IACUCs employ a majority voting system," Hansen, Goodman, and Chandna note, "arithmetic alone places the ultimate authority of the committees in the hands of animal researchers."

Imagine yourself an early-career researcher pressed into service on an IACUC. The colleagues whose proposals you vote on today may be the same individuals who will vote on *your* proposals next month. (I witnessed this issue in play during my brief tenure on a university IACUC.) How could there not be an enormous risk for conflicts of interest? Aren't the animals the ones likely to lose out? In posing these questions I echo the concerns expressed by Pound and Bracken in their *BMJ* article. Ethical shifts in the field of biomedical research, they write, are difficult to achieve because stakeholders, including researchers and those in the research industry, have strong interests, including financial ones, in maintaining the status quo.

Inviting the participation of informed members of the public on IACUCs, as suggested by Hansen et al., strikes me as a good first step toward reform. *Minimum* requirements for membership are set by the IACUC system, but leeway exists beyond that. If transparency is the supposed goal of animal researchers, shouldn't members of the public be trusted to take the evaluation process seriously and to consider both the researchers' goals and the animals' well-being? In *Voracious Science and Vulnerable Animals*, Gluck lays out eleven conditions for IACUCs without which the system can provide little protection.

Gluck calls not only for active resistance against "the tendency to defer to highly placed professionals or university colleagues" but also for evaluation of "the potential for harm" to animals "at all significant contact points." These points begin with acquisition and transport of animals, continue through the experimental phase, and conclude with how the animals' lives end, or are ended.

In a paper cowritten with five others including lead author Hope Ferdowsian, whose book *Phoenix Zones* I have quoted from (see chapter 1), Gluck expands on these potential risks to animals caught up in research labs: "harms associated with breeding and transport; separation from parents, siblings, and other conspecifics; an inability to control access to that which meets one's own basic needs; a lack of safety and security; thwarting of an animal's preferences; an inability to fulfill one's own developmental potential; deprivation of a normal, species-appropriate, natural environment; and being killed." This list was created by people who see lab animals as individuals with lives of intrinsic value, who deserve more than a decent-sized cage or adequate amelioration of pain. It challenges any feel-good notions that institutional review committees grapple seriously with ethical issues—or that biomedical laboratories work seriously toward transparency.

Beginning in 2020, Ferdowsian convened a working group with a goal of producing nothing less than a set of ethical guidelines aimed at animals in ways parallel to those offered by the famous Belmont Report forty years ago. I am pleased to be part of that group. Using the principles of respect for persons, beneficence, and justice, the Belmont Report aimed to protect human subjects, including those from vulnerable populations (e.g., people of color, incarcerated individuals, and children with cognitive challenges), and we aim to set in motion something just as revolutionary for animals. As the Ferdowsian-Gluck team emphasized in their writing, minimizing harms must co-exist with "transparent and rigorous *direct comparison* of the risks of harms and potential benefits." Here the focus should be on potential benefits *to the animals themselves* rather than only to human populations that might or might not be helped in the future—what a welcome notion!

I asked Alka Chandna, one of the coauthors on the IACUC study I reviewed above, what she thought of the notion that the biomedical community is committed to transparency. Chandna is now vice president of laboratory investigation cases at PETA. The very mention of PETA is liable to stir strong feelings one way or the other among readers of this book, so I want to interject a quick aside here. Sometimes, I dislike PETA's provocative public actions, such as when the group uses scantily clad women in its campaigns for animal well-being. As Carol J. Adams and Lori Gruen write in their edited collection *Ecofeminism*, often in single-issue campaigns "the larger political context in which the messages are presented is ignored," as in this case sexism is ignored. Further, PETA's stance that "culling" (killing) is often the kindest response to feral cats in one's community is, in my view, as harmful as it is wrong (see chapter 2). Yet I have positive views too, stemming from years of experience working with PETA scientists and investigators on animal-advocacy campaigns that fight for the well-being of animals, ranging from laboratory monkeys to octopuses served alive in restaurants. I know firsthand that PETA staff members repeatedly bring about superb results for animals in trouble. They also spend a good deal of time rescuing pets in trouble, both in the aftermath of disasters and from situations of neglect or abuse. (The sensationalized claims of PETA killing high numbers of dogs and cats are false.) Further, when reading about animals saved from some cruel situation such as invasive laboratory testing or bad conditions at some "entertainment" venue, frequently I discover that PETA played a leading role in the rescue. Is it necessary to agree 100 percent of the time with decisions made by an organization in order to value that organization's work on behalf of animals? That question I answer with a no.

As one of the most knowledgeable people in the country about transparency in the biomedical field, Chandna pulled no punches in answering the question I posed to her about lab researchers and transparency: "It is *transparently* a public relations ploy," she told me. "From our experience, and we have a fair bit with these institutions, they are not interested in transparency. To us it is laughable that in documents in which they talk about the importance of transparency, when they reference an experiment they might have a generic photograph of a mouse, or a monkey in a generic setting, but they would never ever include a photograph of a mouse or a monkey in a setting true to the experiment they are talking about. They are very good at window-dressing."

After Chandna made these points to me, I explored the website of the group Speaking of Research, through which some scientists advocate for animal models in biomedical research. On the day I looked (November 2, 2018), I found these photographs on the "FAQ about Animal Research" page: two beagles standing on a stainless steel table against a wall, in close social contact; a single mouse standing on what seems to be a scientist's outstretched, gloved arm; a masked and gloved scientist pulling out from a series of boxes a single glass box with two mice in it; and two mice, again in close social contact, sitting on some kind of bedding material. (No species identifications are included with the photographs; some of the animals I identify here as mice could possibly be rats.) Just as Chandna noted, the animal images are pristine. There's no hint of the experimental context in which the animals are used. No mice with mini-microscopes screwed into their heads, jumping away from "noxious stimuli" or coping with induced chronic pain, are visible here.

Finding out what's really going on behind laboratory walls is usually hard. Private institutions, including universities, are under no obligation to make relevant documents available for public scrutiny. FOIA requests like the one that led to Lowrey's scrutiny of VCU's experiments with monkeys (and its false statements about its monkeys heading to sanctuary) may simply go unanswered by these institutions. Public universities and federal research centers do need to provide documents according to FOIA requests. Yet Chandna encounters obstacles even in those cases. "Increasingly what we are seeing," she told me, "is that public institutions are erecting barriers. They may redact a lot of information from the documents and make claims that there are proprietary issues. The other issue that we see is that more and more institutions are charging a lot of money for documents, so that becomes prohibitive."

Bringing about greater access to institutional animal-care and -experiment records is an achievable goal—if only research administrators would buy in. Any institution that receives money from the National Institutes of Health (NIH), Chandna explained, must submit written reports to NIH when they fail to comply with federal animal welfare guidelines. "It would be great if NIH would publish these things in a database that is publicly accessible," Chandna told me. "These are experiments that we [taxpayers] are paying for; we have an interest in knowing whether these animal guidelines which reflect public values are [enforced]."

Chandna is right, of course: taxpayers foot the bill for experiments at federally funded research facilities. This fact points us toward the mission of the bipartisan White Coat Waste Project, the animal advocacy organization that was instrumental in relocating the FDA nicotine-study monkeys to sanctuary in Florida. The organization, founded by conservative political consultant Anthony Bellotti in 2015, explains its mission this way: "Save animals and taxes by cutting the root problem: wasteful government spending." Two-thirds of all animal experimentation in the US is federally funded, and this amounts to a $15—20 billion investment that returns very little. That's according to Justin Goodman, White Coat's vice president for advocacy and public policy, and coauthor with Chandna of that paper about the unbalanced composition of IACUCs.

Animal experimentation is strikingly ineffective on the whole, and the waste of *our* tax dollars is a fresh angle on the problem. "If we wiped out taxpayer-funded animal experimentation," Goodman told me, "we would wipe out two-thirds of the problem" of suffering laboratory animals. There's real hope, Goodman thinks, because the use of animals in biomedical and drug testing is "a nonpartisan issue with wide political support, and you can't say that about any other animal issue." Polling numbers, he told me, show that Republicans and Democrats care equally about this issue. Might forward momentum be achieved, even in Washington gridlock?

White Coat Waste puts most of its energies toward experiments on nonhuman primates, cats, and dogs. This choice is strategic, Goodman acknowledges, based on what most galvanizes people's empathy. "We focus here because we meet people where they are." Rodent advocates may not find that logic fully satisfactory, but unquestionably, light shined on cruelty to kittens creates a space in which diverse constituencies may come together. In 2018 the KITTEN bill, officially the Kittens in Traumatic Testing Ends Now Act of 2018, was introduced to the US House and Senate in response to federally funded animal experiments ongoing since 1982 at a USDA laboratory in Beltsville, Maryland.

Here's the backstory to the bill: Each year, up to one hundred kittens were bred in the USDA laboratory. At eight weeks old, they were fed raw meat containing the parasite that causes a toxoplasmosis infection. From the kittens' infected feces the researchers collected parasites with which they conducted other experiments. The kittens were tools, in the way that beakers or a batch of enzymes are tools. Unlike beakers or enzymes, the kittens can die, and die they did, because two weeks later researchers anesthetized them and then injected ketamine into their hearts.

Over the years, about three thousand kittens have died at the USDA lab in this way. Let's assume for only a moment that these kittens' participation in the experiments was critically necessary. Were their deaths also necessary? Toxoplasmosis infection can be treated, if not cured, in cats. Couldn't the kittens be treated for the parasites introduced into their system, and then adopted out? Regarding adoption, the best answer is "by some people yes, not by others." The Feline Health Center at Cornell University notes that "because cats only shed the organism for a short time, the chance of human exposure via cats they live with is relatively small." Handling the cat poses no risk because the parasite isn't carried on the fur. Nor is the parasite transmitted through a bite or scratch. The "shedding" happens in the cats' feces, and because of this, people at high risk of problems from a toxoplasmosis infection—especially pregnant women and anyone with a compromised immune system—should not take up litterbox duty for these cats. Understandably, then, some families would be, and should be, reluctant to adopt infected kittens. Otherwise, adoption would have been a good outcome all around.

The bill aimed to stop the breeding and use of these kittens in USDA toxoplasmosis research altogether. Sponsored in the House in 2018 by Republican Mike Bishop and Democrat Jimmy Panetta of California in an act of bipartisan collaboration, some months later it was brought to the Senate by Democrat Jeff Merkley. Major media paid attention: dead kittens are news. In April 2019 the USDA announced that the infliction of death would stop: "Toxoplasmosis research has been redirected and the use of cats as part of any research protocol has been discontinued and will not be reinstated." Fourteen cats remaining at the lab, each uninfected, would be adopted by agency employees. In fact, there's no good reason why many lab animals shouldn't be adopted after experimentation, as we saw with Eva Cross's rats. In 2020 the FDA announced a new policy that permits the adoption or retirement of its lab animals once experiments are concluded, and the VA and NIH had previously moved in that same direction.

Together with Brooke the fistulated cow, visible to all who pass by an Illinois university's Dairy Cattle Research Unit and yet described via a highly controlled public narrative; the Oregon monkeys, some of whom are visible and some of whom very much are not; and all the other animals I have written about in this chapter, the USDA kittens tell us something in clear terms. In order to act with compassion toward animals in science, it takes *work* to know what we're dealing with. A stroll through a biomedical laboratory is not an option, a fact that sets this realm apart from what happens in zoos, national parks, or of course our own homes. We can't rely on decades of investigative journalism, and whistleblower or undercover videotape exposés, as increasingly happens in slaughterhouses. *Some* knowledge of what life is like for animals in biomedical laboratories is available to us, to be sure; the more biomedical subjects who retire to sanctuary as Tom the chimpanzee did, the more likely we are to learn their individual histories. At the moment, the hidden or highly controlled nature of what happens to laboratory animals requires extra effort, all the more so for animals such as rats and mice who typically aren't known as individuals.

How then do we help laboratory animals when more often

than not they are kept hidden from our sight? Even here, opportunities exist to be animals' best friends: we might learn as much as we can about experiments with animals at universities and federally funded labs near us; voice protest to institutions that allow lab animals to suffer as part of their sanctioned experiments; write letters to the editor to journals, magazines, or newspapers that mention new research without describing the cost to animals; support alternatives to animal models in biomedical science, including the new approaches I am about to discuss; and aid the work of organizations whose advocacy includes laboratory animals.

Vigilance for animals excluded from the AWA, including rats and mice, is key. On this last point, note that at NIH, the Office of Laboratory Animal Welfare (OLAW) does include rodents in its purview. But this fact sends us full circle back to flaws in the IACUC system. Let's walk through this alphabet soup of the regulatory system: At NIH, it's the overall job of the IACUCs to maintain compliance with the policies of the AWA (which excludes rodents) and the Public Health Service (PHS, which considers rodents). The resulting protections are weak in large part because OLAW does not send inspectors to monitor facilities. "OLAW operates mostly as a pen pal with research facilities," Ryan Merkley of the Physicians Committee for Responsible Medicine (PCRM) explained to me. "If a facility violates PHS policy, it notifies OLAW and explains how it will fix the problem. OLAW responds to thank the facility for notifying it. Research facilities never face serious repercussions, like the withholding of NIH funding, for violations of PHS policy." This jumble of acronyms points to a systematic failure of protection for laboratory rodents.

The sheer number of *different* ways that animals are used in medical science is daunting to consider. The US Navy uses pigs and goats in order to train its medics, who are called corpsmen, in how to treat battlefield trauma. The idea is that "live tissue" of mammals with biology similar to our own provides necessary experience for student medics, who must learn how to deal with organs and arteries undergoing trauma while that trauma is unfolding. In a 2015 technical report of the Naval Health Research Center in San Diego, lead author Stephanie Booth-Kewley and her colleagues explain that the animals are anesthetized during the procedures and once those are finished, they are "euthanized." Students practice hemorrhage control and airway intubation on the animals, a practice that provides feedback to them through the animals' vital signs and other physical responses. Originally healthy, the pigs and goats become surgically altered teaching tools, in the same way that Brooke the fistulated cow became a teaching tool or Tom the chimpanzee became a research tool. And the goats and pigs die as part of the package.

Booth-Kewley's report is a hopeful one, however. Through interviews and surveys carried out with twenty-five active navy service members, it compares the efficacy of the animal training method ("live tissue" using pigs) with a second one ("highly realistic training") that uses no animals. Highly realistic training (HRT) encompasses a suite of methods in which the circumstances of combat are simulated using special effects and live human actors. In this case it refers to an actor who wears what is informally called the Cut Suit. Formally termed the Human Worn Partial Task Surgical Simulator, this device is a type of high-tech "torso" worn on an actor's body, described in this way by the PCRM: "It includes breakable bones, interchangeable organs, and variable blood flow. Wounds are created by the user, and the skin and other organs are repairable, allowing for multiple uses."

When Merkley of the PCRM first told me about the Cut Suit, he sent along a video that mesmerized me. Even knowing that the "pain" and "writhing" emerge from a human actor who actually feels no pain at all, I found the video hard to watch because it simulates the horror of real-world battlefield casualties. As the device's demonstrator explains, the mesh matrix of the Cut Suit allows for surgical cutting through layers of simulated fatty tissue, which causes bleeding to occur, and through the visceral lining right into the organs, which again causes bleeding. In this way the medics-in-training deal with what's called a "conscious casualty," a person whose injury is changing dynamically by the moment even as he or she remains awake and able (until pain medications are available) to feel acutely what is happening.

To its credit, the US Navy wanted to know if this HRT is as effective for its trainees as the live-tissue option, otherwise known as the pig option. The short answer is yes, according to results from the twenty-five subjects of the study—twenty-three corpsmen, one medical doctor, and one physician's assistant, all of whom participated in both types of training. When asked how beneficial live-tissue training or HRT / Cut Suit is for the participant, and to what degree live-tissue training or HRT / Cut Suit has a positive impact on readiness for deployment, no significant differences in ratings occurred between the two methods. The use of pigs did not, in the medics' own eyes, make their training more beneficial or prepare them better for their jobs. Eighty-eight percent of participants felt that the strength of using the pigs in training was "the ability to work on a live animal/patient." Eighty-four percent of participants noted that the HRT prepares them for "high-stress" real-life settings. Weaknesses of both methods were noted as well. Among these for the live-tissue method are a too-high ratio of student to "specimen" (36%) and the controlled, clean, and clinical nature of the setting (36%), the killing of the pigs for the sake of the training (28%), and the differences between a pig's and a person's anatomy (28%). In the HRT method, problems included deficiencies of the Cut Suit such as its bulky and unsturdy nature and deviations from anatomical correctness (32%), along with insufficient medical supplies (24%) and actors who fail to act like real patients (20%).

What ripe ground for compassion! It embraces the pigs and also the navy personnel who deserve to receive care in the field from highly capable medics when a trauma befalls them. It's not that the pigs were *ineffective*. It's that the Cut Suit–wearing actor was *just as effective* in training these medics. Why, then, continue using and killing live pigs (and goats) when technology allows for excellent training without causing animals to die?

Merkley pointed out that since 2016, no live animals are used in medical student training in the US or Canada. They certainly used to be, particularly in the fields of physiology and surgery. Merkley explained: "In a physiology lab a dog or pig would be anesthetized and placed on a table; students would place catheters in the arteries and veins of live, anesthetized animals, block the animals' arteries, and inject them with drugs to see how the drugs affected biometrics like blood pressure. In some physiology labs, students would also open the animals' chest cavities to expose the hearts. In surgery training labs, medical students performed minor procedures on anesthetized animals that might include suturing, knot-tying, and laparoscopy." That these procedures, and the subsequent killing of the animals, no longer happen is testament to the value and validity of non-animal alternatives. The simulators that replace these procedures work well.

Not all recent developments are positive. In an eerie parallel to the recent push for octopus farming (chapter 5), increasing numbers of octopuses are now being held in laboratories. Even as new evidence of these animals' intelligence comes to light by the year (chapter 4), the *Washington Post* ran a piece called "Inside the Grand and Sometimes Slimy Plan to Turn Octopuses into Lab Animals." NPR went with "Why Octopuses Might Be the Next Lab Rats." Both articles focused on research ongoing at the marine biology lab at Woods Hole, Massachusetts, where cuttlefish and squid are involved as well as octopuses. Because these cephalopods are invertebrates, they are not protected in the US from scientific experimentation, and researchers at Woods Hole are interested in their genetics. Octopuses might be helpful models in limb regeneration, the thought goes, but right now the research program is open ended. As Nell Green-fieldboyce put it at NPR, "Knowing all the genes is just a start for researchers interested in these animals. The obvious next step is trying to tinker with those genes, to see what happens if they're disrupted." Already an albino squid has been created.

According to the *Post*, "several thousand" cephalopods are being raised at the Woods Hole lab. In a letter to the editor, published by the *Post*, I mentioned finding this news "chilling," and I still do. My message was to lab managers: "Please think twice. Please learn from the recorded suffering of chimpanzees and monkeys, cats and dogs, and rats and mice whose sacrifices we now know too rarely have led to genuine scientific break-throughs. Invest in alternative, nonanimal models instead, because the cost to our fellow creatures of what you are planning to do is too high. It moves our society precisely in the wrong ethical direction."

How can we turn this cresting tide of unprotected marine animals being used in lab experiments? The octopuses, cuttle-fish, and squid aren't being used as models for specific diseases (as far as I know). Yet the *Post* reports that part of the drive to experiment with these animals is to see if the highly unusual type of enzyme-driven genetic editing (RNA editing) that goes on in their bodies, which results in the construction of new pro-teins, could help humans, for example with pain management.

The sheer diversity of alternatives to animal models fills me with hope for the future. I can illustrate why by describing a case study focused on muscular dystrophy.

Muscular dystrophy (MD) isn't a single disease but a cluster of conditions that, owing to genetic mutations, causes progressive muscle weakness. Although MD can be managed and even slowed, it cannot be cured; eventually it is fatal. The human toll of MD is heartwrenching, especially because children may be severely afflicted. The most common form of the disease, Duchenne MD, is also the most severe form, and it begins as early as age two in children. A toddler may show signs of what seems like clumsiness because his pelvic and leg muscles are weakening. The progressive nature of MD means that before they are teenagers, most children with Duchenne MD must use a wheelchair. Severe breathing problems often accompany the inability to walk, because heart and lung muscles are affected as well. Boys are overwhelmingly likely to be the ones with Duchenne MD. Here's why: The key protein in the body that binds muscle fibers together is called dystrophin. Boys have a single copy of the gene involved with producing dystrophin, because it's found on the X chromosome. Should a mutation be inherited by a boy, no backup second gene exists to produce the protein necessary to keep the muscles healthy. In almost all cases, a girl will have that second backup copy even if she does have a mutation in one dystrophin gene.

In an attempt to help these children, researchers breed dogs in laboratories to show symptoms of MD. A canine version of MD that doesn't fully track with the human version of the disease is induced in the dogs. About a quarter of puppies with MD die soon after birth because of diaphragm abnormalities, for example, which doesn't happen in humans. The sick dogs don't always lose the ability to walk with MD, which *does* happen in humans. The altered dogs suffer, to the extent that *Houston Press* columnist Craig Malisow says their lives are ones "of general misery." Undercover video shot at the canine-MD laboratory at Texas A&M University shows, again according to the *Houston Press*, "dogs living in slat-floor cages furnished only with buckets of water, rapidly pacing and chewing on the cage bars out of frustration. Many of the dogs have weakened jaw muscles and swollen tongues, which makes it difficult to digest anything other than mushy gruel."

Breakthroughs have occurred, but only in helping the afflicted laboratory dogs themselves. It's a hellish vicious cycle: the dogs are caused to come down with a version of a human disease, the research helps some of the dogs who suffer, more dogs are bred, and on it goes. Might a breakthrough come any day now for people with MD because of this research? It's not impossible. Writing in *Science* in 2018, researchers led by molecular biologist Eric Olson of the University of Texas (UT) Southwestern Medical Center in Dallas reported that canine MD has responded to gene editing. Four beagle puppies underwent a gene-editing procedure using the genetic engineering tool CRISPR to correct mutations in the dystrophin gene. When tested six or eight weeks later, their dystrophin levels had risen in a variety of muscles: skeletal, diaphragm, and heart. In the most notable finding, one dog's cardiac muscle was restored to 92 percent of normal dystrophin levels.

Yet this finding is little cause for excitement. In an analysis of this research, Jon Cohen, also writing in *Science*, notes that "the study offers little evidence that dogs regained muscle function" and reports that this fact, coupled with the short duration of the study and the small number of animals included, left some scientists less than enthusiastic. The dogs were killed at the conclusion of the experiment, leaving no way to assess what their long-term progress might have been.

When public pressure builds, positive changes often follow, as we've seen with kittens and monkeys. The Texas A&M laboratory decided in 2019 to stop breeding dogs for its MD experiments. On a larger scale, alternative courses of research that don't damage or kill dogs in the first place show increasing promise. The analytical work of neuroscientist Emily Trunnell and veterinarian Ingrid Taylor on behalf of PETA guided me in reading about these alternative methods: Cells from fetuses shown to have MD mutations can be collected, with stem-cell lines established and the disease studied that way, with an eye to cell maturation and developing pathologies. Stem cells from skin, blood, or urine from children or adults with MD can also be used to establish stem-cell lines for similar purposes. "Bio-artificial muscles," or BAMs, are now engineerable from starter cells over a seven-day period, with potential for becoming a 3D muscle model for intramuscular injections of drugs, which is a crucial aspect of MD research. "Muscles on a chip" are a specialized type of "organ on a chip" gaining in popularity. These 3D platforms allow the study of disease development in human cells and tissues, and in the case of MD provide a way to study both healthy and pathological muscle cells.

Veterinary scientists—not all of them, but enough of them—conclude that dogs are poor surrogates in MD research. Trunnell and Taylor sum up the situation by saying that "the negligible information gained through MD experiments on dogs" completely fails to offset the suffering experienced by these animals. Could the failure of dog research on MD to translate to humans, together with the experimental dogs' physical and emotional distress, be an opportunity for a greater push forward for nonanimal technologies?

In just a few years, the kinds of nonanimal technologies I have mentioned here will be further along in their development, just as both plant-based and cellular meat and dairy products will be. It's not just about MD, either. A disease-by-disease review of effective nonanimal models to treat illness would swell this chapter beyond its boundaries. But try this yourself with an online search engine: input the phrase "alternatives to animal models for [name of disease]," and solid science, from credible sources, regularly pops up.

In the stages of cancer research that precede clinical testing in people, for example, the go-to method is often to grow experimental tumors in rodents. Knowledge about the significance of T-cell responses in treating cancer emerged from this kind of work. Owing to major differences in human and rodent physiology, however, the history of clinical trials in oncology is littered with spectacular failures of drugs in human patients that worked well in mice. As Isabella W. Y. Mak and her colleagues report in 2014 in the *American Journal of Translational Research*, the drug TGN1412, developed to treat certain cancers (as well as other diseases) and tolerated well in mice at extremely high doses, "caused catastrophic systemic organ failure in patients, despite being administered at a sub-clinical dose that was 500 times lower than the dose found safe in animal studies." Rodent models, they write, are characterized by "weaknesses in faithfully mirroring the extremely complex process of human carcinogenesis."

Alternative approaches include phase 0 studies in humans, in which people are given micro-doses of new drugs, less than one-hundredth of a dose thought to be therapeutic. In this way potential treatments are checked for toxicity in human bodies directly. Human tissue-culture models and the very exciting organ-on-a-chip technologies are emerging as useful too in cancer research. In a paper published in the journal *Disease Models & Mechanisms* subtitled "Looking beyond the Mouse," Samuel J. Jackson and Gareth J. Thomas review some of these new approaches. The entrenched biomedical culture of animal models first and animal models always is hard to shift, they ac-

knowledge, but nonanimal approaches, including those stemming from "biobanks" of human tissue, are already altering the
world of cancer research.

*   *   *

Near the start of this book, I wrote about the embodied compassion I felt for confined bile bears on the long night in the
hospital following my cancer surgery. All these years later, I
think frequently of the unseen army of biologists, physicians,
and technicians whose work in hospital and biomedical laboratories paved the way for oncologists to save my life. Every
year at the holidays I write a card of thanks to my oncologist,
describing some events of the past year—quiet times with family at home and exciting times on trips, splendid experiences
observing wildlife up close or through binoculars, a writing or
speaking accomplishment that carried particular meaning for
me—that I lived to experience.

In my mind, that card doubles as a way to thank also those
health-care workers who remain invisible to me. How many
person-years in the lab and hospital did it take for researchers
to discover that aggressive uterine cancer cells are most likely
to die off when subjected to a specific sequence of surgery, chemotherapy, and radiation? It goes far beyond cancer, of course.
How many years of failures and setbacks occurred before scientists learned how to restore a person's sight when her retina
detaches, as mine did years ago after a cataract operation? Who
figured out that keeping my head down for fifty minutes out
of every hour for ten straight days after surgery would ensure
that everything done to my eye—removal of the vitreous, inser-
tion of a gas bubble and buckle—would "take" so that I wouldn't
be blind in one eye? Whose life work allowed me to survive a

top-of-thigh-to-mid-calf blood clot in 2019, a major deep vein thrombosis event that cascaded into a small pulmonary embolism and caused another anxious night at the hospital?

Invisible too are the laboratory animals who have given up so much, with no choice in the matter, and with untold experiences of harm and suffering. The invasions these animals experience are countless as well—invasions to the bodies of rodents implanted with tumors and of kittens infected with toxoplasmosis parasites; to the muscles of dogs weakened in muscular dystrophy research; to the rumen of Brooke the fistulated cow made accessible to human hands; to the integrity of the body and mind of Tom the chimpanzee and of more monkeys in Oregon than we will ever be permitted to see. I don't know how many animal bodies were invaded as part of the biomedical experiments meant to save both my eyesight and my life. I do know that my part-bionic eye flashes to my husband across a dark room. The tiny blueish marks on my hips that outlined the territory for radiation techs to target show my tattoo-bearing Sarah that I'm in the tat club too. The scarred-over holes on my torso and abdomen where the chemo port went in, and where multiple organs came out, stand as icons of a harrowing experience, but not only my own harrowing experience. I live on, and many other animals do not.

In the words John Gluck chose to end his memoir, "The debt we have incurred has yet to be paid." The lives of laboratory animals are inscribed on my body; in seeking a different future, one in which alternatives to animal models are explored and embraced, I honor those lives.

Epilogue

In her biography *Henry David Thoreau: A Life*, Laura Dassow Walls recounts that Thoreau said of a muskrat: "While I am looking at him I am thinking what he is thinking of me. He is a different sort of man, that is all." I am beginning to grasp what Thoreau meant, I think. He wasn't guilty of wildly inappropriate anthropomorphism, assigning human qualities themselves to rodents.

Thoreau was saying, I believe, that there's a fundamental life force, a force often based in thinking and feeling, that runs through animals. When we spontaneously recognize it, or train ourselves to recognize it, our compassion springs to life. Anyone who rescues animals or agitates for better lives for household spiders or oceangoing orcas, zoo-captive seals or dairy cows, "opens up radically to the world" just as Thoreau did with the muskrat.

Cofounder of Vermont's VINE sanctuary pattrice jones notes that for all animals (including us), freedom is "all about bodies," about "eros." That means it is all about desire. Sometimes that desire is sexual (and definitely not always heterosexual). Sometimes it is not. "Salmon want streams that haven't been damned or diverted," jones writes. "Frogs want unpolluted ponds. Chickens want *out* of those battery cages. Dogs want other dogs." And so on. Recognizing these desires, as best we humans can, aids the process of radical opening up.

My own progress has been slower than I would like. Another, more positive way to look at it is this: even though I've been on this road for decades, I have made fresh progress compared to only five years ago. During the summer of 2019, I spent weeks informally observing four orb-weaver spider females (including Portia; see chapter 2) who hunted for a living, each spinning a home in her chosen location around the exterior of our home. These females curated and, when necessary, repaired their web, wrapped and consumed their insect prey, and as summer waned, produced small egg sacs. That means I'll have spider companions again any month now (summer of 2020). My wonder at spider behavior has slowly overtaken my fear. Even indoors I now rescue the once-dreaded wolf spiders on my own; occasionally I even acquiesce to the wishes of those spiders who seem to want to stay indoors and cohabit with me.

While only one example, this arachnological change points to an intentional stance, one in which cultivation of compassionate action becomes a lifelong journey. To take a second example, while I now eat far fewer animal products than ever before, five years from now I expect to be even farther along that path. What I notice is that there's always someone doing more and doing better for animals than I am, and in recognizing this, I can choose to feel inspiration rather than guilt.

*   *   *

In the years when I taught Primate Behavior to undergraduates, I often projected a video segment that was centered on grapes, cucumbers, and two capuchin monkeys. The minute-long clip shows a monkey who gives a small rock to a researcher in exchange for a slice of cucumber. The animal appears content with this trade-off *until* she notices that her partner sitting in the next cage receives a grape in the exact same type of exchange. Grapes are much preferred to cucumbers by these primates. When the first monkey is once again handed a bit of cucumber for a token, her response changes. She hurls the cucumber piece outside her cage, rattles the cage bars, and slaps the ground. Her displeasure is clear.

This clip went viral on the internet, perhaps because many of us can relate instantly to the unfairness to which the first monkey responds. It's not just a single monkey who acts this way, of course; the clip represents a set of experimental trials carried out and written up by Sarah Brosnan and Frans de Waal in de Waal's capuchin lab at Emory University. (This lab is in no sense biomedical; the focus is on behavior and cognition.) The monkeys who rejected cucumber pieces didn't suddenly find those items unpalatable; the cucumber became unsatisfactory only in a very particular context. Writing in *Mama's Last Hug*, de Waal puts it this way: "If you just feed two monkeys different foods, they barely notice, but if both of them work for it, all of a sudden it matters what one gets relative to another."

Switch the species from capuchins to dogs, and unequal treatment goes down no better, de Waal reports. At a dog cognition lab at the University of Vienna, dogs engaged in "handshakes" (pawshakes) quite happily over and over again, with no reward. When researchers rewarded one dog in a pair with food in exchange for a shake, however, the second dog (offered no food) refused to continue participating. In chimpanzees, expression of upset at being treated unfairly, such as when one individual receives a carrot but her partner receives a grape, may be matched by something more: concern over *another* chimpanzee's treatment. If a chimpanzee is offered a grape but sees that her partner gets only a carrot, she will sometimes refuse the grape in solidarity.

Thinking over these series of experiments on fairness, my mind spins a fantasy. What would happen if animals coping with some harmful situation could somehow *know* that others of their species get a better deal? What if a bear kept in a barren cage in a roadside zoo knew that some bears freely roam Yellowstone National Park? What if a baboon or macaque monkey made to undergo invasive experiments in a laboratory could envision a day spent foraging and grooming as part of a social group in the wild? A spider who made the mistake of crawling through a crack into the house of someone who crushes "bugs" on sight could wish he were a spider lucky enough to dwell unnoticed (maybe even admired) outside. A deer family kept constantly on the run at the sight of gun-toting hunters could know that reserves exist in which ungulates cannot be killed for meat or for fun. In his last minutes alive in a slaughterhouse, a pig, sensing the fear of those walking ahead, could conjure up a mental image of pigs at a farm sanctuary who wallow in mud or rest back to back with a friend.

All these animals in my fantasy, and billions more in real life, sacrifice something—their physical well-being, their sanity, their lives—because of our actions and human decisions. And in real life, they cannot become aware of better lives to be led (unless in captivity they retain memories of a happier previous life), which means that it's up to us.

Often the first step is to ask questions that others don't. Speaking at Rhodes College in Memphis in spring 2019, I was reminded of this as person after person wanted to describe for me some issue regarding animal ethics with which they grappled. An undergraduate woman asked me what she should do: In class she was instructed to dissect a frog. As the other students participated in this assigned task, she found herself in tears and needing to leave the laboratory in distress. Though I don't deal out "shoulds" to students, I did thank this woman for her empathy and invite her to think together with me about her dilemma. Virtual models like the one called SynFrog are widely available online as replacement for once-living flesh-and-blood animals in these dissection labs; how did she feel about requesting from her professor the right to gain the knowledge required by this alternative means? Her eyes lit up; a friend of hers at a nearby university was using such a virtual model.

This solution took no special brilliance to propose. Yet the student's emotional dilemma was real. Perhaps she just needed to know that in a local culture where her peers were going along with the status quo, it was okay to reach for a different way. It's sometimes hard to be the only one who questions treatment of animals; speaking up may embolden others to know their concern isn't strange but arises from kindness—and has a whole compassionate community behind it.

A second Rhodes undergraduate, a woman who had arrived in the United States from China only months before as a first-year undergraduate, raised concerns that required a more intricate response. She told me of her ambivalence about eating meat. Reading for the first time about the terrible harm to animals caught up in the factory-farming system, she felt distress. She also knew, she told me, that humans sit at the top of the food chain; that fact was a source of her uncertainty. What was right to do, and what was only natural when it comes to eating meat?

This sort of honest acknowledgment about one's conflicting feelings paves the way for open dialogue and further introspection. Meat eating *did* contribute significantly toward the increase in brain size that helped propel the human lineage in its evolution, I told the student. Claims of a wholly vegetarian past for humanity simply don't fit with the anthropological facts of tool-aided carcass-processing going back two million years, and hunting of big game going back a half million years. Yet it's that very meat-enabled trajectory of biological and cultural evolution over eons that has produced beings—we ourselves—who can think with compassion about our food. No lion confers with her hunting partners about the harms inflicted on the antelope in her sights, nor do orcas weigh the ethical pros and cons when they collaborate to flip a seal off the ice into the sea for consumption. Our brains allow for a blossoming of compassionate action in ways that are, insofar as we know, as unprecedented on Earth as is our species' bent for destruction.

Wherever I go now, whether in person on college campuses or at public science events, or online at Twitter or in conversations with TED video viewers, I encounter a questioning about animals, a yearning to be better and do better for animals. As I have shown in this book, every day of our lives we can recognize or create opportunities to become the best friends of animals in our homes, in the wild, in zoos, considered to be our food, and held in laboratories. The time is now, and the animals are waiting.

Acknowledgments

I thank the scientists and animal advocates who took time to share their knowledge with me: Benjamin Beck, Alka Chandna, Susie Coston, Eva Cross, Jane Desmond, Brittany Fallon, Hope Ferdowsian, Erika Fleury, Dennis French, Justin Goodman, Harry W. Greene, Brandon Keim, William Lynn, Kim Marra, Lori Marino, Jo-Anne McArthur, Ryan Merkley, Sy Montgomery, Clint Perry, Ryan Phillips, Becky Robinson, Jill Robinson, Timothy J. Smith, Elizabeth Tavella, Ingrid Taylor, Scott Terrell, and Emily Trunnell.

My gratitude as well to Marsha Autilio, Pat Autilio, Mark Devries, Diana Gordon, the late Wilson Menashi, Angie Rizzo, Stuart Shanker, Diane Brandt Wilkes, and Stephen Wood, for conversations that enriched the book. A special shout-out to Marsha Autilio and Stephen Wood because their friendship and their willingness to think through hard issues with me—since 1968 and 1976 respectively—has meant everything.

Ellen Geiger of the Frances Goldin Literary Agency is all I could ask for in an agent. Thank you, Ellen.

This is my seventh book overall, my third with the University of Chicago Press, where I have found a delightful publishing home. My editor Alan Thomas's conversations with and notes to me improved my thinking and my writing. This book also benefited from the professionalism of Jenni Fry, Ruth Goring, Nick Lilly, Levi Stahl, and Isaac Tobin.

To all the animals who have taught me how to look and how to see, I hope this book honors you.

To Charlie Hogg and Sarah Elizabeth Hogg, who bring joy to my life, my thanks and my love always.

References

Chapter One: Cultivating Compassionate Action

Eaton, Nate. 2017. "Good Samaritans Frantically Rush to Save Herd of Elk That Fall through Ice into Frigid Water." *EastIdahoNews. com*, December 29. https://www.eastidahonews.com/2017/12 /good-samaritans-rush-into-action-as-herd-of-elk-plunge -through-ice-into-frigid-water/.

Dovey, Dana. 2017. "Helpless Baby Elephant Trapped in Well Rescued by Indian Village in Heartwarming Video." *Newsweek*, November 29. http://www.newsweek.com/helpless-baby-elephant -trapped-well-rescued-indian-village-heartwarming-video -725080.

Ferdowsian, Hope. 2018. *Phoenix Zones: Where Strength Is Born and Resilience Lives*. Chicago: University of Chicago Press.

Robinson, Jill. 2017. Personal communication, email message, June 29.

Animals Asia. 2015. "#BearSeaRescue: Two Rescued Moon Bears Take a Sunset Boat Ride to Freedom." May 31. https://www.you tube.com/watch?v=UW4ttx31Plo.

Animals Asia. 2016. "Rescued alongside Simon Who Died—Now Moon Bear Sam Is Living for Two." February 5. https://www .animalsasia.org/us/media/news/news-archive/rescued -alongside-simon-who-died-%E2%80%93-now-moon-bear-sam -is-living-for-two.html.

Animals Asia. 2017. "The Moment We Knew Damaged Rescue Bear Snow Was Going to Be OK." May 11, 2017. https://www.youtube.com/watch?v=pjKHcBrhM70.

Animals Asia. 2016. "Six Bears Rescued from a Bile Farm in Vietnam." December 9. https://www.animalsasia.org/us/media/news/news-archive/six-bears-rescued-from-a-bile-farm-in-vietnam.html.

Tanenbaum, Michael. 2020. "Obese Black Bear from Pennsylvania Sportsmen's Club Relocated to Colorado Sanctuary." *Philly Voice*, January 24. https://www.phillyvoice.com/obese-black-bear-rescued-pennsylvania-club-relocated-colorado/.

King, Barbara J. 2017. "Bears Can Face Summer Challenges In Roadside Zoos." NPR, August 17. https://www.npr.org/sections/13.7/2017/08/17/543682389/bears-can-face-summer-challenges-in-roadside-zoos.

Vonk, J., and M. J. Beran. 2012. "Bears 'Count' Too: Quantity Estimation and Comparison in Black Bears, *Ursus americanus*." *Animal Behaviour* 84:231–38. DOI: 10.1016/j.anbehav.2012.05.001.

Poulsen, Else. 2009. *Smiling Bears: A Zookeeper Explores the Behavior and Emotional Life of Bears*. Vancouver, BC: Greystone Books, quoted material from 15.

"Aly Raisman's All-Around Routines and Her Parents' Reactions Side by Side." 2016. *NBC News*, August 13. http://archivepyc.nbcolympics.com/news/aly-raismans-all-around-routines-and-her-parents-reactions-side-side.

Gruen, Lori. 2015. *Entangled Empathy: An Alternative Ethic for Our Relationships with Animals*. New York: Lantern Books, quoted material from 67.

Bloom, Paul. 2016. *Against Empathy: The Case for Rational Compassion*. New York: HarperCollins, quoted material from 3, 5.

Ferdowsian, *Phoenix Zones*, 152.

Stoewen, Debbie L. 2015. "Suicide in Veterinary Medicine: Let's Talk about It." *Canadian Veterinary Journal* 56, no. 1 (January): 89–92. https://www.ncbi.nlm.nih.gov/pmc/articles/PMC4266064/.

Galazka, Kasia. 2017. "How Animal Rescuers Are Burning Out Their Empathy." *Nautilus*, January 13. http://nautil.us/blog/how-animal-rescuers-are-burning-out-their-empathy.

Chapter Two: Animals at Home

Walker, Alice. 2011. *The Chicken Chronicles: Sitting with the Angels Who Have Returned with My Memories: Glorious, Rufus, Gertrude Stein, Splendor, Hortensia, Agnes of God, the Gladyses, and Babe—a Memoir*. New York: New Press, quoted material from 136, 139.

Buddle, Christopher M., and Eleanor Spicer Rice. 2018. *Dr. Eleanor's Book of Common Spiders*. Chicago: University of Chicago Press, quoted material from 88.

Bertone, Matt. 2018. "Should I Kill Spiders in My Home? An Entomologist Explains Why Not To." *Conversation*, May 16. https://theconversation.com/should-i-kill-spiders-in-my-home-an-entomologist-explains-why-not-to-95912.

Wilson, E. O. 2018. "The 8 Million Species We Don't Know." *New York Times*, March 3. https://www.nytimes.com/2018/03/03/opinion/sunday/species-conservation-extinction.html.

Rodriguez, Rafael R., R. D. Briceno, E. Briceno-Aguilar, and G. Hobel. 2015. "*Nephila clavipes* Spiders (Araneae: Nephilidae) Keep Track of Captured Prey Counts: Testing for a Sense of Numerosity in an Orb-Weaver." *Animal Cognition* 18:307–14, quoted material from 313.

"Tiny Dancer: When Jumping Spiders Show Their True Colors, UC Biologist Looks through the Lens for the Reasons." 2017. *UC Magazine*, University of Cincinnati. January 23. http://magazine.uc.edu/editors_picks/recent_features/tinydancers.html.

Peckmezian, Tina, and Phillip Taylor. 2015. "A Virtual Reality Paradigm for the Study of Visually Mediated Behaviour and Cognition in Spiders." *Animal Behaviour* 107:87–95.

Selk, Avi. 2018. "The Extraordinary Life and Death of the World's Oldest Known Spider." *Washington Post*, May 1. https://www.washingtonpost.com/news/speaking-of-science/wp/2018/05/01/the-extraordinary-life-and-death-of-the-worlds-oldest-known-spider/.

Frank, Erik T., Marten Wehrhahn, and K. Eduard Linsenmair. 2018. "Wound Treatment and Selective Help in a Termite-Hunting Ant." *Proceedings of the Royal Society* B 285: 20172457. http://dx.doi.org/10.1098/rspb.2017.2457.

Sample, Ian. 2018. "'Paramedic Ants' Observed Treating Injured Comrades." *Guardian*, February 13. https://www.theguardian .com/science/2018/feb/14/nursing-in-nature-matabele-ants -observed-treating-injured-comrades.

Wilson, Edward O. 2020. *Tales from the Ant World*. Advanced reader's copy. New York: Livewright, quoted material from 11.

Montgomery, Sy. 2018. *How to Be a Good Creature: A Memoir in Thirteen Animals*. New York: Houghton-Mifflin, quoted material from 138.

Duranton, Charlotte, Thierry Bedossa, and Florence Gaunet. 2018. "Pet Dogs Synchronize Their Walking Pace with That of Their Owners in Open Outdoor Areas." *Animal Cognition* 21, no. 2: 219–26.

King, Barbara J. 2018. "Keeping a Close Eye: Dogs, Social Referencing, and Evolution." NPR, February 22. https://www.npr.org /sections/13.7/2018/02/22/587997756/keeping-a-close-eye-dogs -social-referencing-and-evolution.

Horowitz, Andrea. 2019. *Our Dogs, Ourselves*. New York: Simon & Schuster.

Merola, I., M. Lazzaroni, S. Marshall-Pescini, and E. Prato-Previde. 2015. "Social Referencing and Cat-Human Communication." *Animal Cognition* 18, no. 3: 639–48.

Banszegi, Oxana, Andrea Urrutia, Peter Szenczi, and Robyn Hudson. 2016. "More or Less: Spontaneous Quantity Discrimination in the Domestic Cat." *Animal Cognition* 19, no. 5: 879–88, quoted material from 886.

Marra, Peter P., and Chris Santella. 2016. *Cat Wars: The Devastating Consequences of a Cuddly Killer*. Princeton, NJ: Princeton University Press, quoted material from 152, 153, 164.

Khadka, Navin Singh. 2019. "Dogs 'Becoming Major Threat' to Wildlife." BBC, February 12. https://www.bbc.com/news/science -environment-47062959.

King, Barbara J. 2016. "Stakes Grow Higher in the Cat–Bird Wars." NPR, September 29. https://www.npr.org/sections/13.7/2016/09 /29/495883093/stakes-grow-higher-in-the-cat-bird-wars.

Robinson, Becky. 2018. Personal communication by telephone, February 19.

Doherty, Tim S., and Euan G. Ritchie. 2017. "Stop Jumping the Gun:

A Call for Evidence-Based Invasive Predator Management." *Conservation Letters* 10:15–22.

Lynn, William S., Francisco Santiago-Avila, Joann Lindenmayer, John Hadidian, Adrian Wallach, and Barbara J. King. 2019. "A Moral Panic over Cats." *Conservation Biology*, May 14. https://doi .org/10.1111/cobi.13346.

Chapter Three: Animals in the Wild

King, Barbara J. 2019. "Grief and Love in the Animal Kingdom." TED talk, April 18, Vancouver, BC, April 18, posted online July 8. https://www.ted.com/talks/barbara_j_king_grief_and_love_in _the_animal_kingdom?language=en.

King, Barbara J. 2013. *How Animals Grieve*. Chicago: University of Chicago Press.

De Waal, Frans. 2019. *Mama's Last Hug: Animal Emotions and What They Tell us about Ourselves*. New York: W. W. Norton, quoted material from 43.

Bearzi, Giovanni, Dan Kerem, Nathan B. Furey, Robert L. Pitman, Luke Rendell, and Randall R. Reeves. 2018. "Whale and Dolphin Behavioral Responses to Dead Conspecifics." *Zoology* 128:1–15.

Jauhar, Sandeep. 2018. "Cardiologists Should Care about Our Love Lives." *New York Times*, September 14. http://sandeepjauhar.com /why-your-cardiologist-should-ask-about-your-love-life-new -york-times/.

Anderson, James R., Donna Biro, and Paul Pettitt. 2018. "Evolutionary Thanatology." *Philosophical Transactions of the Royal Society B, Biological Sciences* 373, no. 1754 (July 16): 20170262. doi.org /10.1098/rstb.2017.0262.

Whitehead, Hal, and Luke Rendell. 2015. *The Cultural Lives of Whales and Dolphins*. Chicago: University of Chicago Press, quoted material from 130.

Mapes, Lynda V. 2018. "A Mother Orca's Dead Calf and the Grief Felt around the World." *Seattle Times*, August 2. https://www .seattletimes.com/seattle-news/environment/a-mother-orcas -dead-calf-and-the-grief-felt-around-the-world/.

Quinton, Sean. 2018. "'I Have Not Slept in Days': Readers React to Tahlequah, the Mother Orca Clinging to Her Dead Calf." *Seattle*

Times, August 5. https://www.seattletimes.com/seattle-news /i-have-not-slept-in-days-readers-react-to-tahlequah-the -mother-orca-clinging-to-her-dead-calf/.

Mapes, Lynda V. 2018. "Orca J50 Presumed Dead but NOAA Continues Search." *Seattle Times*, September 13. https://www.seattle times.com/seattle-news/environment/orca-j50-declared-dead -after-search-southern-residents-down-to-74-whales/.

Mapes, Lynda V. 2018. "Seattle Chef Renee Erickson Takes Chinook Salmon off Menus to Help Ailing Puget Sound Orcas." *Seattle Times*, August 22. https://www.seattletimes.com/seattle-news /seattle-chef-renee-erickson-takes-chinook-salmon-off-menus -to-help-ailing-puget-sound-orcas/.

Lacy, R. C., et al. 2017. "Evaluating Anthropogenic Threats to Endangered Killer Whales to Inform Effective Recovery Plans." *Scientific Reports* 7, no. 1: 14119. https://www.nature.com/articles /s41598-017-14471-0.

Heuer, Karsten. 2008. *Being Caribou: Five Months on Foot with an Arctic Herd*. Minneapolis: Milkweed Editions, quoted material from 196.

Landis, Abbie Gascho. 2018. *Immersion: The Science and Mystery of Freshwater Mussels*. Washington, DC: Island Press, quoted material from 5.

Meloy, Ellen. 2005. *Eating Stone: Imagination and the Loss of the Wild*. New York: Vintage Books, quoted material from 87 (epigraph), 142, 53.

Keim, Brandon. 2017. *The Eye of the Sandpiper: Stories from the Living World*. Ithaca, NY: Cornell University Press, quoted material from 170–71.

Wilson, Edward O. 2018. "The 8 Million Species We Don't Know." *New York Times*, March 4.

Messenger, Stephen. 2018. "Woman Forms Incredible Bond with Bee Who Needed a Friend." *Dodo*, March 21. https://www.the dodo.com/in-the-wild/woman-befriends-wingless-bumblebee.

Loukola, Illi J, Clint J. Perry, Louie Coscos, and Lars Chittka. 2017. "Bumblebees Show Cognitive Flexibility by Improving on an Observed Complex Behavior." *Science* 355, no. 6327: 833–36. DOI: 10.1126/science.aag2360.

Perry, Clint J., Luigi Baciadonna, and Lars Chittka. 2016. "Unexpected Rewards Induce Dopamine-Dependent Positive Emotion-Like State Changes in Bumblebees." *Science* 353, no. 6307: 1529–31.

Perry, Clint. 2018. Personal communication, email message, April 6.

Hansen, Thor. 2018. *Buzz: The Nature and Necessity of Bees*. New York: Basic Books, quoted material from 59.

Gammon, Katherine. 2019. "Los Angeles to Build World's Largest Wildlife Bridge across 10-Lane Freeway." *Guardian*, August 21. https://www.theguardian.com/environment/2019/aug/21/los-angeles-wildlife-bridge-mountain-lions.

Cherry, Cara, Kirsten M. Leong, Rick Wallen, and Danielle Buttke. 2018. "Risk-Enhancing Behaviors Associated with Human Injuries from Bison Encounters at Yellowstone National Park, 2000–2015." *One Health* 6 (May 26):1–6. DOI: 10.1016/j.onehlt.2018.05.003, quoted material from 4.

Greene, Harry W. 2013. *Tracks and Shadows: Field Biology as Art*. Oakland: University of California Press.

Hughes, Trevor. 2018. "2 Grizzlies Killed by Wyoming Wildlife Officials after Hunting Guide Fatally Mauled." *USA Today*, September 16. https://www.usatoday.com/story/news/2018/09/16/grizzlies-killed-wyoming-hunting-guide-fatally-mauled/1330037002/.

Dutcher, Jim and Jamie Dutcher. 2018. *The Wisdom of Wolves: Lessons from the Sawtooth Pack*. Washington, DC: National Geographic.

Deckha, Maneesha. 2018. "Postcolonial." In *Critical Terms for Animal Studies*, edited by Lori Gruen, 280–93. Chicago: University of Chicago Press.

Chiu, Allyson. 2018. "'I Shot a Whole Family of Baboons': Idaho Fish and Game Official Faces Fury after Africa Trophy Hunting Boasts." *Washington Post*, October 15. https://www.washingtonpost.com/news/morning-mix/wp/2018/10/15/i-shot-a-whole-family-of-baboons-idaho-fish-and-game-official-faces-fury-after-africa-trophy-hunting-boasts/?utm_term=.9aac9a90b6d7.

Rutberg, Allen T. 2013. "Managing Wildlife with Contraception: Why Is It Taking So Long?" *Journal of Zoo and Wildlife Medicine* 44, no. 45: S38–S46, quoted material from S40.

Monbiot, George. 2020. "I Shot a Deer—and I Still Believe It Was the Ethical Thing to Do." *Guardian*, February 19. https://www.theguardian.com/commentisfree/2020/feb/19/wildlife-killing-deer-diversity-resources-environment.

King, Barbara J. 2018. "Why Are Iguanas' Skulls Being Crushed in the Name of Science?" NPR, March 20. https://www.npr.org/sections/13.7/2018/03/20/595186291/why-are-iguanas-skulls-being-crushed-in-the-name-of-science.

Bolotnikova, Marina, and Jeff Sebo. 2020. "Stop Treating Animals as 'Invaders' for Simply Trying to Exist." Sentient Media. https://sentientmedia.org/stop-treating-animals-as-invaders-for-simply-trying-to-exist/.

Goldfarb, Ben. 2018. *Eager: The Surprising, Secret Life of Beavers and Why They Matter*. White River Junction, VT: Chelsea Green, quoted material from 10, 55.

Ramp, Daniel, and Marc Bekoff. 2015. "Compassion as a Practical and Evolved Ethic for Conservation." *BioScience* 65:323–27, quoted material from 324, 325.

Treves, Adrian, Francisco J. Santiago-Àvila, and William S. Lynn. 2019. "Just Preservation." *Biological Conservation* 229:134–41.

Santiago-Avila, F. J., W. S. Lynn, and A. Treves. 2018. "Inappropriate Consideration of Animal Interests in Predator Management: Towards a Comprehensive Moral Code." In *Large Carnivore Conservation and Management: Human Dimensions and Governance*, edited by T. Horvardos, 227–51. New York: Routledge.

Deckha, Maneesha. 2018. "Postcolonial," quoted material from 288.

Chapter Four: Animals in Zoos

Montgomery, Sy. 2015. *The Soul of an Octopus*. New York: Simon & Schuster, quoted material from 221, 33.

"The Ultimate Octopus Disguise." 2018. *Planet Earth: Blue Planet II*, BBC America, February 17. https://www.youtube.com/watch?v=GoTk5WofgoE.

King, Barbara J. 2015. "Viewing Octopus Choreography in Captivity." NPR, May 28. https://www.npr.org/sections/13.7/2015/05/28/410209112/viewing-octopus-choreography-in-captivity.

"Scimitar-Horned Oryx." n.d. Smithsonian's National Zoo and Con-

servation Biology Institute. https://nationalzoo.si.edu/animals
/scimitar-horned-oryx.

"The Future of Zoos." 2016. *The Diane Rehm Show*, NPR, June 21.
https://dianerehm.org/shows/2016-06-21/rethinking-zoos.

Grazian, David. 2015. *American Zoo: A Sociological Safari*. Princeton, NJ: Princeton University Press, quoted material from 11,
261–62.

Veasey, Jake S. 2017. "In Pursuit of Peak Animal Welfare; The Need
to Prioritize the Meaningful over the Measurable." *Zoo Biology*
36:413–25.

"Ethics Guide: Introduction to Animal Rights." n.d. BBC. http://
www.bbc.co.uk/ethics/animals/rights/introduction.shtml.

Williams, Kale. 2015. "USDA Fines S.F. Zoo Over Gorilla Baby
Crushed by Door." *SFGate* (*San Francisco Chronicle* online),
October 23. https://www.sfgate.com/bayarea/article/S-F-zoo-hit
-with-fine-in-door-crush-death-of-6587349.php.

Associated Press. 2011. "Tiger That Mauled Three Teens at San
Francisco Zoo Appears to Have Been Provoked, Reports Says."
LA Unleashed, blog at *Los Angeles Times*, February 12. http://
latimesblogs.latimes.com/unleashed/2011/02/tiger-maul-teens
-san-francisco-zoo-provoked-report.html.

Barnes, Hannah. 2014. "How Many Healthy Animals Do Zoos Put
Down?" *BBC News*, February 27. http://www.bbc.com/news
/magazine-26356099.

Fobar, Rachel. 2019. "Hundreds of Zoos and Aquariums Accused of
Mistreating Animals." *National Geographic*, August 15. https://
www.nationalgeographic.com/animals/2019/08/waza-zoos
-accused-of-mistreating-animals wap report/.

McArthur, Jo-Anne. 2017. *Captive*. New York: Lantern Books,
quoted material from 158, 163.

McArthur, Jo-Anne. 2018. Personal communication, email message, October 3.

Terrell, Scott. 2019. Personal communication, email message,
February 15.

Jensen, Eric, Andrew Moss, and Markus Gusset. 2017. "Quantifying
Long-Term Impact of Zoo And Aquarium Visits on Biodiversity-
Related Learning Outcomes." *Zoo Biology* 36:294–97, quoted
material from 294.

Moss, Andrew, Eric Jensen, and Markus Gusset. 2014. "Evaluating the Contribution of Zoos and Aquariums to Aichi Biodiversity Target 1." *Conservation Biology* 29, no. 2: 537–44, quoted material from 537.

Gruen, Lori. 2014. Introduction to *The Ethics of Captivity*, edited by Lori Gruen. Oxford: University of Oxford Press, quoted material from 2.

Rizzo, Angie. 2019. "The Violence of Conservation Science at Zoos." Unpublished paper, Lehigh University.

Aspinall, Damian. Interview by Lesley Stahl. *60 Minutes*, "Back to the Wild" episode, March 15, 2015. https://www.cbsnews.com /news/zoo-gorilla-family-freed-to-wild-60-minutes-lesley-stahl/

Beck, B. B. 2019. Foreword to and summary of *Unwitting Travelers: A History of Primate Reintroduction*. Berlin, MD: Salt Water Media.

Pachirat, Timothy. 2018. "Sanctuary." In *Critical Terms in Animal Studies*, edited by Lori Gruen, 337–55. Chicago: University of Chicago Press, quoted material from 347–48.

AZA. 2016. "Report Shows AZA-Accredited Zoos and Aquariums' Record-Breaking Contribution to Wildlife Conservation." News release, September 27. https://www.aza.org/aza-news-releases /posts/2016-report-shows-aza-accredited-zoos-and-aquariums -record-breaking-contribution-to-wildlife-conserv.

Dehgan, Alex, 2019. *The Snow Leopard Project: And Other Adventures in Warzone Conservation*. New York: PublicAffairs/Hachette.

Fallon, Brittany. 2018. Personal communication, email message, April 22.

Birkett, L. P., and N. E. Newton-Fisher. 2011. "How Abnormal Is the Behaviour of Captive, Zoo-Living Chimpanzees?" *PLoS One*, June 6: e20101. DOI: 10.1371/journal.pone.0020101.

Richmond Metro Zoo. 2018. Personal communication via Facebook Messenger, October 17.

HSUS (Humane Society of the United States). 2014. Factsheet on ZAA (Zoological Association of America), July. https://bigcat rescue.org/wp-content/uploads/2014/07/ZAA-Factsheet.pdf ?fbclid=IwAR2335LT47HZAmDm2LWpyyWopOIQqtxedYYb _PXbo8lXYXOPqZ-Ci3AH_Tg.

Dilonardo, Mary Jo. 2018. "Yellow River Game Ranch Closes Its

Doors." *Mother Nature Network*, January 12. https://www.mnn
.com/earth-matters/animals/stories/closing-doors-yellow-river
-game-ranch,

Coyne, Amanda C. 2018. "Gwinnett Family Re-opening Yellow
River Game Ranch as Animal Sanctuary." *Atlanta Journal-
Constitution*, July 30. https://www.ajc.com/news/local/gwinnett
-family-opening-yellow-river-game-ranch-animal-sanctuary
/VGtG9ZeU5zbmXzCcW6f5II/.

Smith, Timothy J. 2018. Personal communication, email message,
October 29.

Chapter Five: Animals on Our Plates

Pachirat, Timothy. 2011. *Every Twelve Seconds: Industrialized
Slaughter and the Politics of Sight*. New Haven, CT: Yale University Press.

DeMello, Margo. 2014. "Rabbits in Captivity." In *The Ethics of Captivity*, edited by Lori Gruen, 77–89. Oxford: Oxford University
Press, quoted material from 83.

DiVincenti, Louis, and Angelika N. Rehrig. 2016. "The Social Nature of European Rabbits (*Oryctolagus cuniculus*)." *Journal of
the American Association for Laboratory Animal Science* 55, no.
6: 729–36, quoted material from 729.

Best Friends Sanctuary. n.d. "House Rabbit Behavior and Bunny
Body Language." https://resources.bestfriends.org/article/house
-rabbit-behavior-and-bunny-body-language.

Kateman, Brian. 2019. Introductory Remarks. Third Annual Reducetarian Conference, Arlington, VA, September. See https://
reducetarian.org.

Foer, Jonathan Safran. 2019. *We Are the Weather: Saving the Planet
Begins at Breakfast*. New York: Farrar, Straus and Giroux, quoted
material from 71, 154.

Craig W. J., A. R, Mangels, and American Dietetic Association.
2009. "Position of the American Dietetic Association: Vegetarian Diets." *Journal of the American Dietetic Association* 109, no.
7: 1266–82, quoted material from abstract.

Brueck, Julia Feliz, ed. 2017. *Veganism in an Oppressive World: A
Vegans of Color Community Project*. N.p.: Sanctuary Publishers.

Scott, Jennifer. 2017. "Why I Gave Up Being Vegan." BBC, September 5. https://www.bbc.com/news/uk-41158365.

Reese, Jacy. 2018. *The End of Animal Farming: How Scientists, Entrepreneurs, and Activists are Building an Animal-Free Food System*. Boston: Beacon, quoted material from 115.

Gillespie, Kathryn. 2018. *The Cow with Ear Tag #1389*. Chicago: University of Chicago Press, quoted material from 95–97, 215–16.

Foer, Jonathan Safran. 2009. *Eating Animals*. New York: Little, Brown.

King, Barbara J. 2017. *Personalities on the Plate: The Lives and Minds of Animals We Eat*. Chicago: University of Chicago Press.

Leshko, Isa. 2019. *Allowed to Grow Old: Portraits of Elderly Farm Animals from Farm Sanctuaries*. Chicago: University of Chicago Press.

Jenni, Kathie. 2018. "Bearing Witness for the Animal Dead." *Proceedings of the XXIII World Congress of Philosophy* [edited by Konstantinos Boudouris] 12:167–81.

Kaplan, Michele. 2016. "Is Veganism Ableist? A Disabled Vegan Perspective." Vegan Feminist Network, September 7. http:// veganfeministnetwork.com/is-veganism-ableist-a-disabled -vegan-perspective/.

Taylor, Sunaura. 2017. *Beasts of Burden: Animal and Disability Liberation*. New York: New Press, quoted material from 203.

Balk, Josh. 2017. "The Future of Food." In *The Reducetarian Solution*, edited by B. Kateman, 28–31. New York: TarcherPerigee.

Root, Tik. 2019. "Inside the Race to Build the World's First Commercial Octopus Farm." *Time*, August 21. https://time.com /5657927/farm-raised-octopus/.

Jacquet, Jennifer, Becca Franks, Peter Godfrey-Smith, and Walter Sanchez-Suarez. 2019. "The Case against Octopus Farming." *Issues in Science and Technology* 35, no 2. https://issues.org/the -case-against-octopus-farming/.

King, Barbara J., and Lori Marino. 2019. "Octopus Minds Must Lead to Octopus Ethics." *Animal Sentience* 2019.263. https://animal studiesrepository.org/cgi/viewcontent.cgi?article=1495&context =animsent.

UN News. 2013. "The Latest Buzz: Eating Insects Can Help Tackle Food Insecurity, Says FAO." May 13. https://news.un.org/en/story /2013/05/439432.

Lesnik, Julie. 2018. *Edible Insects and Human Evolution*. Gainesville: University of Florida Press, quoted material from 138.

Broad, Garrett. 2016. *More Than Just Food: Food Justice and Community Change*. Oakland: University of California Press.

Goodall, Jane. 2018. "The Most Intellectual Creature to Ever Walk Earth Is Destroying Its Only Home." *Guardian*, November 3.

Carrington, Damian. 2018. "Avoiding meat and dairy is 'single biggest way' to reduce your impact on Earth." *Guardian*, May 31. https://www.theguardian.com/environment/2018/may/31 /avoiding-meat-and-dairy-is-single-biggest-way-to-reduce-your -impact-on-earth.

Poore, J., and T. Nemecek. 2018. "Reducing food's Environmental Impacts through Producers and Consumers." *Science* 360:987– 92, quoted material from 991.

Blanchette, Alex. 2020. *Porkopolis: American Animality, Standardized Life, and the Factory Farm*. Durham, NC: Duke University Press, quoted material from 205, 216, 236.

Potts, Annie and Philip Armstrong. 2018. "Vegan." In *Critical Terms for Animal Studies*, edited by Lori Gruen, 395–409. Chicago: University of Chicago Press, quoted material from. 398, 407.

Phillips, Ryan. 2018. Personal communication, email message, June 18.

Life with Pigs animal sanctuary, run by Ryan Phillips: https://www .lifewithpigs.com/.

Leenaert, Tobias. 2017. *How to Create a Vegan World: A Pragmatic Approach*. New York: Lantern Books, quoted material from 35, 131–32, 168.

Beam, Chris. 2018. *I Feel You: The Surprising Power of Extreme Empathy*. Boston: Houghton Mifflin, quoted material from 79.

McKibben, Bill, 2017. "Meat Is Precious." In *The Reducetarian Solution*, edited by Brian Kateman, 159–60. New York: Tarcher-Perigree.

Friedrich, Bruce. 2019. "The Next Global Agricultural Revolution." TED talk, April 15, Vancouver, BC, posted online May 21. https://

www.ted.com/talks/bruce_friedrich_the_next_global_agricul-
tural_revolution/transcript?language=en.

King, Barbara J. 2018. "Opinion: As Florence Kills Pigs and Millions of Chickens, We Must 'Open Our Hearts.'" NPR, September
24. https://www.npr.org/sections/thesalt/2018/09/24/650437498
/opinion-as-florence-kills-pigs-and-millions-of-chickens-we
-must-open-our-hearts.

Nierenberg, Amelia. 2020. "Plant-Based 'Meats' Catch On in the
Pandemic." *New York Times*, May 24. https://www.nytimes.com
/2020/05/22/dining/plant-based-meats-coronavirus.html.

Adams, Carol J. 1990. *The Sexual Politics of Meat*. New York: Continuum.

Pachirat, Timothy. 2013. *Every Twelve Seconds: Industrialized
Slaughter and the Politics of Sight*. New Haven, CT: Yale University Press.

Marino, Lori. 2017. "Thinking Chickens: A Review of Cognition,
Emotion, and Behavior in the Domestic Chicken." *Animal Cognition* 20:127–47, quoted material from 127, 131, 141.

Shahin, Munira. 2018. "The Effects of Positive Human Contact by
Tactile Stimulation on Dairy Cows with Different Personalities."
Applied Animal Behaviour Science 204:23–28.

Young, Rosamund. 2018. *The Secret Life of Cows*. New York: Penguin.

Wurgaft, Benjamin Aldes. 2019. *Meat Planet: Artificial Flesh and
the Future of Food*. Oakland: University of California Press.

Shapiro, Paul. 2018. *Clean Meat: How Growing Meat without Animals
Will Revolutionize Dinner and the World*. New York: Gallery Books.

Wilson, Bee. 2017. "Wisdom from Margaret Mead." In *The Reducetarian Solution*, edited by Brian Kateman, 148–50. New York:
TarcherPerigee, quoted material from 150.

Save the Redwoods League: https://www.savetheredwoods.org
/redwoods/coast-redwoods/.

Wohlleben, Peter. 2016. *The Hidden Life of Trees: What They Feel,
How They Communicate—Discoveries from a Secret World*. Vancouver, BC: Greystone Books, quoted material from 248.

Powers, Richard. 2018. *The Overstory: A Novel*. New York: W. W.
Norton.

Pennisi, Elizabeth. 2019. "Do Plants Favor Their Kin?" *Science* 363,
no. 6422: 15–16.

Hawthorne, Mark. 2018. *Striking at the Roots: A Practical Guide to Animal Activism*. Washington, DC: Changemakers Books, quoted material from 100.

Chapter Six: Animals in Research Labs

O'Brien, Anna. 2014. "Holey Cow: The Wonderful World of a Fistulated Cow." *Modern Farmer*, September 12. https://modernfarmer.com/2014/09/holey-cow-wonderful-world-fistulated-cow/.

Jacobs, Rebecca. 2014. "Hole-y Cow." *Daily Illini*, December 19. http://rrjacob2.h.media.illinois.edu/jour425/.

Yong, Ed. 2016. *I Contain Multitudes: The Microbes within Us and a Grander View of Life*. New York: Ecco.

Tavella, Elizabeth, and Brandon Keim. 2019. "Inside the (In)visible Life of Fistulated Cows." Paper presented at Living with Animals conference, Eastern Kentucky University, March.

Zemo, Tesfay and James. O. Klemmedson. 1970. "Behavior of Fistulated Steers on a Desert Grassland." *Journal of Range Management* 23, no. 3: 158–63.

Newby, Natalie, et al. 2014. "An Investigation of the Effects of Ketoprofen Following Rumen Fistulation Surgery in Lactating Dairy Cows." *Canadian Veterinary Journal* 55:442–48, quoted material from 442.

French, Dennis. 2018. Personal communication, email message, August 28.

Westoll, Andrew. *The Chimps of Fauna Sanctuary: A True Story of Resilience and Recovery*. Boston: Houghton Mifflin Harcourt, quoted material from 28.

Kaplan, Sheila. 2018. "Citing Deaths of Lab Monkeys, F.D.A. Ends an Addiction Study." *New York Times*, January 26. https://www.nytimes.com/2018/01/26/health/fda-monkeys-nicotine.html.

Fleury, Erika. 2017. "Money for Monkeys, and More: Ensuring Sanctuary Retirement of Non-human Primates." *Animal Studies Journal* 6, no. 2: 30–54.

Fleury, Erika. 2019. Personal communication, email message, January 8.

Grimm, David. 2018. "Opening the Lab Door." *Science* 360, no. 6396: 1392–95. DOI: 10.1126/science.360.6396.1392.

Gordon, Diana. 2018. Personal communication, email messages, July 13 and 18.

O'Brien, Kerri. 2018. "Contrary to Previous Reports, There's No Sanctuary for VCU Monkeys." *ABC Channel 8 Richmond News*, August 16. https://www.wric.com/news/8-investigates/contrary -to-previous-reports-there-s-no-sanctuary-for-vcu-monkeys /1375907312.

Pound, Pandora, and Michael B. Bracken. 2014. "Is animal research sufficiently evidence based to be a cornerstore of biomedical research?" *BMJ*, May 30. https://www.bmj.com/content/348/bmj .g3387, quoted material from 1.

Akhtar, Aysha. 2015. "The Flaws and Human Harms of Animal Experimentation." *Cambridge Quarterly of Healthcare Ethics* 24, no. 4: 407–19. DOI: 10.1017/S0963180115000079.

Merkley, Ryan. 2019. Personal communication, email message, January 15.

Zainzinger, Vanessa. 2018. "Animal Tests Surge under New U.S. Chemical Safety Law." *Science*, May 8. https://www.sciencemag .org/news/2018/05/animal-tests-surge-under-new-us-chemical -safety-law.

Cross, Eva. 2019–20. Personal communication, email messages, January 23 and 25, October 1, March 10.

Reardon, Sara. 2018. "Frustrated Alzheimer's Researchers Seek Better Lab Mice." *Nature*, November 21. https://www.nature.com /articles/d41586-018-07484-w.

Picher-Martel, Vincent, Paul N. Valdmanis, Peter V. Gould, Jean-Pierre Julien, and Nicolas Dupré. 2016. "From Animal Models to Human Disease: A Genetic Approach for Personalized Medicine in ALS." *Acta Neuropathologica Communications* 4 (2016): 70. https://actaneurocomms.biomedcentral.com/articles/10.1186 /s40478-016-0340-5, quoted material from abstract.

Edler, Melissa, et al. 2017. "Aged Chimpanzees Exhibit Pathologic Hallmarks of Alzheimer's." *Neurobiology of Aging* 59:107–20. https://www.sciencedirect.com/science/article/pii/S019745801 7302397?via%3Dihub.

Cohen, Jon. 2020. "From Mice to Monkeys, Animals Studied for Coronavirus Answers." *Science* 368, no. 6488: 221–22, quoted material from 221.

Lakdawala, Seema S., and Vineet D. Menachery. 2020. "The Search for a COVID-19 Animal Model." *Science* 368, no. 6494: 942–43, quoted material from 942.

Corder, Gregory, et al. 2019. "An Amygdalar Neural Ensemble That Encodes the Unpleasantness of Pain." *Science* 363, no. 6424: 276–81. DOI: 10.1126/science.aap8586.

Gluck, John. 2016. *Voracious Science and Vulnerable Animals: A Primate Scientist's Ethical Journey.* Chicago: University of Chicago Press, quoted material from 8.

Graeber, Charles. 2018. *The Breakthrough: Immunotherapy and the Race to Cure Cancer.* New York: Twelve, quoted material from 82, 157.

Chen, Angus. 2018. "Baboons Survive for Half a Year after Heart Transplants from Pigs." *Scientific American*, December 5. https://www.scientificamerican.com/article/baboons-survive -for-half-a-year-after-heart-transplants-from-pigs/.

Hansen, Lawrence A. 2013. "Institution Animal Care and Use Committees Need Greater Ethical Diversity." *Journal of Medical Ethics* 39:188–90.

Hansen, Lawrence A., Justin R. Goodman, and Alka Chandna. 2012. "Analysis of Animal Research Ethics Committee Membership at American Institutions." *Animals* 2:68–75.

Gluck, John. 2016. *Voracious Science and Vulnerable Animals*, quoted material from 279, 296.

Ferdowsian, Hope, et al. 2019. "A Belmont Report for Animals?" *Cambridge Quarterly of Healthcare Ethics.* https://www .cambridge.org/core/journals/cambridge-quarterly-of -healthcare-ethics/article/belmont-report-for-animals /F4518E13F2FE89A7719C5082A7FB44F8?fbclid=IwAR0VIv JAxSEK2C3Qu9aVy2YDZtDVG7fUX6myFQPwjAmhAM5 DWWcr9i16H18, quoted material from 9.

Chandna, Alka. 2018. Personal communication, telephone call, August 29.

Adams, Carol J. and Lori Gruen. 2014. "Groundwork." In *Ecofeminism: Feminist Intersections with other Animals and the Earth*, edited by Carol J. Adams and Lori Gruen, 7–36. New York: Bloomsbury, quoted material from 28.

Goodman, Justin. 2018. Personal communication, telephone call, August 30.

USDA (United States Food and Drug Administration). 2019. "ARS

Announces Toxoplasmosis Research Review, Discontinues Research with Cats." Press release, April 2. https://www.usda.gov /media/press-releases/2019/04/02/ars-announces-toxoplasmosis -research-review-discontinues-research.

Merkley, Ryan. 2018–19. Personal communication, email messages, August 23 and January 15.

"Blood and Guts on Capitol Hill." 2013. Physicians Committee for Responsible Medicine, video of Cut Suit, October 25. https://www .pcrm.org/news/blog/blood-and-guts-capitol-hill.

Booth-Kewley, Stephanie, et al. 2015. "Perceived Strengths and Weaknesses of Highly Realistic Training and Live Tissue Training for Navy Corpsmen." Naval Health Research Center, San Diego, Report 15-12.

Guarino, Ben. 2019. "Inside the Grand and Sometimes Slimy Plan to Turn Octopuses into Lab Animals." *Washington Post*, March 2. https://www.washingtonpost.com/national/health-science /inside-the-grand-and-sometimes-slimy-plan-to-turn-octopuses -into-lab-animals/2019/03/01/c6ce3fe0-3930-11e9-b786 -d6abcbcd212a_story.html.

Greenfieldboyce, Nell. 2019. "Why Octopuses Might Be the Next Lab Rats." NPR, June 3. https://www.npr.org/sections/health -shots/2019/06/03/727653152/why-octopuses-might-be-the-next -lab-rats.

King, Barbara J. 2019. "Don't Use Cephalopods as Lab Animals." Letter to the editor, *Washington Post*, March 8. https://www .washingtonpost.com/opinions/dont-use-cephalopods-as-lab -animals/2019/03/08/c8a6063a-407f-11e9–85ad-779ef05fd9d8_ story.html.

Malisow, Craig. 2017. "Has Texas A&M Ended Its Controversial Dog Experiments?" *Houston Press*, April 5. https://www.houston press.com/news/conflicting-stories-on-the-future-of-texas -aandms-dog-laboratory-9329778

Amoasii, Leonela, et al. 2018. "Gene Editing Restores Dystrophin Expression in a Canine Model of Duchenne Muscular Dystrophy." *Science* 362, no. 6410: 86–91. DOI: 10.1126/science .aau1549.

Cohen, Jon. 2018. "Gene Editing of Dogs Offers Hope for Treating Human Muscular Dystrophy." *Science*, August 30. https://www

.sciencemag.org/news/2018/08/gene-editing-dogs-offers-hope
-treating-human-muscular-dystrophy.

Else, Holly. 2019. "Genomics Institute to Close World-Leading Animal Facility." *Nature*, May 29. https://www.nature.com/articles
/d41586-019-01685-7.

Trunnell, Emily, and Ingrid V. Taylor. 2017. "Muscular Dystrophy
(MD) Studies on Dogs: Time for a Change?" Poster presentation
at World Congress on Alternatives and Animal Use in the Life
Sciences, Seattle, August.

Mak, Isabella W. Y. 2014. "Lost in Translation: Animal Models and
Clinical Trials in Cancer Treatment." *American Journal of Translation Research* 6, no. 2: 114–18, quoted material from 115, 117.

Jackson, Samuel J., and Gareth J. Thomas. 2017. "Human Tissue
Models In Cancer Research: Looking beyond the Mouse." *Disease
Models and Mechanisms* 10, no. 8: 939–42.

Epilogue

jones, pattrice. 2014. "Eros and the Mechanisms of Eco-defense."
In *Ecofeminism: Feminist Intersections with other Animals and
the Earth*, edited by Carol J. Adams and Lori Gruen, 91–106. New
York: Bloomsbury, quoted material from 103.

Walls, Laura Dassow. 2017. *Henry David Thoreau: A Life*. Chicago:
University of Chicago Press, quoted material from 305, 131.

De Waal, Frans. 2013 "Two Monkeys Were Paid Unequally: Excerpt
from Frans de Waal's TED Talk." *TED Blog* video, April 4. https://
www.youtube.com/watch?v=meiU6TxysCg.

De Waal, Frans. 2019. *Mama's Last Hug: Animal Emotions and What
They Tell Us about Ourselves*. New York: W. W. Norton, quoted
material from 210.

Index